Palgrave Macmillan Studies in Banking and Financial Institutions

Series Editor: **Professor Philip Molyneux**

The Palgrave Macmillan Studies in Banking and Financial Institutions are international in orientation and include studies of banking within particular countries or regions, and studies of particular themes such as Corporate Banking, Risk Management, Mergers and Acquisitions, etc. The books' focus is on research and practice, and they include up-to-date and innovative studies on contemporary topics in banking that will have global impact and influence.

Titles include:

Yener Altunbaş, Alper Kara and Öslem Olgu
TURKISH BANKING
Banking under Political Instability and Chronic High Inflation

Paola Bongini, Stefano Chiarlone and Giovanni Ferri *(editors)*
EMERGING BANKING SYSTEMS

Vittorio Boscia, Alessandro Carretta and Paola Schwizer
COOPERATIVE BANKING: INNOVATIONS AND DEVELOPMENTS

Vittorio Boscia, Alessandro Carretta and Paola Schwizer
COOPERATIVE BANKING IN EUROPE: CASE STUDIES

Roberto Bottiglia, Elisabetta Gualandri and Gian Nereo Mazzocco *(editors)*
CONSOLIDATION IN THE EUROPEAN FINANCIAL INDUSTRY

Alessandro Carretta, Franco Fiordelisi and Gianluca Mattarocci *(editors)*
NEW DRIVERS OF PERFORMANCE IN A CHANGING FINANCIAL WORLD

Dimitris N. Chorafas
CAPITALISM WITHOUT CAPITAL

Dimitris N. Chorafas
FINANCIAL BOOM AND GLOOM
The Credit and Banking Crisis of 2007–2009 and Beyond

Vincenzo D'Apice and Giovanni Ferri
FINANCIAL INSTABILITY
Toolkit for Interpreting Boom and Bust Cycles

Peter Falush and Robert L. Carter OBE
THE BRITISH INSURANCE INDUSTRY SINCE 1900
The Era of Transformation

Franco Fiordelisi
MERGERS AND ACQUISITIONS IN EUROPEAN BANKING

Franco Fiordelisi, Philip Molyneux and Daniele Previati *(editors)*
NEW ISSUES IN FINANCIAL AND CREDIT MARKETS

Franco Fiordelisi, Philip Molyneux and Daniele Previati *(editors)*
NEW ISSUES IN FINANCIAL INSTITUTIONS MANAGEMENT

Hans Genberg and Cho-Hoi Hui
THE BANKING SECTOR IN HONG KONG
Competition, Efficiency, Performance and Risk

Carlo Gola and Alessandro Roselli
THE UK BANKING SYSTEM AND ITS REGULATORY AND SUPERVISORY
FRAMEWORK

Elisabetta Gualandri and Valeria Venturelli (editors)
BRIDGING THE EQUITY GAP FOR INNOVATIVE SMEs

Kim Hawtrey
AFFORDABLE HOUSING FINANCE

Otto Hieronymi (editor)
GLOBALIZATION AND THE REFORM OF THE INTERNATIONAL BANKING
AND MONETARY SYSTEM

Sven Janssen
BRITISH AND GERMAN BANKING STRATEGIES

M. Mansoor Khan and M. Ishaq Bhatti
DEVELOPMENTS IN ISLAMIC BANKING
The Case of Pakistan

Anders Ögren (editor)
THE SWEDISH FINANCIAL REVOLUTION

Dominique Rambure and Alec Nacamuli
PAYMENT SYSTEMS
From the Salt Mines to the Board Room

Catherine Schenk (editor)
HONG KONG SAR's MONETARY AND EXCHANGE RATE CHALLENGES
Historical Perspectives

Noël K. Tshiani
BUILDING CREDIBLE CENTRAL BANKS
Policy Lessons for Emerging Economies

The full list of titles available is on the website:
www.palgrave.com/finance/sbfi.asp

Palgrave Macmillan Studies in Banking and Financial Institutions
Series Standing Order ISBN 978-1-4039-4872-4

You can receive future titles in this series as they are published by placing a standing order.
Please contact your bookseller or, in case of difficulty, write to us at the address below with
your name and address, the title of the series and the ISBN quoted above.

Customer Services Department, Macmillan Distribution Ltd, Houndmills, Basingstoke,
Hampshire RG21 6XS, England

New Issues in Financial Institutions Management

Edited by

Franco Fiordelisi
Professor of Banking and Finance, University of Rome III, Italy;
Bangor Business School, Bangor University, UK and
Essex Finance Centre, Essex University, UK

Philip Molyneux
Professor of Banking and Finance, Bangor Business School,
Bangor University, UK

and

Daniele Previati
Professor of Banking and Finance, University of Rome III, Italy

First published 2010 by
PALGRAVE MACMILLAN

Palgrave Macmillan in the UK is an imprint of Macmillan Publishers Limited,
registered in England, company number 785998, of Houndmills, Basingstoke,
Hampshire RG21 6XS.

Palgrave Macmillan in the US is a division of St Martin's Press LLC,
175 Fifth Avenue, New York, NY 10010.

Palgrave Macmillan is the global academic imprint of the above companies
and has companies and representatives throughout the world.

Palgrave® and Macmillan® are registered trademarks in the United States,
the United Kingdom, Europe and other countries.

ISBN: 978-0-230-27810-3 hardback

This book is printed on paper suitable for recycling and made from fully
managed and sustained forest sources. Logging, pulping and manufacturing
processes are expected to conform to the environmental regulations of the
country of origin.

A catalogue record for this book is available from the British Library.

Library of Congress Cataloging-in-Publication Data

New issues in financial institutions management / edited by Franco
Fiordelisi, Philip Molyneux, Daniele Previati.
        p. cm.—(Palgrave Macmillan studies in banking and financial
           institutions)
    ISBN 978-0-230-27810-3 (hardback)
    1. Banks and banking – Europe. 2. Bank management – Europe.
3. Financial institutions – Europe – Management. I. Fiordelisi, Franco, 1972–
II. Molyneux, Philip. III. Previati, Daniele.

HG2974.N49 2010
332.1068—dc22   2010027506

10 9 8 7 6 5 4 3 2 1
19 18 17 16 15 14 13 12 11 10

Printed and bound in Great Britain by
CPI Antony Rowe, Chippenham and Eastbourne

Contents

List of Tables and Figures   vii

Notes on Contributors   xii

Introduction   1
Franco Fiordelisi, Philip Molyneux and Daniele Previati

Part 1   Bank Management, Innovation and Technology

1   Financial Innovation: Theoretical Issues and
    Empirical Evidence in Europe   11
    F. Arnaboldi and B. Rossignoli

2   A New Appraisal of the Structure of
    European Banking Systems   26
    Cristina Ruza, Rebeca de Juan and Marta de la Cuesta González

3   The Performance of Intellectual Capital and Banking:
    some Empirical Evidence from the
    European Banking System   41
    Gimede Gigante and Daniele Previati

4   Traditional and R&D Investments:
    are They really Different?   59
    Paola Brighi and Giuseppe Torluccio

Part 2   Efficiency and Productivity of Financial Intermediaries

5   Incorporating Risk in the Efficiency and
    Productivity Analysis of Banking Systems   91
    Thomas Weyman-Jones, Miguel Boucinha, Karligash Kenjegalieva,
    Geetha Ravishankar, Nuno Ribeiro and Zhi Shen

6   Efficiency and Environmental Factors in
    Investment Banking   106
    Nemanja Radić, Claudia Girardone and Franco Fiordelisi

7   Post-merger Bank Efficiency and Stock Market Reaction:
the Case of the US versus Europe   122
*Dimitris K. Chronopoulos, Claudia Girardone and
John C. Nankervis*

Part 3   Consolidation in the Financial Industry

8   The Impact of Corporate Culture, Efficiency
and Geographic Distance on M&A Results:
the European Case   139
Franco Fiordelisi and Duccio Martelli

9   What does Bank Financial Profile tell Us
about Mergers and Acquisitions in Latin American Banking?   153
Fatima Cardias Williams and Jonathan Williams

10   What are the Determinants of Mergers
and Acquisitions in Banking?   171
Elena Beccalli and Pascal Frantz

Part 4   Corporate Governance Issues

11   An Assessment of Compliance with
the Italian Code of Corporate Governance   203
*Marcello Bianchi, Angela Ciavarella, Valerio Novembre and
Rossella Signoretti*

12   Sources of Risk and Return in Different Bank Business
Models: Comparing Poland with Global Trends   219
Ewa Miklaszewska and Katarzyna Mikolajczyk

13   Does Board Composition Affect Strategic Frames of Banks?   246
Alessandro Carretta, Vincenzo Farina and Paola Schwizer

14   In Search of an Optimal Board of Directors for Banks   260
*Pablo de Andrés-Alonso, M. Elena Romero-Merino,
Marcos Santamaría-Mariscal and Eleuterio Vallelado-González*

15   Value and Governance in the Exchange Industry:
the Case of Diversified Conglomerate Exchanges   274
Maurizio Polato and Josanco Floreani

Index   291

Tables and Figures

Tables

1.1	Financial figures all countries 2005–2008	13
A1.1	Sample composition	21
2.1	Duda & Hart Index	29
2.2	Panel data estimations for the EU-11	30
2.3	Panel data estimations for the EU-2	31
2.4	Benchmarks for the banking structure (by the end of 2004)	33
2.5	Benchmarks for the banking structure (by the end of 2007)	34
2.6	Convergence ratios	35
3.1	Top ten banks in terms of VAIC values and of the VA for Italian sample (2003–2007)	50
3.2	Comparative VAIC analysis of Central Europe: overview of top ten German banks (2003–2007)	51
3.3	Comparative VAIC analysis of Central Europe: overview of the top ten Spanish banks (2003–2007)	53
3.4	Comparative VAIC analysis of Central Europe: overview of the top ten banks in sample (2003–2007)	53
3.5	Comparative VAIC analysis of Northern European banks: overview of the top ten banks (2003–2007)	54
3.6	Comparative VAIC analysis of Eastern European banks: overview of the top ten Eastern banks (2003–2007)	54
4.1	The sources of finance: investments vs. R&D	63
4.2	Rationing and sources of finance: investments vs. R&D	64
4.3	Description of variables	66
4.4	Correlations	72
4.5	Investments vs. R&D: LOGIT model	75
4.6	Investments vs. R&D: OLS model	77
4.7	Investments vs. R&D: SUR model	80
6.1	Sample description: number of banks and average asset size by country	111
6.2	Environmental variable definitions and sources	112
6.3	Correlation matrices for the explanatory variables	116
7.1	Descriptive statistics for the bank merger sample	125

7.2	Time and size distribution of banks included in the estimation of the frontiers	126
7.3	Cumulative daily abnormal returns to stockholders upon merger announcements	130
7.4	Descriptive statistics of the variables used in the univariate analysis	132
7.5	Pearson correlation coefficients: acquirer banks	132
7.6	Abnormal returns and operating efficiency: univariate regressions	133
8.1	Sample description: large M&A deals in European banking between 2000 and 2007	140
8.2	Variables used to investigate short horizon M&A outcomes and their determinants in European banking	145
8.3	The determinants of large successful M&A deals in European banking	146
9.1	Profile of outcomes: Latin America, 1985–2006	157
9.2a	Covariates used in MNLM	160
9.2b	Descriptive statistics, by outcome	161
9.3	Wald tests for combining alternatives outcomes	163
9.4	Wald tests for independent variables	164
9.5	Relative Risk Ratios, by outcome, LatAm	165
10.1	Acquisition likelihood hypotheses and independent variables	175
10.2	Number of M&A deals involving acquirers and targets (by country and by year)	181
10.3	Descriptive statistics	184
10.4	Multinomial logit with hypotheses' variables	187
10.5	Factor analysis – rotated component matrix	190
10.6	Multinomial logit with common factors	194
11.1	The methodology for the assignment of the scores with respect to the two components of the *CoRe* indicator (i.e. the identification of significant RPTs and the procedures adopted for their approval)	208
11.2	Descriptive statistics for the *CoRe* indicator	210
11.3	Comparison between actual and formal compliance by sector	211
11.4	Comparison between actual and formal compliance by market index	211
11.5	*CoRe* indicator and firms' characteristics: test of difference between means	213
12.1	Bank profitability in selected countries: ROE (%)	221

12.2	Evolution of bank organizational structures	223
12.3	Net non-interest income as a percentage of total net income in selected countries	225
12.4	Groups of analysed banks, according to bank business models	228
12.5	Correlation matrix	235
12.6	Regression results: ROA	236
12.7	Regression results: Z-score	237
A12.1	List of analysed Polish banks, by bank types	239
13.1	Roots of verbs or terms indicating strategic actions	251
13.2	Fields for strategic actions and roots of associated verbs or terms	252
13.3	Descriptive statistics	253
13.4	Correlations	253
13.5	Initial cluster centres	254
13.6	Iteration history	255
13.7	Final cluster centres	255
14.1	The main statistics of banking boards	264
15.1	Financial ratios and cost structure for major exchanges	279
15.2	Some performance measures	280
15.3	Trading volumes and revenues in main cash markets	280
15.4	Number of contracts traded and revenues in main derivative markets	281
15.5	Average EV/EBITDA multiples in recent mergers	281
15.6	Exchange value: some comparisons	283
15.7	Estimated post merger values for NYSE Euronext and the LSE Group	284
15.8	Market concentration	286

Figures

1.1	Financial innovation by year (2005–2008)	16
1.2	Total assets and innovation – all banks	18
2.1	Dendogram using average linkage	29
3.1	Sector efficiency analysis in the use of IC in the Italian sample (2003–2007)	48
3.2	Analysis of domestic vs. foreign banks' use of ICE for the Italian sample (2003–2007)	48
3.3	Overview of domestic Italian banks in the VAIC investigation for the period 2003–2007	48

3.4	VAIC: mean for Italian sample during the period 2003–2007	49
3.5	HCE: mean for Italian sample during the period 2003–2007	49
3.6	SCE: mean for Italian sample during the period 2003–2007	49
3.7	CEE: mean for Italian sample during the period 2003–2007	50
3.8	Sector efficiency analysis in the use of IC in the German sample (2003–2007)	52
5.1	Shadow price of equity capital in Portugal (1997–2004)	94
5.2	Shadow price of equity in ten Asian countries (1997–2004)	95
5.3	Total factor productivity in the banking system in Portugal (1997–2004)	96
5.4	Total factor productivity in the banking systems of ten Asian countries (1997–2005)	97
5.5	Total factor productivity in the banking system of Russia (1998–2005)	97
5.6	Managerial utility maximization	101
6.1	Cost and profit efficiency estimates (means) by country (2001–2007)	114
6.2	Cost and profit efficiency estimates by country over time	115
8.1	Number and value of M&A deals concluded by financial institutions (as acquirers): the US vs. Europe	141
8.2	Corporate culture and M&A success in EU banking: a summary of estimated empirical relationships	149
12.1	Total assets write-downs, 2007–1Q2009	223
12.2	Non-depository funding share and non-interest net income share by bank type	229
12.3	Non-depository funding share and non-interest net income share: impact on ROA and Z-score	230
12.4	Non-depository funding share and non-interest net income share: impact on the Sharpe ratio	231
12.5	Trend of ROA and ROE by bank type	232
12.6	Trend of CAR by bank type	233
12.7	Average ratios for different bank business models (2000–2008)	234
14.1	Banking board composition and functioning across countries	264

14.2   Relationships between banks' characteristics
       and their boards' composition   266
14.3   Board composition in civil-law countries vs.
       common-law countries   267
14.4   Relationships between ownership structure and
       board composition   268
14.5   Relationships between market to book ratio
       and board composition   269
15.1   Volumes traded and average costs in major exchanges   278

Contributors

Pablo de Andrés Alonso (PhD in Business Administration, 1995) is Professor of Finance at the Universidad de Valladolid, Spain. His research interests range between corporate governance, corporate finance and real options. He has published his research in such journals as the *Journal of Banking and Finance, Journal of Business Finance and Accounting, Corporate Governance, Universia Business Review* and *Investigaciones Económicas.* He is in charge of the doctoral programme New Trends in Business Administration and he is Executive Editor of the *Spanish Journal of Finance and Accounting.* He was a Visiting Researcher at Harvard University in 2009–10.

Francesca Arnaboldi is Assistant Professor at the Università di Milano, Italy and Visiting Fellow at the Cass Business School, City University, London. Her main areas of interest are banking, corporate governance and financial innovation. She has presented her work at several international conferences and published various chapters in referred books and articles.

Elena Beccalli is currently Associate Professor in Banking and Finance at the Università Cattolica del Sacro Cuore, Italy, and Visiting Senior Fellow in Accounting at the London School of Economics (LSE), UK. She has written books and articles in national and international academic journals in the area of the economics of financial institutions. Her research interests include stochastic efficiency measurement, technology and performance, mergers and acquisitions and analyst forecasts.

Marcello Bianchi is the Chairman of the OECD Corporate Governance Committee. He is also Head of the Regulation Impact Assessment Unit at Consob (the Italian Financial Markets Authority) where he has worked since 1990. At Consob, he has directed several research and regulatory activities concerning corporate governance issues, namely major shareholdings, pyramiding, related party transactions, take-overs and board structure.

Miguel Boucinha has been an economist at the Economic Research Department at the Banco de Portugal since 2007, working in the Financial Stability Division. He has a Licenciatura and an MSc from the Universidade Nova de Lisboa and is currently working on his PhD at the same institution. His main fields of interest are industrial economics, regulation and banking.

Paola Brighi is Associate Professor of Banking and Finance at the Faculty of Economics, University of Bologna in Rimini. She received her MSc from the University of Louvain-la-Neuve and her PhD from the University of Ancona. Her specialty areas include banking, financial markets and corporate finance. Her current research interests include lending technologies, local banking efficiency, R&D financing and credit risk management.

Fatima Cardias Williams holds degrees from Brazil (BSc), the United States (MSc) and the United Kingdom (PhD). Formerly at the Instituto Nacional de Pesquisas da Amazonia – INPA, Manaus, Brazil, Dr Cardias Williams is a scientist at European Plant Science, Bangor, UK. A contributor on several Pan-European and Latin American projects, Dr Cardias Williams publishes scientific and financial papers. Her current research includes discrete choice modelling of banking sector consolidation.

Alessandro Carretta is Full Professor of Economics and Management of Financial Intermediaries at the University of Rome Tor Vergata and Director of the PhD programme in Banking & Finance. His current research interests relate to banking management, asset based lending and corporate culture in financial institutions.

Dimitris Chronopoulos is a Lecturer in Finance at the University of St Andrews School of Management. He completed his PhD in Accounting and Finance from the University of Essex in 2009. His research interests lie in the area of performance measurement in banking and finance, with particular focus on financial conglomeration and mergers and acquisitions.

Angela Ciavarella is an Economist at the Department of Economic Studies of Consob (the Italian Financial Markets Authority). She holds a PhD in Economics from the Università di Napoli "Federico II" and a Master's in Mathematical Economics and Econometrics from the Université de Toulouse. Her research interests comprehend corporate governance, regulatory impact assessment and institutional economics.

Marta de la Cuesta González has a PhD in Economics and Business Management. She is Senior Lecturer at the Department of Applied Economics of the Universidad Nacional de Educación a Distancia, UNED, Madrid. She was Vice-chancellor of Economic Affairs at UNED from 2005 to 2009. Her main research interests are in the area of banking and finance, corporate social responsibility and socially responsible investments. She is teacher at undergraduate and postgraduate levels, and she is responsible for delivering modules in the areas of banking, financial systems and sustainable finance.

Vincenzo Farina is Assistant Professor of Economics and Management of Financial Intermediaries at the Università di Roma "Tor Vergata". His current research interests relate to banking management, focusing on strategy, corporate governance, culture and organizational change.

Franco Fiordelisi is Professor of Finance and Banking in the Faculty of Economics at the Università di Roma III, Italy. He is also Visiting Research Fellow at Bangor Business School, Bangor University, UK, and the Essex Finance Centre of Essex University, UK. His recent books include *Shareholder Value in European Banking* (Palgrave Macmillan, 2006), *New Drivers of Performance in a Changing Financial World* (Palgrave Macmillan, 2008) and *Mergers and Acquisitions in European Banking* (Palgrave Macmillan, 2008). He has published various articles in national and international academic journals in the area of the economics of financial institutions.

Josanco Floreani is a Lecturer in Banking and Finance at the Faculty of Economics of the Università di Udine, Italy, from which he graduated in Economics and received a PhD in Business Sciences. His main research interests are related to the economics and governance of the securities industry and the regulation of financial markets.

Pascal Frantz has an MSc in applied physics (ENSPG, Grenoble), an MBA (LBS) and a PhD in Accounting and Finance (LBS). He is currently a Lecturer in Accounting and Finance at the London School of Economics. His research interests include economic analysis in the areas of accounting, corporate governance and mergers and acquisitions.

Gimede Gigante has a PhD in Banking and Finance from the Università di Romà "Tor Vergata," Italy. He also has an ITP (International Teachers Program) qualification from SDA Bocconi in 2008. He has been a Visiting Scholar at NYU's Stern School of Business and Visiting Researcher in Finance at Columbia Business School, New York. He is currently a Research Fellow at the Università di Roma III, Italy. His research interests lie in the area of intellectual capital in the banking sector.

Claudia Girardone is Reader in Finance at the Essex Business School, Essex University. Her research focus is on modelling bank efficiency and productivity and competition issues in banking. Her recent work includes a textbook entitled *Introduction to Banking* (FT Prentice Hall, 2006) and articles on efficiency, integration and market power in banking markets. She has published widely in these areas, and her recent publications appear in *Review of Development Economics, Economics Letters, Journal of Business, Finance and Accounting* and the *Journal of Banking and Finance*.

Rebeca de Juan is Lecturer in Economics at the Universidad Nacional de Educación a Distancia (UNED), Madrid. A graduate of UNED in 1993, she has a PhD in Economics from UNED and a Master's in Economics Analysis from the Escuela de Hacienda Pública. She received a Young Economists' Essay Competition Award in the 26th EARIE. Her research interests are industrial organization, banking and micro-econometrics. She has published several papers in the *International Journal of Industrial Organization, Review of Industrial Organization, The Economic and Social Review* and *Revista de Economía Aplicada*.

Karligash Kenjegalieva is a Lecturer in Economics at the Department of Economics of Loughborough University. She previously worked in capacity of Cost Effectiveness Modeller at the University of Sheffield and as a Research Associate at Loughborough University. Her main research interests and publication record cover a range of topics on efficiency and productivity analysis; banking and transition economics; parametric, semi-parametric and non-parametric econometrics and bootstrapping, Markov chain and Monte-Carlo simulations.

Duccio Martelli obtained a PhD in Banking and Finance from the Università di Roma "Tor Vergata", Italy. His research interests relate to real estate, corporate culture and asset management.

Ewa Miklaszewska is Professor of Finance and Banking at the Uniwersytet Ekonomiczny w Krakowie and Associate Professor of Economics in the Department of Management and Public Communication at the Uniwersytet Jagielloński. She has held several visiting positions in Polish and foreign universities and Polish regulatory bodies. She specializes in strategic developments in the global banking industry.

Katarzyna Mikolajczyk is Assistant Professor of Finance at the Uniwersytet Ekonomiczny w Krakowie. She has published heavily on the outcomes of privatization programmes in transition countries and on the impact of structural changes in the banking industry (including mergers and acquisitions) on bank efficiency.

Phil Molyneux is currently Head of Bangor Business School and Professor of Banking and Finance. His main area of research is on the structure and efficiency of banking markets and he has published widely in this area. He has also published a variety of texts on banking areas and has acted as a consultant to a wide range of organizations including the European Commission, UK Treasury, Citibank Private Bank, McKinsey & Co, Credit Suisse and various other international banks and consulting firms.

John Nankervis is Professor in Finance and Research Director at the Essex Business School, Essex University. His research interests are primarily in the area of financial econometrics and, in particular, autocorrelation testing and bootstrap methods in time series. He has published in leading journals such as *Econometrica, Journal of Econometrics, Econometric Theory, Journal of the American Statistical Association, Journal of Business and Economic Statistics* and *International Economic Review.*

Valerio Novembre is an Economist at the Department of Economic Studies of Consob (the Italian Financial Markets Authority). He holds a PhD in Economics, Markets and Institutions from the IMT Institute for Advanced Studies in Lucca and an MSc in Finance and Regulation from the London School of Economics. His research interests cover financial regulation, regulatory impact assessment and institutional economics.

Maurizio Polato is an Associate Professor in Banking and Finance at the Faculty of Economics of the Università di Udine, where he teaches Securities Exchange Economics. He graduated in Economics from Università di Venezia 'Ca' Foscari and received a PhD in Business Economics from the same university. His main research interests are related to the economics and governance of the securities industry, banking economics and risk management.

Daniele Previati is Professor of Banking and Finance in the Faculty of Economics at the Università di Roma III, Italy. He has widely published in a large number of academic journals. His research focuses on stakeholder management in banking and other financial institutions.

Nemanja Radić (PhD) is Lecturer in Banking and Finance at the London Metropolitan Business School. His key teaching areas are Domestic and International Banking, International Corporate Finance, Introduction to Financial Services, Policy Issues in Financial Services (dissertation supervision), International Banking (dissertation supervision) and International Banking and Finance (dissertation supervision). His specialist area focuses on efficiency, risks and competition in banking.

Geetha Ravishankar is Research Associate at Loughborough University, UK. Her current research interests focus on efficiency and productivity analysis using Data Envelopment Analysis and econometric methodologies, as applied to the banking and financial services industry.

Nuno Ribeiro works in the Economic Research Department of the Banco de Portugal in capital markets, financial systems and financial stability issues. Currently, he is the head of the Financial Stability Division. His main fields of interest are financial stability, banking, industrial organization and corporate finance.

M. Elena Romero-Merino is Professor of Finance at the Universidad Europea Miguel de Cervantes (Spain). Born in Palencia in 1978, she obtained her Bachelor's degree in Economics and Business and her PhD in Business Administration at the Universidad de Valladolid. Her academic research focuses on corporate governance, non-profit organizations and financial institutions. She has published her research in such journals as the *British Journal of Management, Universia Business Review* and *Nonprofit and Voluntary Sector Quarterly*.

Bruno Rossignoli is Professor of Banking and Finance at Università di Milano, Italy and member of CEFIN, Centro Studi di Banca e Finanza, Università di Modena e Reggio Emilia, Italy. He is author, co-author and editor of numerous books and articles. His main research interest is in the area of credit and banking.

Cristina Ruza y Paz-Curbera is an economist and graduate with a Master's degree in Banking and Finance from the University of Bangor, and in Public Finance and Taxation from the Centro Colegio de Economistas de Madrid and Escuela de Hacienda Pública (Instituto de Estudios Fiscales) y Universidad de Alcalá de Henares, both with distinction grade, and she was awarded PhD in 2004 by the Universidad Nacional de Educación a Distancia (UNED). Nowadays she is a PhD lecturer in the Applied Economics Department (UNED) at undergraduate and postgraduate levels, and she also participates in a master module in the areas of banking and sustainable finance.

Marcos Santamaría-Mariscal is Professor of Finance at the Universidad de Burgos, Spain. Born in Burgos (1975), he obtained his Bachelor's degree in Economics and Business from the Universidad Nacional de Educación a Distancia (UNED), Spain and his PhD in Business Administration at the Universidad de Burgos. His academic research focuses on corporate governance, corporate finance and financial institutions. He has published his research in such journals as *Corporate Governance* and *Universia Business Review*.

Paola Schwizer is Full Professor of Economics and Management of Financial Intermediaries at the Università de Parma. Her current research interests relate to banking strategies and organization, corporate governance and internal control systems, Basel 2 and risk management.

Rossella Signoretti is an Economist at the Department of Economic Studies of Consob (the Italian Financial Markets Authority). She holds a PhD in Banking and Finance from the Università di Roma "Tor Vergata". Before joining Consob, she was research assistant in finance at the Università di Roma III. Her research interests cover corporate governance, regulatory impact assessment and institutional economics.

Giuseppe Torluccio (MbA, PhD) is Professor in Banking and Finance at the Faculty of Economics of the Università di Bologna, Italy where he is also coordinator of the Banking and Finance PhD programme. He has been Visiting Researcher at the State University of Arizona and that Olin Business School, Washington University, St Louis. His research interests are related to financial institutions, focusing on credit risk, SME financing, ICT and research and development.

Eleuterio Vallelado-González is Professor of Finance at the Universidad de Valladolid. Born in Laguna de Duero (Spain), he obtained his Bachelor's degree in Economics and Business, his PhD at the Universidad de Valladolid and an MBA from New York University. He is author of several books, and his articles can be found in the *Journal of Banking and Finance, Applied Economics, Financial Review, Abante*, the *Spanish Review of Finance and Accounting* and *Cuadernos de Economía y Dirección de Empresas*, among others. His research interests include corporate finance, corporate governance in banks and behavioral finance.

Thomas Weyman-Jones has been Professor of Industrial Economics at Loughborough University in the UK since 1995. His research interests include efficiency and productivity analysis and applied microeconometrics, and how these techniques can be used to inform regulatory policy. His published research work has examined the economic performance of European and Asian banking systems, and has also been applied to European airlines, energy and water supply networks and climate change.

Zhi Shen has completed his PhD at the Department of Economics at Loughborough University. His research interests are mainly on efficiency and productivity analysis in banking industries. His work on cost efficiency analysis in Asian banking industries has been published in the *Journal of Chinese Economic and Business Studies* and presented at several international conferences including the fifth North American Productivity Workshop, 2008.

Jonathan Williams is Professor in Banking and Finance at Bangor University, UK. His research interest focuses on banking sector deregulation. He has written on bank privatization, foreign banks, governance, efficiency and productivity, competition and risk, market power, management behaviour and mergers and acquisitions. His recent empirical work includes discrete choice modelling of bank failure and consolidation in Latin American banking sectors.

Introduction

Franco Fiordelisi, Philip Molyneux and Daniele Previati

This text comprises a selection of papers that focus on recent developments in the financial sector and drawn from the European Association of University Teachers of Banking and Finance Conference (otherwise known as the Wolpertinger Conference) held at the Università di Roma III, Italy in September 2009. The text is divided into four topical themes that cover: management, innovation and technology in the financial sector; efficiency and productivity; consolidation and finally various corporate governance issues.

Part 1 Bank Management, Innovation and Technology

In Chapter 1 Francesca Arnaboldi (Università di Milano, Italy) and Bruno Rossignoli (Università di Milano and Università di Modena e Reggio Emilia, Centro Studi di Banca e Finanza, Italy) examine the role of financial innovation in the financial sector with a particular emphasis on the UK and Italy. Their interesting study focuses on various financial innovations introduced by domestic banks listed on Euronext (the Amsterdam, Brussels, Lisbon and Paris markets), London Stock Exchange and Borsa Italiana over the 2005 to 2008 period. Their analysis of banks' corporate accounts shows that specific organizational units in charge of research and development (R&D) are not mentioned and that in most cases in which R&D activity is described it is combined with products, sector information, marketing policies, organizational measures and ICT. Innovations also appear to be concentrated mainly in the product area. This, the authors argue, could be because of differences in the "life cycles" of innovations and by the various operational conditions of banks in all systems.

Changes in technology, innovation and other factors impact on the structural features of banking markets. This is considered in Chapter 2, in which Cristina Ruza, Rebeca de Juan and Marta de la Cuesta (all Universidad Nacional de Educación a Distancia, UNED, Spain) analyse the main determinants of financial system structures for the European Union countries (EU-25 countries) between 1999 and 2007. The authors classify EU banking systems according to their financial structures and compare these with the financial features of the new EU Member States. The main findings suggest a convergence of financial structures in Europe, although the speed of convergence appears to have gradually diminished since 2004.

Among the key features of service companies are its employees and the intellectual capital embodied in the firms' activities. In Chapter 3 Gimede Gigante and Daniele Previati (both Università di Roma III, Italy) measure the intellectual capital performance of European banks. They note that while physical capital is essential for banks to operate, it is intellectual capital that determines the quality of services provided to customers. The authors use parametric techniques to investigate the efficiencies of banks in utilizing their intellectual capital. After considering the the Italian banking market they also analyse banks in a number of other European countries. Using the value-added approach they seek to disentangle intellectual capital from other drivers of value. Their main conclusion is that intellectual capital appears to be just as important as other more traditional drivers of bank performance.

Chapter 4 by Paola Brighi and Giuseppe Torluccio (both Università di Bologna, Italy) examines the different roles played by the financing of (R&D) and traditional investments by Italian firms. Using information from Capitalia's Survey of Italian Firms the authors investigate which factors (firm structure, information asymmetries and credit market structure) influence the pattern of R&D financing. They go on to investigate whether R&D investments face greater difficulties in gathering external financial resources than is the case with traditional investments. An interesting finding is that the level of R&D financing appears to relate to the level of public subsidies provided aimed at encouraging such activity.

Part 2   Efficiency and Productivity of Financial Intermediaries

A number of contributions to this text examine efficiency and productivity issues in banking, and Chapter 5 by Thomas Weyman

Jones, Karligash Kenjegalieva, Geetha Ravishjankar, Zhi Shen (all Loughborough University, UK), Miguel Boucinha and Nuno Ribeiro (both Banco de Portugal) links bank risk to efficiency issues. It has long been recognized that an important issue concerns how to take account of bank risk-taking when modelling efficiency and productivity. This chapter examines three different approaches to the incorporation of risk in measuring the efficiency and productivity performance of banking systems: the use of equity capital as an explanatory variable, the role of scale efficiency change as an indicator of risky behaviour and, finally, the use of second moment statistics to measure risk. The first two approaches are indirect measures of risk in contrast to the third, which is a direct measure. The authors argue that while the direct approach is theoretically superior, it faces very challenging and possibly insurmountable empirical problems in terms of linking risk to bank efficiency and productivity measures.

While there is a large literature concerning examining the efficiency of commercial banks, relatively little work to date has been done on other financial institutions. Here Chapter 6 by Franco Fiordelisi (Università di Roma III, Italy), Claudia Girardone (University of Essex, UK) and Nemanja Radic (Università di Roma "Tor Vergata", Italy) makes a contribution by examining the efficiency of investment banks. They estimate cost and profit efficiency for a large sample of investment banks operating in the G7 countries (Canada, France, Germany, Italy, Japan, the UK and the US) and Switzerland over the period 2001 to 2007. The modelling approach also includes a variety of environmental factors (macroeconomic, institutional and regulatory) so as to examine the extent to which these are associated with estimated efficiency scores. Our results show that with only a few exceptions, cost and profit efficiency scores are generally higher for investment banks operating in non-EU countries. In most cases the relationship between efficiency and environmental variables is highly significant.

Chapter 7, by Dimitris Chronopoulos, Claudia Girardone and John C. Nankervis (all University of Essex, UK), examines whether bank efficiency is embodied in market returns surrounding merger and acquisition (M&A) announcements. First the chapter analyses whether whether bank mergers have different effects on shareholders' wealth in the US and Europe. Second, it examines whether changes in operating efficiency, as a result of bank mergers, are priced in the stock markets. The assumption is that changes in a bank's cost and profit efficiency, following a merger, are likely to affect its cash flows, which in turn should be valued in the stock markets – in particular they should be reflected in the market valuation of the acquirer. The results show that European bank mergers enhance the value of the combined entity and that acquiring shareholders in Europe earn significantly greater returns than their US counterparts. There is also evidence that changes in profit efficiency are positively associated with the abnormal returns.

Part 3   Consolidation in the Financial Industry

M&A activity has been a major feature of many financial systems over the last 20 years or so and there has been an extensive literature looking at the determinants and effects of the consolidation process. Chapter 8, by Franco Fiordelisi (Università di Roma III, Italy) and Duccio Martelli (Università di Roma "Tor Vergata", Italy), puts a new spin on the established literature by seeking to link corporate culture issues to the bank M&A process. There is a lack of empirical evidence about the relationship between M&A results and the culture of banks involved in deals. The authors use textual analysis to investigate a variety of official documents (e.g. reports to shareholders and financial statements) to evaluate various corporate features. Overall, their results show that if the attitude of the target banks' employees regarding cooperation with each other or loyalty towards the executive is higher than for the acquirer banks (i.e. a positive power-oriented culture gap), this is positively linked to acquirer shareholder returns. Conversely, if target banks have a less flexible organizational structure (e.g. more bureaucratic or hierarchical) than the acquirer companies (i.e. a positive gap in corporate culture role-orientation), this has a negative link with acquirer banks' shareholder returns. In addition, if target banks view the human resource contents as a key part of the corporate culture and the acquirer banks consider this less critical, this situation has a negative impact on the M&A success from the standpoint of the target bank shareholders

Chapter 9, by Jon Williams and Fatima Cardias Williams, (both Bangor University, UK), examines the financial features of Latin American banks in order to examine the determinants of M&A activity in the region. Using a sample of banks from Argentina, Brazil, Chile and Mexico between 1985 and 2006 they apply a multinomial logit model to identify the probabilities of a bank belonging to one of six selected discrete outcomes associated with the consolidation process against it not being involved in any M&A activity. Their findings show evidence of a too-big-to-fail policy which can explain why some banks were restructured and others failed; the targets of domestic and foreign banks have different characteristics, implying heterogeneity of banking strategy, and efficiency motives offer an explanation for M&A activity. An interesting finding, which conflicts with the idea of a market power motive for consolidation, is that more competitive banks have participated in M&A activity.

On a similar theme Elena Beccalli (Università Cattolica S. Cuore, Italy, and London School of Economics, UK) and Pascal Frantz (London School of Economics, UK) examine the determinants of the likelihood of banks being involved in M&A activity. Using a sample of 777 deals involving EU acquirers and 312 deals involving targets located throughout the world over the period 1991–2006, the authors use two approaches for the identification of the relevant M&A determinants (traditional determinants drawn from the extant literature and factor analysis). The results obtained from the multinomial logistic regression indicate that a higher likelihood to be acquirers is found for larger banks, banks with a history of high growth, banks with higher cost efficiency and banks with lower capital strength. Banks are more likely to be targets if they have lower free cash flow, efficiency, capital and liquidity. The alternative approaches to variable selection (hypotheses development and factor analysis) provide different results for the influence of regulatory/institutional and specialization variables.

Part 4   Corporate Governance Issues

Corporate governance issues in the corporate world have been of paramount importance since the high profile collapses of Enron, WorldCom and Parmalat (to name a just a few) as well as the recent global banking crises. Chapter 11, by Marcello Bianchi, Angela Ciavarella and Valerio Novembre and Rossella Signoretti (all Consob, Italy), examines the compliance of Italian listed companies (banks and non-banks) to the country's corporate governance code. In order to improve corporate governance, several self-regulatory codes have been issued across countries. Such codes are sets of recommendations on the different items that characterize a proper system of governance. They set standards regarding the role and composition of the board of directors, the structure and functioning of internal committees, directors' remuneration and related party transactions. Such codes are usually based on voluntary compliance and adopt the "comply or explain" principle whereby firms are required to state clearly the reasons for non-compliance. In particular the authors examine one of the most important features of the code, namely how companies manage transactions for which the interests of insiders and outsiders are most likely to be in conflict (i.e. related party transactions, RPTs). They examine all the 262 companies listed on the Italian market at the end of 2007. Their results show that the adoption of best practices suggested by the code for dealing with potential conflicts of interests arising from RPTs is markedly weaker and much more differentiated than is formally declared in company reports. In spite of a declaration of high compliance, listed companies show poor results in terms of actual compliance with the code's best practices.

The choice by banking firms of the most appropriate business model to adopt has gained great importance post-crisis – particularly as major losses appeared to come from the securities activities of banks and not their traditional lending business. This has led from calls in some quarters for the reintroduction of separate commercial and investment banking. Chapter 12, by Ewa Miklaszewska and Katarzyna Mikolajczyk (both Uniwersytet Ekonomiczny w Krakowie, Poland), examines the sources of risk and return in various bank business models and compares Polish bank experiences with global trends. They note that the the financial crisis has redefined the strengths and weaknesses of bank business models by highlighting the riskiness of the universal (conglomerate) model, in which bank expansion is based on non-depository funding and focused on non-interest incomes. It also suggests that, in many cases, the benefits from diversification away from traditional banking have been overstated. The chapter compares the risk-return fetaures of Polish banks and links this to business model structures. The main conclusion from the empirical evidence is that despite differences in market development and structure, similar tendencies concerning efficiency and risk in different bank models were also characteristic of Polish banks.

The next two chapters focus on the composition of bank boards and the final one looks at stock exchange business models. Chapter 13, by Vincenzo Farina, Alessandro Carretta (both Università di Roma "Tor Vergata", Italy) and Paola Schwizer (Università di Parma, Italy), examines how board composition influences strategic frames (i.e. the knowledge structures used by top decision-makers in formulating strategic guidelines). For example, do larger boards and/or boards with more executive directors and/or more interlocking directors make a difference in formulating strategies? Based on a sample representative sample of 27 listed Italian banks in 2007 the authors propose a procedure for measuring strategic frames in the banking industry. The results suggest that as the number of board members, non-executive directors and interlocking directorates increases, strategic frames become increasingly complex. Moreover, the results show that larger banks are associated with more complex strategic frames, since their greater size exposes them to a broad range of competitive options.

Chapter 14, by Marcos Santamaría Mariscal (Universidad de Burgos, Spain), Pablo de Andrés Alonso (Universidad de Valladolid, Spain), M. Elena Romero Merino (Universidad Europea Miguel de Cervantes, Spain) and Eleuterio Vallelado-Gonzàlez (Universidad de Valladolid, Spain), studies the determinants of board composition for an international sample of commercial banks. They first outline the main board characteristics and then analyse the possible endogenous relationships between the entity's idiosyncrasy and the board's composition. They find important differences in the composition of banking boards across countries. Large boards are related to bigger banks with high leverage and of greater age. It is also noted that concentrated ownership is negatively connected to board size and independence. When there is a major shareholder who can monitor activity, or when the costs of controlling managers are too high, the bank's board reduces its monitoring role, and this means that fewer members and outsiders are required.

Chapter 15, by Maurizio Polato and Josanco Floreani (both Università di Udine, Italy), examines changes in the business models of exchanges. They first examine governance reforms in the exchange industry and then identify major economic drivers for exchange value. Finally, they outline the key threats posed by mergers and the implications for the governance of networks. It is noted that M&A in the securities industry underlies some opportunities related to cost reductions as trading volumes increase. From a strategic standpoint, after M&As exchanges are able to expand their offer and control almost all the phases related to exchange trading. Mergers are not only aimed at improving liquidity but also at diversifying business models. Diversifying the business model permits exchanges to stabilise revenues and exploit cross selling opportunities. However, in some cases observed, mergers seem to relate more to the opportunistic goals of controlling shareholders than to clear economic and strategic needs.

Part 1

Bank Management, Innovation and Technology

1
Financial Innovation: Theoretical Issues and Empirical Evidence in Europe

F. Arnaboldi and B. Rossignoli

1. Introduction

Financial innovation has always characterized the evolution of financial activities to a varying extent, but this has become more and more evident in the past 15 years, particularly as a consequence of technological innovation and deregulation. Acceleration of speed and alterations of formats can be envisaged, with changes – sometimes radical – in the processes and organizational structures of financial firms, the creation of more and more complicated financial instruments and of secondary markets for trading and the development of products aimed at the transfer and subsequent allocation of specific risk types.

In this work empirical evidence is provided on the financial innovation introduced by domestic banks listed on Euronext (the Amsterdam, Brussels, Lisbon and Paris markets), the London Stock Exchange and Borsa Italiana over the 2005–2008 period, as inferred from the consolidated annual reports. Forty-six banks are reviewed, covering most of the respective markets in terms of total assets. Section 3 contains the conclusions and a few hints for discussion.

2. Empirical analysis of European listed banks

There is no single definition of financial innovation. For Frame and White (2002), "Financial innovation represents something that reduces costs, reduces risks or provides an improved product/service/instruments". Many authors work on the topic, and it is hard to mention all contributors to the debate. Among the others, Silber (1975, 1983),

Merton (1992), Finnerty (1992) and Llewellyn (2009), suggested different factors or functions for identifying financial innovation.

If defining financial innovation is troublesome, identifying it is even more difficult. Unlike industrial companies, where the R&D function can be clearly identified in terms both of organizational units and of costs/resources allocated to it, as well as of outputs (registered patents), innovation in a financial company can hardly be "isolated". Measures of innovation more focused on banking have been proposed (Pavitt 1984; Anderloni and Bongini 2009).

Based on the above preliminary statements, in order to check the forms and extent of financial innovation in the past few years, we started our analysis from banks' consolidated annual reports.

Five banks are members of banking groups, whose holdings are listed. To prevent any duplication resulting from the internal transfer of innovation, these were considered together with their holdings.

In the period under scrutiny, M&As took place among the listed banks, which resulted in the delisting of ten banks and into the listing of three new ones. With a view to ensuring continuity of the analysis and to collecting information, the financial statements of these ten banks were also considered, attributing the innovations conventionally to the respective banks as listed at the end of 2008. Seven further banks were delisted in the period for various reasons. They were not considered in the sample since innovation could not be clearly attributed to domestic banks primarily listed on the markets under scrutiny. Finally, 16 banks were excluded since the listed securities are other than ordinary shares. Over the period 2005–2008 the sample thus consists of 46 domestic banks compared to the 66 listed at the end of 2008 (Table A1.1 in the Appendix).

Analysis of the sample, albeit with the limitations imposed by the relatively small number of banks considered, would allow identification of any "common trends" in innovation, whatever the features of the system as a whole. The average total assets of the sample span from €280.6bn in 2005 to €415bn in 2008. In the same period, the deposits and short term funding rise from €140.6bn to €172.6bn on average. As for the costs and revenues, the cost to income ratio increases from 66.8 per cent to 70 per cent, while average return on assets (ROA) decreases from 0.8 per cent to almost zero. This picture is mainly due to bad economic results in 2008. In fact, at the end of 2007, the average cost to income ratio (CI) amounts to 62.5 per cent and ROA to 1 per cent. Banks in the sample have been negatively affected by 2008's turmoil. This is especially true for Belgian banks, which show the greatest increase in

Table 1.1   Financial figures all countries 2005–2008

Country	Number of banks (all years)	Total assets (€ thousands – avg)	Total deposits (€ thousands – avg)	CI (%)	ROA (%)
2005					
Belgium	3	521,185,500	296,017,604	58.91	0.62
Portugual	5	33,547,940	19,836,100	63.91	0.85
Netherlands	1	17,971,600	12,167,100	57.32	0.88
France	7	556,520,371	223,919,329	61.80	0.64
UK	8	647,556,923	385,496,995	100.83	0.13
Italy	22	94,691,285	48,438,618	59.77	1.11
2006					
Belgium	3	555,790,667	312,520,667	57.15	0.74
Portugual	5	37,072,841	22,912,040	63.89	0.93
Netherlands	1	18,739,301	12,244,400	57.53	1.01
France	7	632,043,586	258,033,143	58.65	0.68
UK	8	724,284,212	381,087,908	94.57	0.36
Italy	22	101,067,764	52,107,054	58.54	1.02
2007					
Belgium	3	610,446,667	330,478,000	56.58	0.65
Portugual	5	42,145,081	25,429,780	61.64	0.96
Netherlands	1	21,718,801	15,501,200	64.00	0.94
France	7	708,172,914	275,339,643	66.17	0.53
UK	8	933,732,585	469,565,422	74.92	−0.24
Italy	22	106,199,817	54,042,162	57.48	1.69
2008					
Belgium	3	366,397,667	189,715,000	89.64	−0.44
Portugual	5	45,714,601	26,966,440	69.38	−0.03
Netherlands	1	20,691,900	15,709,900	85.52	0.14
France	7	944,762,917	338,652,250	91.02	0.17
UK	8	1,139,235,655	470,113,200	67.24	−0.88
Italy	22	121,829,702	60,404,400	60.60	−0.40

Source: Bankscope.

CI in the period. In contrast, UK banks have strongly reduced their CI on average (from 100 per cent to 67.24 per cent) and Italian ones stay almost stable. On the revenues side, the situation worsened in all countries. However, if we stop at 2007, trying to separate banks' revenues trends from effects due to the financial crisis, ROA decreases only in France and the UK.

The review of the annual reports begins with R&D, which is one of the assumptions for innovation. In the financial statements of banks R&D expenses are usually not mentioned clearly and separately. Moreover, how fixed intangible assets are aggregated and enterered in balance sheets does not allow the identification of any capitalized R&D costs.

Since the size of the invested resources could not be quantified, we focus instead on qualitative issues, as inferred from the report on operations.

In non-financial companies, where R&D is a strategic asset, their reports contain, in a dedicated part, rich information on the organization, on the contents and aims of the projects and on product and project innovation.[1]

Such information is not contained in reports on the operations of banks, despite their repeated claims to focus on innovation. As mentioned above, innovation does not necessarily require R&D, at least in the approach which characterizes financial companies. Technology transfer from production sectors, the often poor inclusion of process and product innovation, as well as the lack of any requirement for patentability and, finally, the fact that the layout of financial statements does not provide for the entry of such expenses could be good reasons to account for differences in the information provided.

The first aspect concerns the existence – or not – of specific organizational units. The reports do not provide significant information, except the mention – by some banks – that product innovation is among the responsibilities of their business divisions.

This obviously does not mean that the organizational structure necessarily lacks an R&D function. In this respect, reference can be made to the findings of a survey carried out in January 2008 by the ABI Lab on innovation management in 17 Italian banks, whose branch office network covers a total market share of 62 per cent. The survey highlights that a specific organizational entity for innovation is in place in 61 per cent of cases, represented by an office (41 per cent) or a dedicated team (17 per cent). Such activity is mostly included in the tasks of the information systems function (75 per cent) or in the organization function (25 per cent). Only 33 per cent of banks provide for the allocation of a dedicated budget to R&D, in that innovation investments usually represent an item of expense for ICT (Cammino and Pellegrino 2008).

The second aspect concerns the identification of R&D content. Only few banks include in their reports, at least for one year, a specific section with the words "research and development" in the title.

A careful reading of reports, however, highlights different ways of describing R&D content. Actually, while a few banks provide a specific section on R&D, others include this same information in different parts of their reports. Hence, they do not provide entirely homogeneous and directly comparable information. This is the case, for example, for details on risk measurement and control initiatives or new product offers.

In the majority of banks, where no R&D section is included, the information is often spread throughout the text and requires readers to search for it.

These observations go beyond formal aspects of the reports to include the objective identification of innovations. A collection of all the information contained in the reports allowed identification of the possible innovations of the 46 banks under study. Consideration was given only to the initiatives for which it turned out to be feasible to identify three distinctive features: strong discontinuity, actual improvement of customer service and positive impacts on the profit and loss account. Innovations introduced to comply with legal provisions or supervision and those that imply cooperation among all banks, as in the case of the payment system, were deliberately excluded from the study. This is certainly a solution which, without any specific guidelines, grants the reader some freedom of interpretation, but in the given conditions allows us to highlight useful elements for the current analysis.

Based on this criterion, innovations were classified according to the following groups: (1) group organizational model, (2) organizational structure, (3) operating systems, (4) ICT, (5) delivery channel and (6) product. Innovative changes referring to the group structure are included in the first category (e.g. the acquisition of an asset management company or a leasing company by a banking group not yet involved in either of these activities through its subsidiaries or organizational units, or the establishment of new legally autonomous divisions). The group of innovations in the organizational structure includes innovative organizational changes which have no direct impact at group level, but imply a new structure for the individual bank. The third set includes innovations in operating systems, processes and internal controls, provided these changes are not tied to amendments in rules or regulations. The ICT category includes innovations with a primarily technological content (e.g. new voice recognition software for phone banking). Any major product focused on innovation (e.g. the introduction of a new functionality for mortgages or home banking) is included in the last group. While technological innovation can span the different groups, it is included in the fourth group only if the technology is clearly identifiable and prevalent in the concerned innovation.

The analysis of the data obtained through the above-described classification highlights a prevalence of product innovations in the four-year period in all countries. Seventy-seven per cent of the banks surveyed made innovations in their product portfolios, while the ICT was modified in 52 per cent of cases. Finally, innovations in organizational structure concern 44 per cent of banks. The above information on various type of financial innovation and their distribution per year is summarized in Figure 1.1 below.

It should be noted that the different innovation types might have different "life cycles". Product innovation, easier for competitors to imitate, may have a relatively short life cycle. It can be repeated over multiple periods, and also over a limited time horizon, like the one considered in the analysis. If existing products are substantially modified, then the

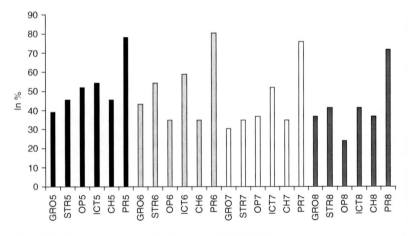

Figure 1.1   Financial innovation by year (2005–2008)

Notes:
GRO   group organizational model
STR   organizational structure
OP   operating systems
ICT   ICT
CH   delivery channel
PR   product

marginal cost of innovation is also limited. Other innovations, including those referring to organizational structure, may have a longer life cycle and may not be repeated at close time intervals. Some innovations are more recurrent when in combination with certain events, including the M&As which characterized the system from 2005 onwards. Other innovations, such as in products, may develop at all times of everyday activity.

Differences exist between countries. We compute the average number of innovations per country. Innovation has been measured by the number of times (frequency) banks innovate in the six above-mentioned areas over the four-year period. Portuguese banks can be considered as the most innovative. From 2005 to 2008 we reported on average 17 innovations out of a possible 24 (six areas of innovation in each of four years). French banks and the Dutch one innovate on average 15 times, and Belgian banks 13. The Italian and UK banks seem the less innovative in the sample with averages equal to 9.4 and 9.1 respectively. We will now compare the first and the last countries in the sample: Portugal and the UK. This result may be influenced by the degree of accuracy and detail in the information given in the annual reports. For example, Portuguese statements give a wide range of information on the banks' activity. For the scope of our analysis, areas of innovation can be easily identified. In contrast, information on innovation given in UK banks' annual reports is often vague, leading to greater difficulties in identifying it. Thus, another possible explanation of the result is that UK banks may be just as innovative as the others but do not disclose information as effectively, leading to an underestimation of their areas of innovation.

The findings seem consistent in all markets. The primary innovation for banks is always related to products. However, the gap between the number of banks which innovated in this area and those which substantially changed their ICT or organizational structure (the second-ranked innovative areas in Italy, Euronext and the UK) is higher in the UK than in the other two markets (88 per cent of UK banks innovate in the product area and 38 per cent in organizational structure). Innovation would therefore seem to be more focused on an individual area, namely products. On the other hand, in Italy especially the focus on innovation of product is not as strong, and seems more widespread among different areas.

The most innovative areas in all countries apart from the UK appear to include products and ICT, where outside influences, such as technological development or changing customer needs, would be particularly felt. Innovations in the organizational structure and in operating systems, albeit significant in number, could instead be mostly motivated by forces within the bank.

The relationship between bank innovation and some of the individual bank's features is also analysed. Bank innovation is measured by the number of times (frequency) each bank innovates in the six areas from 2005 to 2008. In addition, the size (natural log of total assets), the dynamics of profitability (percentage variation in ROA over the four-year period) and the incidence of operating costs (percentage variation in CI, also over the four-year period) are considered. These indicators, while showing a few limits, are widely adopted in the literature. Data are drawn from Bankscope, the database of the Bureau VanDijk which provides homogeneous and comparable accounting information for the different countries concerned. The following figure shows the relationship between bank size and innovation in the four-year period (Figure 1.2). The relationship is positive with R^2 equal to 28 per cent. We obtain similar results by using the natural log of total deposits as a proxy for bank size ($R^2 = 29$ per cent). Evidence for all countries seems to confirm the theory of Tufano (1989), according to which larger banks are more innovative. He found that banks promoting innovations, at

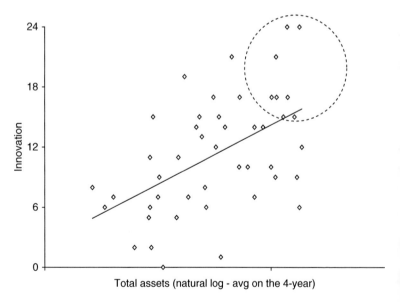

Figure 1.2 Total assets and innovation – all banks

least in the field of securities, were the strongest as well as the largest. Our result particularly holds for France where the top banks for innovation are also the largest (three banks out of six circled – Figure 1.2).

On the other hand no clear relation seems to exist between innovation, the variation in CI and the change in ROA. Moreover, testing the average level of CI and ROA in the four-year period does not lead to significant result. Finally, in general, in all the countries innovation showed a decline during the four-year period. The number of innovative events falls from 145 in 2005 to 116 in 2008. The total of 62 innovative events observed for the 16 Euronext banks in 2005 fell to 56 events in 2008. In the case of the UK, they drop from 24 to 12 for the eight banks. In Italy the decline was evident up to 2007 (from 59 to 46); however, in 2008 the number of innovative events rose to 48. The annual decrease in the number of innovations amounts to 10, 50 and 19 per cent during the four-year period. This does not correspond to a greater focus in innovation, because the number of innovation areas remained unchanged. In fact, among the Euronext countries, the differences are remarkable. In Belgium the decrease in the number of innovative events is 40 per cent. A similar situation can be envisaged in Portugal (–30 per cent) and for the single Dutch bank (–25 per cent). In contrast, French banks show a greater number of innovative events (from 21 in 2005 to 28 in 2008; +33 per cent). It has to be added that the number strongly increased from 2005 to 2006, and then stayed almost stable in 2007 and 2008 (27 and 28 innovative events). As mentioned above, one explanation could be that certain types of innovation occur "once and for all" and are not easily/necessarily repeated. Furthermore, it should be noted that starting since the last quarter of 2007 banks have been facing a deep financial crisis in place since August of the same year. This could have downsized the role of innovation within the strategies of banks, forcing them to adopt more conservative policies.

3. Conclusions

The analysis of the financial statements of a group of 46 domestic banks listed on Euronext, the London Stock Exchange and Borsa Italiana carried out in the 2005–2008 period shows first that specific organizational units in charge of R&D are not mentioned. However, the existence of an R&D function involving different organizational units cannot be excluded. In most cases, when R&D activity is described in dedicated sections of the management reports, it is combined with products, sector information, marketing policies, organizational measures and ICT.

Marketing, technological advance and the design and offering of new products could therefore be the areas that most often incorporate the R&D function.

Second, innovation seems to be mainly concentrated in the product area, in all of the six countries considered. This could be accounted for by the difference in the "life cycles" of innovations and by the different operational conditions of banks in all systems. Product innovation, which competitors can more easily imitate, has a relatively short life cycle. Other innovations, including those referring to the organizational structure or to operating systems, can hardly be replicated at short intervals and are typical of situations of significant change for the bank.

Thus the phenomenon seems to follow similar paths in all countries, albeit with their respective peculiar economic and financial differences. There are at least two possible explanations. Competition in the retail sector of the UK banking system could persuade banks to offer innovative services and products, so as to maintain and expand their existing client bases, more frequently than is the case in other countries. An analysis of UK banks' financial statements points to ongoing product innovation and the acquisition of new market shares. Such a trend can also be observed in banks listed on Euronext and Borsa Italiana, but to a lesser extent. Moreover, the reorganization resulting from certain significant aggregation processes in the Italian and French banking systems in the four-year period could have led banks in these countries to innovate more in other fields, such as the group organizational structure, operating systems and the transition to new ICT systems.

The third conclusion concerns the characteristics of more innovation-focused banks. The evidence seems to highlight that larger banks are more innovative, in all countries, especially in France. No clear relationship between innovation and cost reduction/revenue increase seems to exist.

Finally, we may wonder if the choice not to establish a specific organizational unit dedicated to R&D could be effective in the medium to long term. Perhaps a review of resource allocation, with a view to developing a true culture focused on R&D, could be profitable in terms of lower costs/higher profitability and allow banks to play a role less subject to "outside" innovations and therefore to be more proactive.

Appendix

Table A1.1 Sample composition

Listed banks on 31 December 2008	Banks belonging to listed banking groups — Innovation counted to the holding	Delisted banks following M&As included in the sample — Innovation counted to the new listed bank	Other delisted banks out of the sample — Innovation not counted	Banks in the sample over the period 2005–2008
Italian listed banks on Borsa Italiana				
Banca Carige				Banca Carige
Banca Finnat				Banca Finnat
Banca Generali				Banca Generali
Banca Ifis				Banca Ifis
Banca Intermobiliare				Banca Intermobiliare
Banca Italease				Banca Italease
Banca Monte dei Paschi di Siena				Banca Monte dei Paschi di Siena
Banca Popolare Emilia Romagna	Banco di Sardegna			Banca Popolare Emilia Romagna
Banco di Sardegna				
Banca Popolare dell'Etruria e del Lazio				Banca Popolare dell'Etruria e del Lazio
Banca Popolare di Milano				Banca Popolare di Milano
Banca Popolare di Spoleto				Banca Popolare di Spoleto
Banca Popolare di Sondrio				Banca Popolare di Sondrio
Banca Profilo				Banca Profilo
Banco di Desio e della Brianza				Banco di Desio e della Brianza
Banco Popolare	Credito Bergamasco	Banca Popolare Verona e Novara		Banco Popolare

Continued

Table A1.1   Continued

Listed banks on 31 December 2008	Banks belonging to listed banking groups Innovation counted to the holding	Delisted banks following M&As included in the sample Innovation counted to the new listed bank	Other delisted banks out of the sample Innovation not counted	Banks in the sample over the period 2005–2008
		Banca Popolare Italiana		
Credito Bergamasco				
Credito Artigiano				Credito Artigiano
Credito Valtellinese	Credito Artigiano			
Credito Emiliano				Credito Emiliano
Intesa SanPaolo		Banca Intesa		Intesa SanPaolo
		San Paolo Imi		
		Banca Fideuram		
		Banca Cr Firenze		
Mediobanca				Mediobanca
Meliorbanca				Meliorbanca
UBI Banca		Banche Popolari Unite		UBI Banca
		Banca Lombarda e Piemontese		
Unicredit		Capitalia		Unicredit
			Banca Popolare di Intra[1]	
			Banca Antonveneta[2]	
UK banks listed on London Stock Exchange				
Barclays				Barclays

Continued

Table A1.1 Continued

Listed banks on 31 December 2008	Banks belonging to listed banking groups Innovation counted to the holding	Delisted banks following M&As included in the sample Innovation counted to the new listed bank	Other delisted banks out of the sample Innovation not counted	Banks in the sample over the period 2005–2008
European Islamic Investment Bank				European Islamic Investment Bank
HBOS				HBOS
HSBC HLDGS				HSBC HLDGS
Islamic Bank of Britain				Islamic Bank of Britain
Lloyds TBS Group				Lloyds TBS Group
Royal Bank of Scotland Group Plc				Royal Bank of Scotland Group Plc
Standard Chartered				Standard Chartered
			Alliance & Leicester[3]	
			Bradford & Bingley[4]	
			Egg[5]	
			Northern Rock[6]	
Dutch banks listed on Euronext (Amsterdam)				
Van Lanschot N.V.			ABN Amro Holding	Van Lanschot N.V.
Belgian banks listed on Euronext (Brussels)				
Dexia				Dexia
Fortis				Fortis
KBC		Almancora		KBC

Continued

Table A1.1   Continued

	Banks belonging to listed banking groups	Delisted banks following M&As included in the sample	Other delisted banks out of the sample	
Listed banks on 31 December 2008	Innovation counted to the holding	Innovation counted to the new listed bank	Innovation not counted	Banks in the sample over the period 2005–2008

Portuguese banks listed on Euronext (Lisbon)

Banco BPI				Banco BPI
Banif				Banif
Banco Espirito Santo				Banco Espirito Santo
BCP				BCP
Finibanco				Finibanco

French banks listed on Euronext (Paris)[7]

Banque Tarneaud				Banque Tarneaud
BNP Paribas	Banca Nazionale del Lavoro			BNP Paribas
Banque de la Réunion				Banque de la Réunion
CIC				CIC
Crédit Agricole				Crédit Agricole
Natexis BQ. Popul	Banque de la Savoie			Natexis BQ. Popul
Banque de la Savoie				
Société Générale				Société Générale

[1] Acquired by Veneto Banca. Excluded since Veneto Banca is not listed.
[2] Acquired by ABN Amro. Excluded since ABN Amro has been delisted.
[3] Acquired by Santander which is a Spanish bank.
[4] Acquired by Alliance & Leicester.
[5] Acquired by Prudential, which is an insurance company.
[6] Delisted and nationalized.
[7] 16 Caisses Regionales de Crédit Agricole Mutuel have been excluded. They do not list ordinary shares but Certificates Coopératifs d'Investissement (CCI).

Note

1. See, by way of example, the financial statements of Fiat Group, Enel and Bayer.

References

ABI Lab (2008) "Scenario e trend di mercato ICT per il settore bancario" Italy, March.

Anderloni, L., and Bongini, P. (2009) "Is financial innovation still a relevant issue?" In Anderloni L., Llewellyn, D.T., and Schmidt, R. (eds) *Financial innovation in retail and corporate banking*, Edward Elgar, Cheltenham.

Cammino, B., and Pellegrino, M. (2008) "Il nuovo che avanza" *Bancaforte* 5, ABI, Italy.

Finnerty, J.D. (1992) "An overview of corporate securities innovation" *Journal of applied corporate finance* 4 (4): 23–39.

Frame, W.S., and White, L.J. (2002) "Empirical Studies of Financial Innovation: Lots of Talk, Little Action?" *FRB of Atlanta Working Paper* 2002–12.

Llewellyn, D.T. (2009) "Financial innovation and the economics of banking and the financial system" In Anderloni, L., Llewellyn, D.T., and Schmidt R. (eds) *Financial innovation in retail and corporate banking*, Edward Elgar, Cheltenham.

Merton, R. (1992) "Financial innovation and economic performance" *Journal of applied corporate finance* 4 (4) 12–22.

Pavitt, K. (1984) "Sectoral patterns of technical change: towards a taxonomy and a theory" *Research Policy* 13, 343–373.

Silber, W. (1975) *Financial Innovation* Lexington Books, MA, USA.

Silber, W. (1983) "The process of financial innovation" *American Economic Review* 73, 89–95.

Tufano, P. (1989) "Financial innovation and first mover advantages" *Journal of financial economics* XXV, 213–240.

2
A New Appraisal of the Structure of European Banking Systems

Cristina Ruza, Rebeca de Juan and Marta de la Cuesta González

1. Introduction

Over the last few years, the accession of new candidates to the European Union has posed an additional difficulty for the process of convergence towards a single European financial system. The official accession candidates, most of them with underdeveloped financial systems, have made some reforms in order to become more market orientated.

The aim of this chapter is to analyse empirically the process of convergence of the new EU members towards the European Union countries (EU-15 countries) in financial terms during the period 1999–2007.

The main results are as follows: first, the new EU Member States were close to a banking-based structure in both 2004 and 2007, even though there were significant cross-country differences, and second, the empirical results unambiguously point out the existence of financial convergence among European banking sectors in terms of the credit institutions assets, number of institutions, number of branches and number of employees. However, we found that the speed of convergence gradually diminished after 2004.

The rest of the chapter is organized as follows. Section 2 introduces the data and testing strategies, Section 3 presents the main empirical results and Section 4 contains some concluding remarks.

2. Data and testing strategies

Studies like Demirgüç-Kunt and Levine (1999), in order to analyse financial structures, classified countries as either market-based or bank-based by constructing a conglomerate index of financial structure based on measures of size, activity and efficiency. In this paper we use cluster analysis because it allows us to specify different groups of countries in terms of their financial structure.[1]

The analysis will proceed as follows. First of all, we will identify which of the EU-15 countries belong to each of the financial structures considered – bank-based or market-based – by applying cluster analysis. In the second stage, we apply panel data techniques to ascertain the primary determinants of the observed financial structure in the EU-15 countries. In the third stage, we apply these estimated coefficients to the new EU Member States, in order to obtain benchmarks for the efficiency of the structure of their financial systems. A comparison of benchmarks and the actual values provides us with a basis for evaluating the state of development of these countries and the degree of convergence towards a single European financial system across time.[2]

To estimate the main determinants for financial development for each of the cluster groups, an empirical form has to provide to the financial structure of each country. Thus, we specify the financial structure per country in each year as a dynamic equation of the form:

$$y_{it} = \sum_{k=1}^{q} \alpha_k y_{i(t-k)} + \beta' x_{it} + \gamma_t + \eta_i + v_{it} \qquad (1)$$

$$(t=q+1, \dots \dots, T;\ i=1, \dots \dots, N)$$

where y_{it} represents the financial structure per country i at year t, the vector x_{it} contains the set of explanatory variables, β indicates the parameters to be estimated and q is the maximum lag in the model. The specification also contains a time effect γ_t that is common to all the countries, a fixed but unobservable first-specific effect η_i and an error term v_{it} that is assumed to be serially uncorrelated with zero mean. We estimate the Eq. (1) using the "system" generalized method of moments (GMM).

Once the α and β parameters are estimated for the two clusters, we replace them with their estimates in Eq. (1) to obtain the benchmarks for the efficient structure of the new EU Member States' banking systems. Then, we compare these benchmarks to the actual data to measure their relative efficiency and appraise their banking system convergence across time.

In order to measure banking system development we would consider that banking assets may be housed in few or many institutions, with or without a large branch network and with a higher or lower labour force intensity. So, we consider four alternative variables to measure banking system development: (i) total assets of credit institutions (*Assets*), (ii) number of credit institutions (*Banks*), (iii) number of branches of credit institutions (*Branches*) and (iv) number of employees of credit institutions (*Employees*).

For capturing the cross-country differences (components of $x$it) that may affect the demand for financial services we consider the following set of variables: (a) number of inhabitants (*Population*), (b) population density (*Density*), (c) gross domestic product (*GDP*) and (d) ratio of gross savings to GDP (*GSR*).

3. Empirical results

3.1. Cluster analysis

Now we apply cluster analysis[3] in order to identify countries with similar financial structures. We carry out this analysis for the EU-15 countries for the year 2004 because in that year the ten new Member States joined the EU.[4] The levels of banking intermediation and stock market capitalization are used to group the countries with highly similar financial structure.

The method that we use to form clusters is *agglomerative hierarchical clustering*,[5] using as criteria the *average linkage between groups method* and the *centroid method* in a two-dimensional space defined by the following variables: (1) the ratio of total assets of credit institutions (henceforth CIs[6]) to GDP and (2) the ratio of stock market capitalization to GDP (see the dendogram in Figure 2.1).

Following the Duda and Hart (1973) index (Table 2.1) indicates that the third-group solution is the most distinct from this hierarchical cluster analysis. One cluster is formed by 11 countries (Belgium, Denmark, Germany, Greece, Spain, France, Italy, Austria, Portugal, Finland and Sweden), the second cluster is formed by two countries (the UK and Netherlands) and the third by one isolated country (Ireland).

3.2. Estimation of banking system development

In this section we present the empirical results for the model explained above.

Table 2.2 reports the results of the panel data estimations corresponding to the first cluster formed by the EU-11 countries – the more bank-dominated ones – over the period 1999–2007. The number of observations is 99. The same structure is replicated in Table 2.3, where the results correspond to the EU-2 cluster of two more market-oriented countries. Almost all coefficients for the set of explanatory variables are significant and show plausible signs.[7]

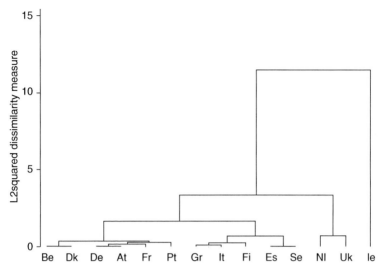

Figure 2.1 Dendogram using average linkage
Source: Own estimations.

Table 2.1 Duda & Hart Index

Number of clusters	Duda/Hart	
	Je(2)/Je(1)	pseudo T-squared
1	0.0316	398.07
2	0.5077	11.64
3	0.5529	8.89
4	0.3147	19.60
5	0.0000	–
6	0.1993	12.05
7	0.4110	5.73
8	0.4706	2.25
9	0.1982	4.05
10	0.1505	5.64

Source: Own estimations.

Table 2.2   Panel data estimations for the EU-11

Estimation procedure[1]: System GMM

	Dependent variables[2]			
Variables	**Assets[3]**	**Banks**	**Branches[3]**	**Employees[3]**
y_{it-1}	1.50 (13.62)	1.21 (9.71)	0.37 (3.00)	0.71 (5.87)
y_{it-2}	−0.48 (−3.81)	−0.32 (−3.04)	0.56 (0.94)	0.01 (0.05)
y_{it-3}			0.23 (0.4)	0.20 (1.11)
Population	−22.84 (−2.56)	1.87 (1.71)	−0.22 (−1.32)	−1.31 (−1.34)
Density	−1.95 (−0.99)	−0.05 (−0.20)	−0.14 (−5.64)	0.38 (2.16)
Density[2]				−0.001 (−2.89)
GDP	0.99 (2.68)	0.02 (0.77)	0.017 (3.34)	0.06 (3.50)
GSR	10.71 (2.11)	3.72 (2.77)	0.13 (0.84)	0.087 (0.15)
Constant		−79.85 (−2.09)		
Statistics				
Sargan test[4] (degrees of freedom)	54.79 (32)	36.15 (32)	47.8 (28)	37.44 (28)

Notes:
Number of countries: 11.
Sample period: 1999–2007.
Number of observations: 99.
[1] For the GMM method in this context see Arellano and Bover (1995) and Blundell and Bond (1998).
[2] t-ratios in brackets.
[3] Time dummies are included in the equation.
[4] The Sargan statistic is a test of the over-identifying restrictions, asymptotically distributed as χ_j^2 under the null, where j is the number of over-identifying restrictions as indicated in parenthesis.

Source: Own estimations.

Table 2.3 Panel data estimations for the EU-2

Estimation procedure[1]: System GMM

Variables	Dependent variables[2]			
	Assets[3]	Banks[3]	Branches[3]	Employees[3]
y_{it-1}	0.68 (2.58)	1.03 (26.24)	0.35 (2.82)	0.13 (0.51)
y_{it-2}	−0.93 (−2.97)		0.49 (3.20)	0.70 (1.67)
y_{it-3}	−0.69 (−1.52)			
Population	3714.49 (9.15)	−1.85 (−2.30)	0.04 (1.02)	−66.12 (−3.01)
Density	−54.07 (−1.45)	−0.57 (−2.47)	−0.014 (−3.33)	
Area				13.21 (3.92)
GDP	1.05 (0.35)	0.06 (6.52)	0.00012 (0.11)	0.21 (1.65)
GSR	117.35 (2.68)	6.27 (2.18)	0.18 (3.08)	0.38 (0.19)
Constant				425.09 (3.06)
Statistics[4]				
m_2		−1.28		
m_3			−1.41	
Sargan test[5]	0.76			4.34
(degrees of freedom)	(1)			(11)

Notes:
Number of countries: 2.
Sample period: 1999–2007.
Number of observations: 18.
[1] For the GMM method in this context see Arellano and Bover (1995) and Blundell and Bond (1998).
[2] t-ratios in brackets.
[3] Time dummies are included in the equation.
[4] m_2 and m_3 are a test for second-order and third-order serial correlation, respectively, in the first difference residuals, asymptotically distributes as N(0,1) under the null of no serial correlation.
[5] The Sargan statistic is a test of the over-identifying restrictions, asymptotically distributed as χ_j^2 under the null, where j is the number of over-identifying restrictions as indicated in parenthesis.

Source: Own estimations.

After estimating the α and β coefficients for the two clusters considered, the benchmark values for the new EU Member States are obtained by replacing the parameters with the estimated coefficients in Eq. (1). The results are presented in Table 2.4, where the *"Actual"* column shows the real value of the variables in the new EU candidates, while *"Benchmark"* reflects both the results of applying the estimated coefficients from Tables 2.2 (EU-11) and 2.3 (EU-2), respectively, to the actual data values in 2004. These benchmarks show how the banking structure would have been, if the banking sector of the new EU Member States had followed the general pattern of either the EU-11 or the EU-2 groups. Table 2.5 follows the same structure and presents the results obtained by the end of 2007.

These empirical results remarks that the new EU Members States were close to a banking-based structure in both 2004 and 2007.

A plausible explanation for this result comes from the profound transition process, which involved fundamental institutional and structural changes that have dramatically turned former planned economies to market economies.

Another factor influencing this bank-dominant structure could be divergences in countries' legal system traditions (following the line of though of La Porta et al. 1997).[8] If we look at the new EU Member States, we can see that they carried out improvements in the domestic legal system during the 1990s that considerably reduced credit risk, thereby promoting the credit supply.[9]

In general terms, the relative size of the new EU Member States credit institutions still lags behind the most developed financial systems in the EU, but they are closer to the levels of the EU-11 than to the whole EU average.[10] Therefore, the two-step procedure of first classifying EU-15 countries and thereafter estimating the model had proved to be useful because we are closer to appreciating the real picture of the new EU candidates.

Table 2.6 shows the main empirical findings in terms of convergence.

In making these findings, we have calculated the absolute deviation from actual values to benchmarks, and defined a convergence ratio as follows:

$$Convergence\ Ratio = 1 - abs\left(\frac{Benchmark - Actual}{Actual}\right) \qquad (2)$$

where it can take the following values:

$\begin{cases} \\ \\ \\ \end{cases}$
1   Perfect convergence (Benchmark = Actual)
0   The current deviation equals 100 per cent of Actual value
−1   The current deviation is more than 100 per cent of Actual value

Table 2.4 Benchmarks for the banking structure (by the end of 2004)

Country	Assets (€ millions)			Banks			Branches			Employees		
	Actual	Benchmark¹		Actual	Benchmark¹		Actual	Benchmark¹		Actual	Benchmark¹	
		EU-11	EU-2		EU-11	EU-2		EU-11	EU-2		EU-11	EU-2
Czech Republic	87,104	78,812	–41,170	70	82	145	1785	1807	1454	38,666	37,187	34,348
Estonia	8537	7118	2348	9	9	140	203	214	202	4455	3878	4234
Latvia	11,167	9347	3139	23	18	141	583	635	513	9655	8049	8080
Lithuania	8553	7232	8484	74	45	148	152	86	121	7266	7223	7946
Hungary	64,970	61,066	4050	217	196	277	2987	3298	2537	35,558	32,547	30,185
Poland	141,571	111,822	13,809	744	634	667	8301	9671	7280	150,037	145,062	135,447
Slovenia	24,462	22,769	–11,250	24	35	146	706	722	637	11,602	10,851	10,411
Slovakia	30,834	24,135	–4505	21	18	90	1113	1060	892	19,819	18,299	16,224

Note: ¹ These benchmarks have been rounded to the nearest lower integer.

Source: Own estimations.

Table 2.5 Benchmarks for the banking structure (by the end of 2007)

Country	Assets (€ millions)			Banks			Branches			Employees		
	Actual	Benchmark[1] EU-11	EU-2	Actual	Benchmark[1] EU-11	EU-2	Actual	Benchmark[1] EU-11	EU-2	Actual	Benchmark[1] EU-11	EU-2
Czech Republic	140,004	123,819	−41,330	56	79	130	1862	1958	1582	40,037	34,997	32,296
Estonia	20,603	17,462	−478	15	10	123	266	248	231	6319	4986	5199
Latvia	30,816	26,615	2053	31	15	118	682	654	529	12,826	10,323	9983
Lithuania	23,817	19,748	5526	80	51	143	324	190	214	10,303	7668	7538
Hungary	108,504	102,817	19,971	206	189	254	3387	3473	2687	41,905	35,415	32,390
Poland	236,008	205,601	17,235	718	704	744	11,607	11,336	8796	173,955	146,699	133,872
Slovenia	43,493	37,916	−15,590	27	44	139	711	699	619	12,051	10,872	10,320
Slovakia	50,318	44,374	−11,020	26	32	98	1169	1192	999	19,779	18,129	17,125

Source: Own estimations.

Note: [1] These benchmarks have been rounded to the nearest lower integer.

Table 2.6 Convergence ratios

Country	Model I Credit Institutions' Assets (Benchmark-Actual)[1] 2004	2007	Convergence Ratio 2004	2007	Model II Number of Credit Institutions' (Benchmark-Actual)[1] 2004	2007	Convergence Ratio 2004	2007	Model III Number of Branches (Benchmark-Actual)[1] 2004	2007	Convergence Ratio 2004	2007	Model IV Number of Employees (Benchmark-Actual)[1] 2004	2007	Convergence Ratio 2004	2007
Czech Republic	-8292	-16,185	0.90	0.88	12	23	0.82	0.58	22	96	0.99	0.95	-1,479	-5,040	0.96	0.87
Estonia	-1419	-3141	0.83	0.85	0	-5	1.00	0.67	11	-18	0.95	0.93	-577	-1,333	0.87	0.79
Latvia	-1820	-4201	0.84	0.86	-5	-16	0.80	0.50	52	-28	0.91	0.96	-1,606	-2,503	0.83	0.80
Lithuania	-1321	-4069	0.84	0.83	-29	-29	0.61	0.64	-66	-134	0.56	0.59	-43	-2,635	0.99	0.74
Hungary	-3904	-5687	0.94	0.95	-21	-17	0.90	0.92	311	86	0.90	0.97	-3,011	-6,490	0.92	0.85
Poland	-29,749	-30,407	0.79	0.87	-110	-14	0.85	0.98	1,370	-271	0.83	0.98	-4,975	-27,256	0.97	0.84
Slovenia	-1693	-5577	0.93	0.87	11	17	0.52	0.37	16	-12	0.98	0.98	-751	-1,179	0.94	0.90
Slovakia	-6699	-5944	0.78	0.88	-3	6	0.84	0.77	-53	23	0.95	0.98	-1,520	-1,650	0.92	0.92

Note: [1] Results have been rounded to the nearest lower integer.
Source: Own estimations.

The ratio can be interpreted as means of "convergence degree" between the EU countries and the new candidates. It measures the percentage change that is required in the dependent variable to achieve convergence to the benchmark. The ratios are calculated at two points in time corresponding to the year when the new Member States joined the EU, and the last year for which data is available, in order to appraise the convergence process across time. The convergence ratios are shown in Table 2.6.

3.2.1. Model I. Credit institutions' assets

We begin the discussion with credit institutions' assets. The size of banking systems in the new EU Member States at the two points in time considered is relatively high compared to the benchmark estimated, even though the position is quite close to that reflected in the convergence ratios.

These facts are the result of the deep process of convergence that took place before 2004 and required profound reform of the banking system in particular and the financial system as a whole.[11] During this period two main types of event occurred: (1) the entry of a high number of foreign banks and foreign direct investors into the banking system[12] and (2) numerous mergers and acquisitions among banking institutions, prompted by the existence of potential profitable growth opportunities, which were taken up by foreign institutions.

During the next period – from 2004 until 2007 – the process of convergence continued at the almost same pace, considering that the whole EU during this period had gone through a process of great expansion of the banking systems as well.

3.2.2. Model II. Number of CIs per country

On the whole it can be appreciated that the new EU Member States were closer to the estimated benchmarks in 2004 than at the end of the period analysed. This can be explained by considering the great efforts made for EU convergence carried out before 2004 in order to meet and comply with all the EU requirements. Afterwards, convergence efforts continued but at a relatively slow pace.

The overall picture for the new EU Member States was that the number of banks has declined due to consolidation or exit, mainly of domestically owned banks. However, in terms of distance the new EU candidates have gradually approximated to EU standards, but there is still further scope for restructuring in the credit institutions sector.

In parallel, the general tendency of the EU-11 credit institutions was to respond to structural changes and increased levels of competition by consolidating their activities in order to increase in size and scope.

Overall, two factors – the enormous effort of the new EU candidates to consolidate their banking system and the second force of EU-15 institutions becoming engaged in a wave of M&A processes – were acting in opposite directions.

3.2.3. Model III. Number of branches of CIs per country

The results presented in Table 2.6 also depict the convergence process in terms of the number of branches. Almost all new EU Member States showed a completely different situation in 2004 and 2007 in terms of sign.

The prevailing situation by the end of 2004 was that of a lower branch intensity as compared to the EU-11, whereas the picture by the end of 2007 was almost the opposite.

Nevertheless, what can be argued is that at these two points in time the position of the new EU candidates was very close to the benchmark as is shown in the convergence ratio column, with levels higher than 0.9 in almost all cases in both 2004 and 2007.

Two different forces had jointly been operating: on the one hand, the efforts of new EU Member States to increase the network of CIs branches across the territory, mainly as a result of the prevailing model of universal banking and a major focus on retail banking, which by its nature is more branch intensive than wholesale banking, and on the other hand, the consolidation process that took place among the EU-15 countries reduced the overall number of branches.[13]

Taking into consideration the dimensions of the countries, the number of bank branches relative to the size of population does not suggest that the new EU candidates were "over-banked".[14]

3.2.4. Model IV. Number of employees of CIs per country

Table 2.6 summarizes the situation of CIs in terms of the number of employees. In both 2004 and 2007 the situation reveals that new EU Member States' banks were employing more people than EU-11 banks in order to manage the same amount of assets.

What we demonstrate is that this excess capacity was lower in 2004 than in 2007, so the reforms that had taken place between these years had been in the right direction for fostering labour productivity at the beginning of the period analysed, while afterwards it appears that the pace of structural reforms had diminished.

4. Concluding remarks

The general aim of this study has been to characterize the existing relationship of banking structures in the EU-15 members and then apply this characterization to develop efficiency benchmarks for the new EU candidates.

The main empirical results are the following:

1. Overall, the new EU Members States are close to a banking-based structure in both 2004 and 2007, even though there are significant cross-country differences.
2. The relatively high level of banking assets in the new EU Member States can be explained by an exponential growth in lending activity, which has led to a situation of highly leveraged institutions; this also occurred across the EU countries for the period analysed.
3. In general terms, the number of credit institutions in the new EU Member States is still larger, so there is scope for further consolidation within the banking system in order to improve their efficiency.
4. Considering the greater convergence in terms of the number of branches we can argue that the new candidates are well advanced in translating the demand for payment services into a supply of branches, because the infrastructure of the payment system already existed under the previous regime of central planning. However, more advances are required in terms of sophisticated investment services for more customers with more specialized demands. The key segments for development of the banking sector in the new EU Member States will be retail banking, insurance banking and lending to small and medium-sized businesses, as these areas allow best use of existing branch networks.
5. In terms of numbers of employees, the factors behind the lower labour productivity in the banking sector in the new EU Member States can be partially attributed to higher interest rates and overheads costs, caused by over-staffing and a low application of modern technology in these countries. However, some progress had already been made during the transition process.[15]

Therefore, the results unambiguously point to the existence of financial convergence among the European banking sectors, even though the speed of convergence gradually diminished after 2004. However, after 2005 this situation was partially reversed and foreign investors were more cautious about the convergence process and were paying more attention to the credit quality standards of investment opportunities.

In general terms the empirical findings of this study are in line with Jaffee and Levonian's (2001) study, which reveals that the greatest convergence of banking institutions occurred in Central and Eastern Europe and the Baltic States. Even though we have presented evidence supporting the idea that the new European Member States had made substantial progress catching up with the EU-15 in financial terms, we should bear in mind that the convergence process has not been concluded, since there also appears to be further scope for structural reforms in the financial sector.

Notes

1. The two main data sources used in this paper are provided by the European Central Bank (report on EU Banking Structure) and by Eurostat. As a complementary source, we have also used the Annual Reports of the EU New Member States provided by the Central Banks of each of these countries. The data cover the EU-25 countries, consisting of EU-15 countries and EU-10 new Members States. The data refer to the period 1999–2007.
2. Aghion et al. (2005) showed evidence that financial development helps an economy converge faster, but that there is no effect on steady-state growth.
3. See Chatfield and Collins (1980) and Aldenderfer and Blashfield (1984) for a more detailed explanation,
4. It is important to remark that we have dropped Luxembourg from the sample due to the fact that it serves as an international banking centre and presents a high percentage of total banking assets to its low GDP. Thus, it can not be compared with the financial structure of the other countries analysed.
5. See the chapter on cluster analysis in the STATA 10.0 manual.
6. CIs are banks, savings banks and loan undertakings (cooperative banks).
7. The Sargan tests of overidentifying restrictions give support to these specifications. Residual time autocorrelation is as expected in a first differences estimation that is obtained by transforming a model with uncorrelated disturbances in levels.
8. In ECB (2008), the chart on page 29 depicted the legal efficiency ratio for the set of EU Member States.
9. For instance, the figures show that in terms of GDP, bank assets in the EU-15 reached more than 200 per cent in 2004 (an increase of 17 per cent compared with 1995), whereas for the new EU candidates the ratio reached 85 per cent in 2004, representing an increase of 27 per cent since 1995, so there is still room for further banking development in the latter countries.
10. In Hagen and Dinger's (2005) study they compared various measures of the size of the CEE banking sectors with those of several "old" European countries and they found that traditional measures tend to produce downward biased results when applied to transition economies. Instead of GDP-based measures they related the banking size to financial wealth.
11. As we have previously mentioned, in 2004 these countries were committed to comply with the Athens Treaty.

12. An important percentage of many EU banks' revenues comes from their operation in the Eastern European countries, especially banks from Germany, France and Austria. Indeed, in the last named country loans to the Central and Eastern countries represents around 70 per cent of GDP. The picture in the Baltic States is that their banks are far more dependant on the Swedish banking system.
13. CIs in the EU countries had evolved in favour of more specialized financial activities which required a less intensive branch structure and technological development.
14. See also the findings in Riess et al. (2002).
15. See Boning et al. (2005) and Fries and Tacit (2005).

References

Aghion, P., Howitt, P., and Mayer-Foulkes, D. (2005) "The Effect of Financial Development on Convergence: Theory and Evidence", *Quarterly Journal of Economics*, 120 (1), 173–222.

Aldenderfer, M.S., and Blashfield, R.K. (1984) *Cluster Analysis* (Sage, New York).

Arellano, M., and Bover, O. (1995) "Another Look at the Instrumental Variable Estimation of Error-Components Models," *Journal of Econometrics*, 68, 29–52.

Blundell, R., and Bond, S. (1998) "Initial Conditions and Moment Restrictions in Dynamic Panel Data Models," *Journal of Econometrics*, 87 (1) 115–143.

Boning, J.P., Hasan, I., and Wachtel, P. (2005) "Bank performance, efficiency and ownership in transition countries", *Journal of Banking and Finance*, 29, 31–53.

Chatfield, C., and Collins, A.J. (1980) *Introduction to Multivariate Analysis* (Chapman and Hall, London).

Demirgüç-Kunt, A., and Levine, R. (1999) *Bank-Based and Market-Based Financial Systems: Cross-Country Comparisons*, Policy Research Working Paper Series, The World Bank, 2143, 1–72.

Duda, R.O., and Hart, P.E. (1973) *Pattern Classification and Scene Analysis* (John Wiley & Sons, New York).

European Central Bank (2009) *Financial Integration in Europe*, April, 1–106.

Fries, S., and Tacit, A. (2005) "Cost efficiency of banks in transition: Evidence from 289 banks in 15 post-communist countries", *Journal of Banking and Finance*, 29, 55–81.

Hagen, J., and Dinger, V. (2005) *Banking Sector (under?) development in Central and Eastern Europe*, Working Paper B06, ZEI Centre for European Integration Studies, 58.

Jaffee, D., and Levonian, M. (2001) "The structure of banking systems in developed and transition economies", *European Financial Management*, 7 (2), 161–181.

LaPorta, R., Lopez de Silanes, F., Shleifer, A., and Vishny, R.W. (1997) "Legal determinants of external Finance", *Journal of Finance*, 52, 1131–1150.

Riess, A., Wagenvoort, R., and Zajc, P. (2002) "Practice makes perfect. A review of banking in Central and Eastern Europe", *EIB Papers*, 7 (1), 31–53.

3
The Performance of Intellectual Capital and Banking: some Empirical Evidence from the European Banking System

Gimede Gigante and Daniele Previati

1. Aims and structure of the study

The aim of this study is to measure the intellectual capital performance of European market banks. Although physical capital is essential for banks to operate, it is intellectual capital that determines the quality of services provided to customers. As an explanatory study, ours also employs an international cross-analysis to investigate the efficiencies of banks in utilizing their intellectual capital. After an in-depth analysis of the Italian banking market, we analyse the following countries and their respective banking systems: Germany, Spain and Italy for Central Europe; Finland, Sweden, Denmark and Norway for Northern Europe and Bulgaria, Poland, the Czech Republic, Hungary, Ukraine and Slovenia for Eastern Europe. The object is to investigate the impact of IC (through the VAIC coefficient described below and its components) on banking performances using a parametric model. A non-parametric model is also engaged in the second part of the study.

2. Review of the literature

Adopted from Roos, et al. (1997), intellectual capital (IC) is the combination of human and structural (particularly relational) resources in an organization. In recent years companies have needed to merge investment decisions concerning physical and financial assets with those concerning intellectual resources.

Human capital, according to Bontis et al. (2000), is the collection of intangible resources that are implanted in individual members of an organization. These resources can be of three main types: competencies (including skills and know-how), attitude (motivation and leadership qualities of the top management), intellectual agility (the ability of organizational members to be "quick on their intellectual feet"), innovation and entrepreneurship (the ability to adapt and cross-fertilize, etc.). Similarly, Hudson (1993) defines human capital as the combination of genetic inheritance, education, experience and attitudes about life and business. *Structural capital* is "... everything that remains in the company after 5 o'clock," according to a definition by Leif Edvinsson et al. (1997). It is the knowledge that stays within a firm after the working day has ended. It is comprised of organizational routines, procedures, systems, cultures, databases, etc. Structural capital can further be divided into relational capital (regarding external actors such as suppliers, customers, allies, local communities, government, shareholders, etc.), organization (including structure, culture, routines and processes) and renewal and development (all projects for the future, including new plant, new products, etc.).

3. Methodology

3.1. Model: Value Added Intellectual Coefficient (VAIC)

The Value Added Intellectual Coefficient (VAIC), developed by Ante Pulic (see Pulic 1997), is an analytical tool for measuring the performance of a company. VAIC measures the total value creation efficiency in a company. The subordinate concept of VAIC, intellectual capital efficiency (ICE) describes the efficient use of intellectual capital within a company. This method is built on the premise that value creation is derived from two primary resource bases: physical capital resources and intellectual capital resources. Actually, VAIC indicates the total efficiency of value created from all resources employed, and ICE reflects the efficiency of value created by the intellectual capital employed. The better a company's resources are utilized, the higher its value creation efficiency will be. The execution of this method is quite simple. Data needed for the calculation can be found in the official financial statements of the firms analysed. As already mentioned, the method is based on two resources: capital employed (CE) and intellectual capital (IC). The former consists of equity, the accumulation of profit-adjusting entries and liabilities with interest. The latter consists of human and structural capital (defined this way in the context of VAIC). The basic proposition is that the higher the VAIC and ICE, the better management has utilized the existing potential of the resources employed in creating value.

The formulas for an evaluation of components of the model are as follows.

$$\text{Value Added (VA)} = \text{Output-Input} \tag{1}$$

Where Output = Gross Income, Input = Operating Expenses (excluding personal costs).

$$\text{Human Capital (HC)} = \text{Personnel Cost} \tag{2}$$

Where Human Capital is viewed as an investment and consider the total expenditure on employees.

$$\text{Capital Employed (CE)} = \text{Physical Capital} + \text{Financial Capital)}$$
$$= \text{Total Assets} - \text{Intangible Assets} \tag{3}$$

$$\text{Structural Capital (SC)} = \text{VA} - \text{HC} \tag{4}$$

Where SC can be considered as an appropriate proxy for structural capital, a result of human capital's past performance.

$$\text{Human Capital Efficiency (HCE)} = \text{VA} \div \text{HC} \tag{5}$$

$$\text{Structural Capital Efficiency (SCE)} = \text{SC} \div \text{VA} \tag{6}$$

Intellectual Capital Efficiency (ICE) is obtained by adding up the partial efficiencies of human and structural capital:

$$\text{ICE} = \text{HCE} + \text{SCE} \tag{7}$$

Intellectual capital cannot create value alone. Therefore, we need information about capital employed efficiency, which can be calculated in the following manner:

$$\text{CEE} = \text{VA} / \text{CE} \tag{8}$$

Where CEE is determined as capital employed efficiency coefficient and CE is determined as book value of the net assets for a company. In order to enable comparison of overall value creation efficiency, all three indicators need to be added up:

Value Added Intellectual Coefficient
$$\text{(VAIC)} = \text{HCE} + \text{CEE} + \text{SCE} \tag{9}$$

3.2. Parametric regression

3.2.1. *Research hypothesis*

Using VAIC as a measure for corporate intellectual ability, the following hypothesis can be posted:

> ✓ *H1a: Companies with greater IC tend to have greater ratios of market/ book value, ceteris paribus.*

VAIC is also an aggregate measure of corporate intellectual ability: if investors place different values in the three components of VAIC described in Eq. (9), the model using the three components of VAIC will have greater explanatory power than the model using just the aggregate measure. Therefore:

> ✓ *H2-1a: Companies with greater physical capital efficiency tend to have greater market/book value ratios, ceteris paribus.*

> ✓ *H2-2a: Companies with greater human capital efficiency tend to have higher market/book value ratios, ceteris paribus.*

> ✓ *H2-3a: Companies with greater proportions of structural capital in the creation of added value tend to have higher market/book value ratios, ceteris paribus.*

In addition to the investigations relating intellectual capital to firms' values, we explore the relationship between intellectual capital and firms' financial performance, and whether intellectual capital may be indicative of firms' future financial performances:

> ✓ *H3-1a: Companies with greater IC tend to have better financial performances contemporaneously, ceteris paribus.*

> ✓ *H3-2a: Companies with greater proportions of CEE, HCE and SCE tend to have better financial performances in the following years, ceteris paribus.*

3.2.2. *Regression Models*

We examine the relationship between market/book value (M/B) and the aggregate measure of intellectual capital VAIC and its three major components: SCE, CEE and HCE.

$$M/B_{it} = \alpha_0 + \alpha_1 \, VAIC_{it} + \varepsilon_{it} \tag{10}$$

$$M/B_{it} = \alpha_0 + \alpha_1 \, CEE_{it} + \alpha_2 \, HCE_{it} + \alpha_3 \, SCE_{it} + \varepsilon_{it} \tag{11}$$

In addition to the dependent variable market/book value, similarly to some other studies (e.g. Muhammad and Ismail (2009), we investigate whether intellectual capital is associated with firms' financial performance and whether it can be a leading indicator for firms' future performance. The dependent variables are: ROAA, ROAE, EP, CI Ratios and Pre-Tax Operational Income.

3.2.3. Variable definitions

a) Independent variables are the VAIC and its individual components (CEE, HCE and SCE).

Determination of the VAIC and its components is calculated from data retrieved from Bankscope/Amadeus and OSIRIS.

Value added represented in Eq. (1) can be recalculated starting from the banks' accounts as follows:

$$VA = TOI - TOE + PE \tag{1a}$$

Where (TOI) is Total Operating Income, (TOE) Total Operating Expense and PE Personnel Expenses in particular:

$$
\begin{aligned}
TOI = {} & \text{Interest Income} - \text{Interest Expense} = \text{Net Interest} \\
& \text{Revenue} + \text{Net Commission Revenue} + \text{Net Trading} \\
& \text{Revenue} + \text{Other Operating Income}
\end{aligned} \tag{1b}
$$

$$
\begin{aligned}
TOE = {} & \text{Personnel Expenses} + \text{Other Admin. Expenses} + \text{Other} \\
& \text{Operating Expenses} + \text{Loan Loss Provisions}
\end{aligned} \tag{1c}
$$

Value added is a totally objective indicator of business success, and it shows the ability of a company to create value. After VA has been calculated, the computation of the resource efficiency (intellectual and financial capital) is a matter of simple mathematical calculation. All the expenditures for employees are embraced in human (rather than structural) capital. What is new about this concept is that salaries and wages are no longer included as INPUT and HC of Eq. (2) is equal to the sum of total salaries, wages and other expenses for personnel taken from the evidence of balance sheets.

b) Dependent variables:

(b1) Market/book value ratios (M/B).

$$M/B = \text{market value/book value of the common stock.} \tag{12}$$

Market value of common stocks = number of shares outstanding stock price at the end of the year.

(b2) Financial performances:

$$ROAE = NET\ INCOME/\ EQUITY\ AVRG*100 \tag{13}$$

ROAE (return on average equity) is an adjusted version of the return on equity (ROE) measure of company profitability, in which the denominator, "shareholders' equity", is changed to "average shareholders' equity".

$$ROAA = NET\ INCOME/TOTAL\ ASSETS*100 \tag{14}$$

ROAA (return on average assets) is a measure of profits relative to size that is most commonly used in analysing banks and finance companies.

$$EP = PRE\text{-}TAX\ INCOME/No\ of\ EMPLOYEES \tag{15}$$

EP (employees' productivity) is a measure of the net value added per employee.

3.3. Non-parametric investigation

This component of the study has been designed to describe the intellectual capital performance of quoted banks in Italy through a non-parametric investigation.

Starting from the equation of the VAIC in Eq. (9), in order to find out what portion of intellectual capital is transformed into profitability an input-oriented analysis has been applied – the Data Envelopment Analysis (DEA) Model. Due to its benchmarking power, DEA provides a competitive analysis by comparing actual practice (the IC ratio not transformed into profitability of the banks in the sector) with reference goals (the IC ratio of the best performing bank in the related sector).

The data required for the research have been obtained from the Bankscope Dataset (that regarding the measures of performance) and from Datastream (that regarding the evaluation of market value).

The effect of intellectual capital on profitability for the Italian banking sector has been calculated as yielding the highest returns among the three portfolios constructed (P1, P2 and P3).

For Portfolio 1 (Intangible Assets Effects) = VAIC as input values

For Portfolio 2   (Tangible Assets Effects) = CEE or VA as input values
For Portfolio 3   (Financial Assets) = Market Value/Book Value as
                                        input values

Output values for the three portfolios consist of three variables: ROAE, ROAA and LDR (Loan on Deposit Ratio).

4. Data analysis and presentation of the results

Our investigations were conducted over a period of three years (2003–2007) on a total sample of analysis covering 267 banks. In particular, we have analysed a sample of 59 banks for the Italian market, a sample of ten banks in Spain and 51 in Germany, for a total cluster of analysis of 120 banks in the region of "Central Europe". We analysed a sample of 31 Danish, 13 Swedish, nine Finnish and 26 Norwegian banks, for a total cluster of 79 representing the "North Europe" region. We then analysed a sample of three Bulgarian, 11 Polish, eight Czech, ten Ukrainian and ten Hungarian banks for a total cluster of 51 constituting the "East Europe" region.

4.1. Italian banking market perspective

We have produced an analysis of intellectual capital efficiency within the Italian banking system.

   In particular, the study has addressed synthetic values for the following sectors (Figure 3.1):

(a) Savings banks
(b) Commercial banks
(c) Cooperative banks
(d) Mid and long-term credit institutions

Also worth noting is the comparative analysis between foreign and domestic banks (Figure 3.2). The former have a medium VAIC equal to 2.47 against a mean of 2.60 for domestic Italian banks.

   The raw data have been consolidated, and the analysis of the VAIC and its components has been applied to a restricted sample of 61 banks during the period of 2003–2007 as synthesized here below in Figures 3.3, 3.4, 3.5, 3.6 and 3.7).

   In Table 3.1 we report the ten highest values obtained for the sample analysed (in the same table there is also a comparison between the

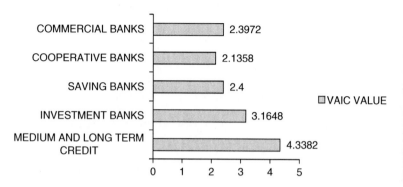

Figure 3.1 Sector efficiency analysis in the use of IC in the Italian sample (2003–2007)

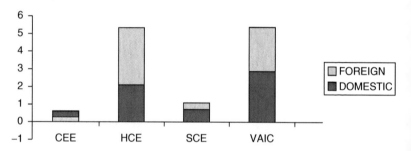

Figure 3.2 Analysis of domestic vs. foreign banks' use of ICE for the Italian sample (2003–2007)

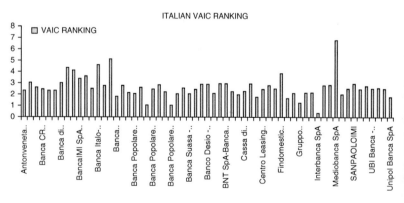

Figure 3.3 Overview of domestic Italian banks in the VAIC investigation for the period 2003–2007

ITALIAN BANKING MARKET VAIC

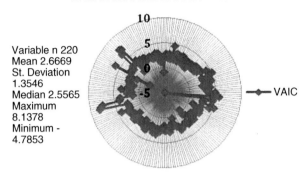

Variable n 220
Mean 2.6669
St. Deviation
1.3546
Median 2.5565
Maximum
8.1378
Minimum -
4.7853

Figure 3.4   VAIC: mean for Italian sample during the period 2003–2007

ITALIAN BANKING MARKET IICE

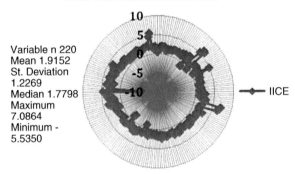

Variable n 220
Mean 1.9152
St. Deviation
1.2269
Median 1.7798
Maximum
7.0864
Minimum -
5.5350

Figure 3.5   HCE: mean for Italian sample during the period 2003–2007

ITALIAN BANKING MARKET SCE

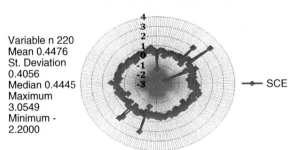

Variable n 220
Mean 0.4476
St. Deviation
0.4056
Median 0.4445
Maximum
3.0549
Minimum -
2.2000

Figure 3.6   SCE: mean for Italian sample during the period 2003–2007

ITALIAN BANKING MARKET CEE

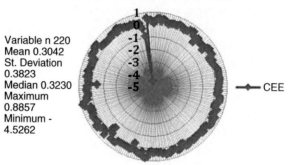

Variable n 220
Mean 0.3042
St. Deviation
0.3823
Median 0.3230
Maximum
0.8857
Minimum -
4.5262

← CEE

Figure 3.7   CEE: mean for Italian sample during the period 2003–2007

Table 3.1   Top ten banks in terms of VAIC values and of the VA for Italian sample (2003–2007)

VAIC ranking	Name of bank	VAIC	VA rank	Name of bank	VA
1	Mediobanca SpA	6.820	1	UniCredit SpA	13.644
2	Banca Mediolanum SpA	5.148	2	Intesa	11.559
3	Banca Fideuram SpA	4.339	3	SANPAOLO IMI	4.026
4	Banca Ifis SpA	4.113	4	Capitalia SpA	2.968
5	Findomestic Banca SpA	3.824	5	UBI Banca	2.720
6	Banca Intermobiliare vestimenti e G	3.583	6	Gruppo Monte dei Paschi de Siena-Banca M	2.691
7	Banca IMI SpA d'Intermediazo	3.395	7	Banco Popolare di Verona e Novara	1.739
8	Banca di Credito Cooperativo dell'Alta P.	2.979	8	Banca Nazionale del Laboro SpA – BNL	1.543
9	Banca Agricola Popolare di Ragusa SCARL	2.954	9	Mediobanca SpA	1.253
10	SANPAOLO IMI	2.942	10	Banca popo-lare dell'Emilia Romagna	1.123

ranking of the first ten banks in terms of VAIC values and of the value added calculated in the same period of investigation).

4.2. European perspective analysis

We also analysed ICE in the rest of Europe. In particular, the investigation was conducted for the following geographic areas: Northern Europe, Central Europe and Eastern Europe.

4.2.1. Central Europe

In the "Central Europe" region, German and Spanish banks were studied.

4.2.1.1. German banks

There were 52 banks in the German sample. The consolidation of these data has yielded the values in Table 3.2 for the top ten German banks in terms of VAIC during the period of investigation:

Considering the sectors of activity (Figure 3.8), we have confirmed that what had already been discovered for the Italian banking system was also true for the German system: the sectors with the highest VAIC levels are the medium and long-term institutions, followed by the investment banks. It is worth observing that the cooperative banks are all clustered around the third position.

Table 3.2 Comparative VAIC analysis of Central Europe: overview of top ten German banks (2003–2007)

VAIC ranking	Name of bank	Mean VAIC
1	Düsseldorfer Hypothekenbank AG	7.468
2	Concord Investmentbank AG	5.505
3	Wüestenrot & Württembergische	5.327
4	Union Asset Management Holding AG	5.306
5	Sparda-Bank Baden-Württemberg eG	4.900
6	HSBC Trinkaus & Burkhardt AG	4.660
7	LBS Ostdeutsche Landesbausparkasse AG	4.305
8	DAB Bank AG	4.297
9	Sparda-Bank München eG	4.184
10	NordFinanz Bank AG	4.181

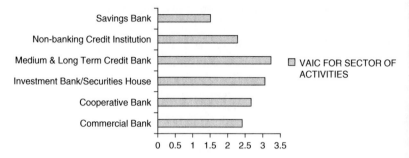

Figure 3.8   Sector efficiency analysis in the use of IC in the German sample (2003–2007)

4.2.1.1. *Spanish market*

Spanish banks have high levels of efficiency in the use of their knowledge capital. We addressed our analysis with a raw sample, calculating the values of VAIC for ten banks (Table 3.3). The VAIC coefficient for Spanish banks is, with a mean equal to 2.88, higher than that measured for Italian and German banks (respectively 2.66 and 2.56).

The VAIC coefficient for Central European banks is, as a mean, equal to 2.67 (Table 3.4).

4.3. Northern European banks

4.3.1. Comparative analysis of Northern European banks

Making an overhead comparison of the four countries analysed for the top ten Northern banks in terms of VAIC (Table 3.5), the highest level of VAIC is found for Pohjola Pankki Oyj-Pohjola Bank plc, with a value of 21, followed by a Swedish bank, the Venantius AB (VAIC value equal to 17.95). The VAIC coefficient for Northern banks is, as a mean, equal to 4.

4.4. Eastern European banks

4.4.1. *Comparative analysis of Eastern European banks*

The VAIC coefficient for the top 50 Eastern banks is, as a mean, equal to 2.78. Making an overhead comparison of the countries (Table 3.6), and considering only the top ten banks in terms of VAIC, the highest level of VAIC is found for MKB Unionbank AD, with a value of 6.30.

4.7. Empirical results

4.7.1. *Parametric model*

The analysis of Italian banks during the period of investigation shows a mean for the market value to book value (M/B) of about 1.7, which

Table 3.3 Comparative VAIC analysis of Central Europe: overview of the top ten Spanish banks (2003–2007)

VAIC ranking	Name of bank	Mean VAIC
1	Banco Español de Crédito SA, BANESTO	7.497
2	Banco Bilbao Vizcaya Argentaria SA	3.480
3	Banco de Sabadell SA	3.321
4	Banco Popular Español Sa	2.816
5	Caja de Ahorros de Calicia – Caixa Galic	2.683
6	Caja de Ahorros de Castilla La Mancha	2.668
7	Banco Santander SA	2.633
8	Banco Guipuzcoano SA	2.438
9	Bankinter SA	2.217
10	Caja de Ahorros de Valencia Castellon	1.033

Table 3.4 Comparative VAIC analysis of Central Europe: overview of the top ten banks in sample (2003–2007)

VAIC ranking	Name of bank	Mean VAIC	Country
1	Banco Español de Crédito SA, BANESTO	7.497	Spain
2	Düsseldorfer Hypothekenbank AG	7.468	Germany
3	Mediobanca SpA	6.820	Italy
4	Concord Investmantbank AG	5.505	Germany
5	Wüstenrot & Württembergische	5.327	Germany
6	Union Asset Management Holding AG	5.306	Germany
7	Banca Mediolanum SpA	5.148	Italy
8	Sparda-Bank Baden-Württemberg eG	4.900	Germany
9	HSBC Trinkaus & Burkhardt AG	4.660	Germany
10	Banca Fideuram SpA	4.339	Italy
Mean VAIC	On the total of 129 central group of banks	2.668,223,358	Three countries

Table 3.5   Comparative VAIC analysis of Northern European banks: overview of the top ten banks (2003–2007)

VAIC ranking	Name of bank	Mean VAIC	Country
1	Pohjola Pankki Oyj-Pohjola Bank plc	21.408	Finland
2	Venantius AB	17.958	Sweden
3	Norvestia Oyj	10.616	Finland
4	Realkredit Danmark A/S	8.165	Denmark
5	Finance for Danish Industry A/S – FIH Gr	7.264	Denmark
6	Kaupthing Bank Oyj	6.477	Finland
7	KommuneKredit	6.040	Denmark
8	ABG Sundal Collier Holding ASA	5.055	Norway
9	Handelsbanken Finans AB	4.183	Sweden
10	Finnvera Plc	4.643	Finland

Table 3.6   Comparative VAIC analysis of Eastern European banks: overview of the top ten Eastern banks (2003–2007)

VAIC ranking	Name of bank	Mean VAIC	Country
1	MKB Unionbank AD	6.304	Bulgaria
2	Bulbank AD	5.688	Bulgaria
3	Komercni Banka	4.578	Czech Republic
4	HVB Bank Czech Republic AS	4.526	Czech Republic
5	OTP Bank Plc	4.305	Hungary
6	PrivatBank	4.160	Ukraine
7	Ceskoslovenska Obchodni Banka – CSOB	3.935	Czech Republic
8	PPF banka a.s.	3.923	Czech Republic
9	KDB Bank (Hungary) Ltd	2.823	Hungary
10	Inter-Europa Bank ZRT	3.822	Hungary

suggests that about 43 per cent of a firm's value is systematically not reflected in its financial statements. The descriptive statistics analysis shows, for the European sample, a mean value of the M/B equal to 2.0183, which indicates that, for European competitors, more than 50 per cent of the value of banks is not evident in official statements.

The correlation analysis shows that financial performance, ROAA is positively correlated to VAIC and, in particular, to its two components: structural capital efficiency (SCE) and human capital efficiency (HCE), which suggests that a firm's market value is positively associated with corporate intellectual ability (ICE). The correlation analysis shows that the financial performance, ROAE, is positively correlated to VAIC and its components.

The results of regression models on M/B show that the coefficient on VAIC is significantly positive in the first model (H1), and that all three components of VAIC are also significantly positive in model 2 (H2). The results support the hypotheses H1 and H2 – that investors place higher value on firms with greater intellectual capital, and that all three components of VAIC are recognized as valuable intellectual capital. Noticeably, the adjusted R^2 increases substantially from model 1 (H1) to model 2 (H2), suggesting that investors may place different levels of emphasis on each of the three components of VA efficiency and, thus, the exploratory power for the value of firms in model 2 (H2) is substantially greater than in model 1 (H1).

Similar to the results obtained for M/B, the R^2 adjusted for the financial performances (ROAE and ROAA) is substantially greater in model H3 (regression on components of VAIC) than that in model in H2 (regression on VAIC).

We have also investigated the relationship between VAIC and another bank financial performance value: that of employer productivity. The model shows an R^2 equal to 58 per cent.

4.7.2. Non-parametric model (DEA analysis)

The portfolio based on intellectual capital has a return on profitability equal to 0.23. The highest annual returns are represented by the portfolio based on capital employed (technical efficiency equal to 0.557) and the portfolio based on financial effects (technical efficiency equal to 0.545).

5. Conclusions

The VAIC method measures and monitors value creation efficiency in companies using accounting-based figures. The better a company's resources (capital employed and intellectual capital) are employed, the higher its value creation efficiency will be (human capital is the decisive value creation factor for modern businesses). Our research has shown that, on the one hand, this results in an increase of value added and, on the other, it determines market value.

We have discovered that in many cases the value added approach is a more objective indicator of business performance than is profit. Banks analysed during the period of investigation, while gaining just the same levels of profit, showed very different levels of value added. This means that, in certain cases, despite a considerable increase in profit, little value was actually created. This is a common situation in many companies. Traditional indicators create an illusion of success, while value is actually being destroyed. We may conclude that, in modern business, value is created only if the efficiency of resources is leveraged. If value creation is falling, then value is being destroyed.

The international cross analysis within different banking markets tells us that Italian banks are generally less efficient in the use of IC than their Spanish and Northern European counterparts.

It is reasonable to consider intellectual capital as a fundamental investment factor. In fact, this study provides empirical evidence to support assumptions about the relationship between it and profitability. In particular, the results support the hypothesis that firms' intellectual capital has an impact on market value and financial performance, and that it may be an indicator for future financial performance.

5.1. Strengths of the study

The depth of analysis in this paper (at a local but also an international level) could help the managers of banks in determining their positions regarding intellectual capital. It might also assist policy-makers in formulating and implementing intellectual capital development plans, aid investors in modifying investment strategies and allow banks to benchmark themselves in order to improve their value creation capabilities. The regression analysis results provide empirical evidence that investors place a higher value on firms with better intellectual capital efficiency, yielding greater profitability. Furthermore, it underlines the importance of intellectual capital in enhancing company profitability. This paper is an experiment in the literature of intellectual capital because it studies the effects of intellectual capital performance on profitability in the banking sector using both VAIC and DEA. Using VAIC as the principle model engaged in this investigation provides several benefits (apart from the benefit of enabling one to decipher the value added efficiency of country's banking systems and IC resources).

First, it provides a standardized and consistent basis of measurement. This allows one to conduct an international comparative analysis using a large sample size and across various industrial sectors more effectively. Alternative IC measures are limited[1] in that they: (1) utilize information associated with a select group of companies/nations (for example stock data), (2) involve unique financial and non-financial indicators that can readily be combined into a single comprehensive measure and/or (3) are customized to fit the profiles of individual companies/ nations. Consequently, the ability to apply alternative IC measures consistently across a large and diversified sample for comparative analysis is diminished.

Second, all data used in the VAIC calculation are based on audited information. Therefore, such calculations can be considered objective and verifiable (other IC measures have been criticized for the subjectivity of their underlying indicators).

Third, VAIC is a straightforward technique that enables ease of calculation by various internal and external stakeholders.

5.2. Limitations of the study

Our study fails to consider the European banking system in its entirety and, moreover, it includes only three years' worth of analysis. Another objective of this paper was to calculate intellectual capital using the VAIC model, and to test the effects of intellectual capital on profitability by applying the DEA approach. The data required were obtained from the listed markets of the countries for which the analysis has been developed. The biggest limitation of this investigation is that, in order to perform the DEA, every input and output value of the numeric data has to be available and positive. As a result of this rule, any banks that had negative input or output values were not included in this part of the analysis. Although, after a laborious review process, we determined that VAIC is an indicator able to capture and measure the intellectual capital stock and flow of each company accurately, it is not exempt from criticism, especially given that it uses only basic financial information in its composition. Thus, our study should be considered an exploratory work, with the aim of building upon available literature covering this issue. We embraced an innovative methodological approach in more depth than has been done before, and our results will potentially pave the way for further analyses in a similar vein.

Note

1. See also for reference Kaplan and Norton (2004).

References

Bontis, N., William, C.C.L., and Richardson, R. (2000) "Intellectual capital and business performance in Malaysian industries" *Journal of Intellectual Capital,* 1 (1), 85–100.

Edvinsson, L. and Malone, M.S. (1997) *Intellectual Capital – Realizing your company's true value by finding its hidden brainpower,* Harper Collins, New York, 94–95.

Hudson W. (1993) *Intellectual Capital: How to Build it, Enhance it, Use it* Wiley, New York, 16.

Kaplan, R.S., and Norton, D.P. (2004) *Strategy Maps: Converting Intangible Assets into Tangible Outcomes* Harvard Business School Press, Boston, MA.

Muhammad, Nik Maheran Nik (corresponding author) and Ismail, Md Khairu Amin (2009) "Intellectual Capital Efficiency and Firm's Performance: Study on Malaysian Financial Sectors", *Journal of Economics and Finance,* 1 (2) (August).

Pulic, A. (1997) The physical and intellectual capital of Austrian banks. available at: http://irc.mcmaster.ca (last access11 June, 2004).

Roos, G., Roos, J., Edvinsson, L., and Dragonetti, N.C. (1997) *Intellectual Capital Navigating in the New Business Landscape* New York University Press, New York.

4
Traditional and R&D Investments: are They really Different?

Paola Brighi and Giuseppe Torluccio

1. Introduction

The aim of this chapter is to identify the different role of financial funds in traditional and R&D investments in Italian manufacturing firms using information from Capitalia's latest Survey of Italian Firms. R&D, defined as a creative activity implemented to improve know-how and its utilization in new applications, is quite distinct because of its high rate of information opacity. Coherently with the asymmetric information theory, R&D thus implies that firms will have greater difficulty in finding external financial funding. The higher risk related to R&D projects could entail some form of financial constraint. However, signalling mechanisms such as self-financing could correct such a market imperfection.

The purpose of our study is twofold. First, we investigate which indicators (firms' structural characteristics, information asymmetries and credit market structure) can define the pattern of the R&D financing scheme. Second, we investigate whether R&D investments face greater difficulty in attracting external financial resources compared to traditional investments.

The decision to fund an R&D investment through informed debt or self-financing is initially tested through a simple logit and OLS analysis and, thereafter, through seemingly unrelated regression (SUR) models. The study includes both traditional and R&D investments, and the outcomes enable a comparative analysis of the particularity of R&D financing versus traditional investments. As highlighted by Himmelberg and Petersen (1994: 38):

> this approach allows us to compare our findings to the existing literature on physical investment under capital market imperfections.

Second, it is inappropriate to view the firm as having access to separate financing sources for R&D and physical investment. Finally, as argued by Schumpeter, new knowledge must be incorporated in the production process through investments in new plant and equipment. Hence, the financing of physical investment for R&D-intensive firms are more prone to moral hazard and adverse selection problems.

The remainder of the chapter is organized as follows. Section 2 briefly looks into the main theoretical and empirical literature on SME financial preferences. Sections 3 and 4 describe the dataset, while the econometric analysis and the main results follow in section 5. Section 6 contains the conclusions.

2. Theoretical background and empirical issues

Traditionally, firm market value and real decisions are considered independently from financial structure and financing policies, given that in the theoretical context, based on Modigliani and Miller's model (1958), financial markets are perfect and characterized by fiscal neutrality, and thus external funds and internal funds are considered perfectly substitutable. However, the absence of information asymmetry implies conclusions that cannot appropriately explain the different SME financial preferences involved in traditional investments as compared to those in R&D. As a result of high information opacity, firms involved in R&D investments have greater difficulty in obtaining external funds than others do. As suggested by Myers and Majluf (1984), information asymmetries lead to a hierarchical preference for internal financial resources, and this justifies the observed higher R&D self-financing rates compared to traditional investment rates (Hall 2002).[1]

According to the pecking order theory, the cost of funding increases in line with the increase of information asymmetries. The cost of information asymmetries – more reliable in the case of SMEs – implies that firms choose the less expensive form of financing in terms of information disclosure (Bhattacharya and Chiesa, 1995).[2] As a consequence, new investments are initially financed with internal capital and further by low-risk bank credit, followed by bonds and, only as a last option, through share issues. Likewise, Berger and Udell (1998) reiterate that firms' financial demands change with the transformation of their information capacities. Small, new and innovating firms primarily make use of internal capital and commercial loans. The development of such firms requires higher information transparency, which thus makes it easier to obtain external equity. The hierarchy of financial resources, partially oriented towards growth, is best adapted to SMEs investing in R&D.[3]

Atzeni and Piga (2007) provide a further interpretation, focusing on the role of self-financing as a way of addressing the problems arising from information asymmetry and thus from the potential risk of credit rationing. However, a high rate of self-financing could cause the project to be extremely confidential and conversely create the undesired effect of limiting access to external financial resources. Furthermore, credit rationing depends on the R&D investment intensity rate. Firms strongly oriented towards R&D activities apparently do not experience credit constraint problems and vice versa.[4] This result is also confirmed by Herrera and Minetti (2007), who demonstrate that there is no clearly defined correlation between R&D investments and credit rationing: firms with low R&D investment intensity are actually inclined to ask for lower loans and, as such, appear to be rationed to a greater extent than those with a high R&D intensity.[5] Moreover, Herrera and Minetti show that relationship lending has a positive effect on the probability that firms engage in innovation, even identifying measures of local financial development. This result is in line with the view that sound banking relationships can foster firms' innovation. The authors find that strong relations benefit innovation not just by fostering R&D but also by channelling funds for the introduction and acquisition of new technologies.[6]

Another important argument linked to R&D investment refers to the lack of collateral, which could partially or entirely cover the project default risk. Bester (1985) argues that there is no rationing if banks compete amongst themselves by simultaneously establishing the collateral level and interest rate. The firm's choice of one contract over another is a self-selection mechanism. For instance, a firm with a low insolvency probability is ready to provide higher collateral in exchange for a lower interest rate as compared to those with higher risk.[7] As suggested by Ozkan (2002: 827) "one important distinction between R&D investment and investment in physical capital is that the result of R&D investment can not serve as collateral, as it may be impossible to put a lien on R&D capital." R&D investment generally has little rescue value: at the R&D stage, investments consist mostly of salaries and intangible assets; at the adoption stage, assets that embody new technology are specific to the firm. This implies that collateral has a limited role in mitigating incentives to add risk (cf. Herrera and Minetti 2007: 227). Evidence suggests that collateral is more likely to be pledged in the presence of significant information asymmetries between borrowers and lenders. However, the theory cannot easily be verified in the case of R&D since intangible assets are difficult to collateralize (cf. Gonas et al. 2004).

Finally, another strand of literature shows that public subsidies to R&D alleviate debt and equity gaps for small firm innovation projects. Innovations are expected to generate positive external effects, but since firms can appropriate only private returns they will launch only privately profitable innovation projects. Thus, underinvestment in R&D entails the risk that socially useful projects are not privately implemented. The absence of collateral from physical assets implies that banks and other debt holders are reluctant to finance projects involving substantial R&D investments. These arguments therefore justify public market interventions in R&D. As suggested by Czarnitzki (2002: 1) the positive external effects argument is usually considered as regards funding basic research, while the second argument on the wedge between the internal and external cost of capital is used as a rationale for supporting SME activities.

R&D activities can be regarded as an investment in a firm's knowledge capital and thus, in several studies, estimations of R&D investment equations are compared with investment in physical assets. Investment in intangible assets, such as R&D, tends to be both riskier and more difficult to collateralize than investment in physical assets. The results of Hall's (2002) study, one of the first on this topic, can be summarized as follows: (1) small and start-up firms in R&D industries face higher costs of capital than larger firms; (2) the financing gap for large firms is more difficult to establish, but it seems clear that these firms prefer internally generated funds for R&D investment; (3) the venture capital solution to the problem of R&D financing has some limitations – primarily because it tends to focus on only a few industries with a minimum size of investment that is too large for start-ups in some fields – and (4) public subsidies are an important source of finance for R&D investments and need to be further investigated.

3. Data and sample analysis

Our study uses the SME Observatory[8] Survey of Italian Manufacturing Firms (hereafter Capitalia 2005), which is a key source of mainly questionnaire-based information. The survey is conducted on firms with 11 to 500 employees and as a full census for larger firms. The

Bureau van Dijk databases complete the financial statement data for Italian firms targeted by the Survey (4139) and provide a greater historic depth. Some 1357 firms declared expenditure in both R&D and other investments and these constitute our sample. To compare the determining factors of R&D expenditure and traditional investment self-financing,[9] we build a homogeneous sample with respect to all the variables, except for the decision to spend on R&D and/or other investments.

The sample is strongly characterized by small firms,[10] and companies in the first quantile are on average five years old.

We focus on the financing source survey sections of the questionnaire,[11] inquiring into the percentage breakdown of the use of different finance investment channels.

Our study focuses on the section[12] dedicated to the different contributions of each financial source to investment, technological innovation and research and development for both R&D expenditure[13] and traditional investments (cf. Table 4.1).[14]

Table 4.1 The sources of finance: investments vs. R&D

Sample: 1 > 0 and R&D > 0 (n = 1357)		
Variable	**Traditional investments**	**R&D expenses**
Private equity	1.32	0.81
Internal funds	50.87	79.70
Short term loans	6.38	–
Long term loans	11.68	5.85
Leasing	14.21	–
Subsidized interest loans	6.67	3.50
National and European funds	3.25	–
Tax incentives	–	6.00
Subsidized loans	3.67	2.84
Intergroup loans	1.63	–
Other firms' loans	0.10	–
Other	0.21	1.29
Total	**100**	**100**

Source: Our computation based on Capitalia's dataset.

4. Descriptive analysis

Table 4.1 shows that self-financing is on average much more important in R&D expenditure than in traditional investments.[15]

In traditional investments, leasing and banking debt are the most significant alternatives to self-financing. In R&D, in contast, credit appears to be just as important as public funding among external sources of financing.[16]

We investigate both the determinants of the choice to self-finance and the importance of internal financial sources where applicable. The aim of the empirical verification is twofold: (1) to verify if financial constraints exist (external rationing) and force firms to self-finance R&D above alternative traditional investments and (2) to define the determinants of self-financing (the structural characteristics of the firm, informative asymmetries and loan market structure).

Table 4.2   Rationing and sources of finance: investments vs. R&D

Sample: 1 > 0 and R&D > 0 (n = 1357)

	Traditional investments		**R&D expenses**	
Variable	Yes	No	Yes	No
Private equity	3.60	0.92	1.85	0.61
Internal funds	**38.52**	**52.83**	**74.55**	**78.13**
Short term loans	9.57	5.87	–	–
Long term loans	15.89	11.08	9.27	5.23
Leasing	5.87	6.85	2.78	3.48
Subsidized interest loans	3.55	3.17	–	–
National and European funds	–	–	6.47	5.94
Tax incentives	3.82	3.70	1.8	3.10
Leasing	16.57	13.71	–	–
Intergroup loans	1.97	1.60	–	–
Other enterprise loans	0.09	0.10	–	–
Other	0.54	0.16	3.28	3.51
Total	**100**	**100**	**100**	**100**

Source: Our computation based on Capitalia's dataset.

Table 4.2 shows that firms asking for more credit are more inclined towards self-financing in R&D (74.55 per cent) than for other investments (38.52 per cent). There is an *ex ante* self-selection effect that suggests that if a firm decides to invest in R&D, it probably already has enough internal resources to finance it.

While this result seems to suggest greater external rationing, in the case of R&D expenditure it shows that credit constraints are much less severe than for traditional investments.

Empirical evidence suggests that the impact of credit rationing is different in traditional investments compared to R&D expenditure. We observed the following results where external rationing occurred: (1) self-financing of traditional investments is higher than in the absence of credit rationing (+14.31 per cent); (2) this difference is marginal (+3.58 per cent) in the R&D case; (3) the financial structure of the source of financing in R&D expenditure is quite similar both in credit rationing and in its absence and (4) the banking channel is marginal in R&D investments both when credit rationing occurs and when it does not.

The data demonstrate that credit rationed firms have fewer self-financing possibilities in both traditional and R&D investments. The difference is, however, less evident in the case of R&D self-financing.

4.1 Specification of independent variables

The independent variables are summarized in Table 4.3. First, with reference to the variables describing the financial and structural firm characteristics, we defined a proxy of INTERNAL RATIONING comparing the cash flow at year t–1 (FDC_{t-1}) and expenditure in traditional and R&D investments at year t ($INV_t+R\&D_t$). If at the end of year t–1 there are enough funds to finance traditional and R&D investments entirely internally then no form of internal rationing was observed, i.e. $FDC_t-1>(INV_t+R\&D_t)$. In the opposite case, the following different degrees of internal rationing were defined:

- $FDC_{t-1}<(INV_t+R\&D_t)$ for one year only, indicates low internal rationing,
- $FDC_{t-1}<(INV_t+R\&D_t)$ for two years, indicates medium rationing,
- $FDC_{t-1}<(INV_t+R\&D_t)$ for three years, indicates high internal rationing.[17]

Likewise, CURRENT RATIO represents a way to calculate the potential internal liquidity sources in the short term, but is also one of the most widely used bank indicators in the loan application evaluation process (i.e. credit rating).[18]

Table 4.3 Description of variables

	Source	Year	Observations	Mean	Std. Dev.	P25	Median	P75
Dependent variables								
INV_SELLFIN_A	Capitalia	2003	1,357	0.78	0.42	1.00	1.00	1.00
Dummy variable; = 1 if self-financed investments > 0.								
INV_SELLFIN_B	Capitalia	2003	1,357	0.53	0.50	0.00	1.00	1.00
Dummy variable; = 1 if self-financed investments > 50%.								
INV_SELLFIN_C	Capitalia	2003	1,357	0.25	0.43	0.00	0.00	1.00
Dummy variable; = 1 if investments are fully self-financed.								
R&D_SELLFIN_A	Capitalia	2003	1,357	0.87	0.34	1.00	1.00	1.00
Dummy variable; = 1 if self-financed R&D > 0.								
R&D_SELLFIN_B	Capitalia	2003	1,357	0.76	0.43	1.00	1.00	1.00
Dummy variable; = 1 if self-financed R&D > 50%.								
R&D_SELLFIN_C	Capitalia	2003	1,357	0.58	0.49	0.00	1.00	1.00
Dummy variable; = 1 if R&D is fully self-financed.								
INV_SELLFIN_%	Capitalia	2003	1,357	0.51	0.40	0.10	0.50	1.00
Proportion of investment covered by self-financing.								
R&D_SELLFIN_%	Capitalia	2003	1,357	0.77	0.36	0.60	1.00	1.00
Proportion of R&D covered by self-financing.								
Explanatory variables								
Firm's financial and structural characteristics								
INTERNAL RATIONING	Capitalia	2003	1,100	1.17	1.14	0.00	1.00	2.00
Categorical variable:								
= 0 if Cash flow$_{t-1}$ > (Investments$_t$ + R&D$_t$) for three years;								
= 1 if Cash flow$_{t-1}$ > (Investments$_t$ + R&D$_t$) for two years;								

= 2 if Cash flowt-1 > (Investmentst + R&Dt) for one year;

= 3 if never verified.

CURRENT RATIO	Current assets / Current liabilities.	Aida	2001–03	1,278	1.53	1.06	1.05	1.24	1.68
LEVERAGE	Debt / Total assets.	Aida	2001–03	1,267	0.71	0.18	0.59	0.75	0.86
PUBLIC SUBSIDIES	Dummy variable = 1 if the firm received fiscal or public subsidies.	Capitalia	2003	1,357	0.64	0.48	0.00	1.00	1.00
TURNOVER	% turnover variation in 2002–2003.	Aida	2002–03	1,267	3.51	83.61	-0.11	0.00	0.08
ROI	Return on investment.	Aida	2001–03	1,052	5.37	5.01	2.61	4.80	7.41
ROI_SD	ROI standard deviation 1996–2003.	Aida	1996–03	1,249	2.83	2.62	0.96	2.02	3.75
TOTAL ASSETS	Ln of total assets.	Capitalia	2003	1,357	9.54	1.30	8.71	9.40	10.33
AGE	Ln of the years of the firm.	Capitalia	2003	1,330	3.37	0.56	3.00	3.37	3.76
GROUP	Dummy variable; = 1 if the firm belongs to a group.	Capitalia	2003	1,355	0.41	0.49	0.00	0.00	1.00
HI-TECH	Dummy variable; = 1 if the firm belongs to Hi-Tech industry.	Capitalia	2003	1,357	0.07	0.25	0.00	0.00	0.00
HIGH_R&D	Dummy variable = 1 if R&D / Total asset > 4,5%.	Capitalia	2003	1,354	0.10	0.28	0.00	0.00	0.00
HIRING	Dummy variable = 1 if the firm hired people in 2001–2003.	Capitalia	2003	1,357	0.91	0.28	1.00	1.00	1.00
Relationship lending and information asymmetries									
MULTIPLE BANKING	Number of bank relationships.	Capitalia	2003	1,344	6.66	3.88	4.00	6.00	9.00

Continued

Table 4.3 Continued

		Source	Year	Observations	Mean	Std. Dev.	P25	Median	P75
LOCAL BANK	Dummy variable = 1 if local bank has registered office in the same province as firm.	Capitalia	2003	1,357	0.52	0.50	0.00	1.00	1.00
MAIN BANK	Proportion of debt with the main bank.	Capitalia	2003	1,260	31.01	24.50	15.00	30.00	44.50
DURATION	Age of relationship with the main bank.	Capitalia	2003	1,306	17.00	12.30	8.00	15.00	24.00
CREDIT RATIONING	Dummy variable = 1 if the firm would desire more credit.	Capitalia	2003	1,357	0.15	0.35	0.00	0.00	0.00
OPACITY	Intangible assets / Tangible assets.	Aida	2001–03	1,278	0.47	0.16	0.36	0.47	0.58
Banking market characteristics									
BRANCHES	Number of branches by region.	Bank of Italy	2003	1,357	3,260	1,787	2,218	3,148	5,841
HHI_LOANS	Loans Herfindal index by region.	Bank of Italy	2003	1,357	0.07	0.02	0.07	0.07	0.08

As suggested by some previous empirical analyses,[19] public funding is an important source of financing in sustaining R&D activities. In our study, the dichotomic variable is PUBLIC SUBSIDIES.[20] The question was addressed without distinction to all firms, regardless of the type of investment made, and public subsidies would appear more relevant in R&D than in traditional investments.

Amongst income variables, we first considered the TURNOVER that also measures the capacity to produce resources and, indirectly, is self-financing. Similarly, the return on investment (ROI) measures the firm's capacity to generate resources; however, a high return variability measured by the STD ROI is generally linked to a greater difficulty in obtaining external financial sources.

We constructed the HIGH_R&D dichotomous variable (equal to 1 if the R&D expenditure over the total asset is greater than 4.5 per cent).[21] Since R&D is heavily dependent on human capital, another proxy of the degree of R&D intensity can be attributed to the rate of recruitment in the last year, HIRING.[22]

The degree of the lending/information asymmetry relationship between the bank and the firm can be summarized in the following set of variables: (1) the number of banks from which the firm borrows, i.e. MULTIPLE BANKING; (2) the main bank's share of total banking debt, i.e. MAIN BANK; (3) the functional distance between the bank and the firm, i.e. LOCAL BANKING; iv) the duration of the relationship with the main bank in years, i.e. DURATION; v) CREDIT RATIONING, for credit constrained firms[23] and (4) the degree of OPACITY proxied the ratio between intangibles over tangible.

Finally, the degree of banking competition was measured by the number of bank branches per region, BRANCHES, and by the loan regional-market concentration, HHI_LOANS, which could alter information gathering and loan economic profitability.

5. Methodology and results

The SELFFIN A, B, C, dependent variables[24] on the decision to self-finance are described in Table 4.3 and defined as follows:

- SELFFIN_A (presence of self-financing)
- SELFFIN_B (self-financing as the main source)
- SELFFIN_C (full self-financing)

Self-financing was also measured by the variables INV_SELFFIN_% and R&D_SELFFIN_%, which express the firm's overall trend to self-finance. These were obtained as a relation between the amount of money used in self-financing for investment purposes (or for R&D) and the size of the firm. Both these variables were applied, in order to analyse the potential existence of correlations between the decision to self-finance investments and those of R&D expenditure. Where such a correlation was negative, a crowding out effect was observed, whereas a common feature of the use of self-financing was observed where the correlation was positive.

The general equation to be estimated can be written as follows:

$$Y = f(K_j, Z_y, B_r, W_q) \tag{1}$$

where the dependent variable **Y** is, alternatively, **SELFFIN A, B, C** or **SELFFIN_%** both for traditional investments and R&D expenses; **K** summarizes the firm's structural and financial characteristics; **Z** summarizes the information asymmetries and relationship lending characteristics; **B** summarizes the bank markets characteristics and **W** summarizes the "symmetric" effects (INV_SELFFIN_% and R&D_SELFFIN_%) that were computed by considering directly the answers given in the questionnaire relating to traditional and R&D investment funding choices (see Tables 4.3 and 4.4).

We use three different models to address the following questions:

First, we investigated the determinants of the self-financing decision related to traditional and R&D investments.[25] INV_SELFFIN A, B, C and R&D_SELFFIN A, B, C were estimated using logit specifications:

$$\Pr(SELFFIN_i = 1) = \frac{1}{(1 + \exp(-X_{ij}\alpha))} \tag{2}$$

where X_{ij} contains the explanatory variables and **j=K,Z,B,W** denotes dependent variables while α is a set of coefficients to be estimated.[26]

Table 4.5 presents the estimation of our LOGIT model with three relevant results. First, PUBLIC SUBSIDIES negatively impacts on all self-financing decisions. Public subsidies, *ceteris paribus*, may reduce internal funding or debt financing. Exclusive self-financing (SELFFIN_C) is also strongly conditioned by the presence of public incentives in traditional and R&D financing choices.[27] Second, the relationship lending variables (MULTIPLE BANKING, LOCAL BANK, MAIN BANK and DURATION) as well as CREDIT RATIONING, OPACITY, BRANCHES and HHI LOANS do not appear to affect R&D self-financing decisions. These results are only partly confirmed in self-financing of traditional investments. According to the theoretical predicted sign, the MULTIPLE BANKING and HHI_LOAN variables appear to be statistical significant. On the one hand, investment self-financing decreases (i.e. banking debt increases) as the bank increases the number of banking relationships; on the other, as the banking market becomes more concentrated firms have greater opportunities for external funding and thus self-financing decreases. Finally, we found that "symmetric" variables (the R&D expenditure self-financing rate in the case of investments and, speculatively, the rate of self-financing in the case of R&D expenditure) are strongly and significant.

This result requires exploration of a possible relation, and interaction, between internal funds used to finance R&D and/or traditional investments. We expected self-financing of investments to decrease as self-financing for R&D expenditure increases (the crowding out effect), since both variables depend on the same availability of internal sources. However, with reference to the sample analysed in this study, the evidence suggests quite the opposite (the inertia effect). Firms with higher self-financing of investments are also those that self-finance R&D expenditure to a larger extent even if the relevance differs.

Second, we investigated the relevance of self-financing to R&D expenditure and investments. The continuous dependent variables INV_SELFFIN_% and R&D_SELFFIN_% were estimated based on the following OLS specifications:[28]

$$INV\_SELFFIN\_\% = F\ (K,\ Z,\ B,\ W) \tag{3}$$

$$R\&D\_SELFFIN\_\% = F\ (K,\ Z,\ B,\ W) \tag{4}$$

Consistently with all previous specifications, the PUBLIC SUBSIDIES variable is statistically significant and its presence implies lower self-financing usage in both the traditional and in the R&D cases (Table 4.6). Therefore, public incentives appear to be a useful "support" to those firms that have limited internal financial sources. The internal rationing variable has a negative and significant sign on investment self-financing while it is not relevant in the alternative, R&D, case. From a financing point of view, the presence of public subsidies is linked to a less binding internal constraint. In addition, public subsidy in R&D constitutes a necessary condition, whereas self-financing

Table 4.4   Correlations

	1	2	3	4	5	6	7
1 INTERNAL RATIONING	1						
2 CURRENT RATIO	−0.275*	1					
3 LEVERAGE	0.258*–0.320*		1				
4 PUBLIC SUBSIDIES	0.079	−0.088		1			
5 TURNOVER		−0.127*			1		
6 ROI	−0.300*	0.196*	−0.296*	−0.081	0.088	1	
7 ROI SD	−0.073	0.182*	−0.138*		−0.159*	0.117*	1
8 TOTAL ASSETS	−0.125*		−0.088		0.084	−0.147*	−0.106*
9 AGE		0.141*	−0.080		−0.063		−0.060
10 GROUP			−0.068		0.070	−0.124*	
11 HI-TECH	0.078	0.061					
12 HIGH R&D	0.291*			0.092*			
13 HIRING						0.073	−0.077
14 MULTIPLE BANKING		−0.245*	0.246*	0.083			−0.181*
15 LOCAL BANK		0.061					
16 MAIN BANK		−0.086	0.141*			−0.129*	
17 DURATION		0.126*	−0.086				−0.093
18 CREDIT RATIONING	0.171*	−0.209*	0.238*		−0.069	−0.150*	
19 OPACITY	0.060	−0.176*		0.132*		−0.177*	−0.112
20 BRANCHES				−0.060			
21 HHI_LOANS							
22 INV_SELFFIN_%	0.085	0.168*	−0.293*	−0.063	0.106*	0.171*	
23 R&D_SELFFIN_%	0.256*	0.088				0.113*	0.077

8	9	10	11	12	13	14	15	16
1								
0.127*	1							
0.234*	−0.067	1						
0.060		0.099*	1					
−0.106*			0.200*	1				
0.156*		0.078		0.077	1			
0.295*	0.103*	0.142*		−0.064	0.134*	1		
	0.079	−0.071		−0.078			1	
−0.107*						−0.137*	−0.059	1
	0.299*	−0.147*					0.196*	
−0.095*								0.084
0.162*	−0.058	0.078	−0.062	−0.059		0.127*		0.074
	0.100*							
								0.059
0.116*	0.096*			0.059		−0.068		−0.105*
−0.144*			0.144*	0.289*	0.065	−0.095*		

Continued

Table 4.4 Continued

	17	18	19	20	21	22	23
1 INTERNAL RATIONING							
2 CURRENT RATIO							
3 LEVERAGE							
4 PUBLIC SUBSIDIES							
5 TURNOVER							
6 ROI							
7 ROI SD							
8 TOTAL ASSETS							
9 AGE							
10 GROUP							
11 HI-TECH							
12 HIGH R&D							
13 HIRING							
14 MULTIPLE BANKING							
15 LOCAL BANK							
16 MAIN BANK							
17 DURATION	1						
18 CREDIT RATIONING		1					
19 OPACITY			1				
20 BRANCHES				1			
21 HHI_LOANS			0.084	−0.293*	1		
22 INV_SELFFIN_%	0.095*	−0.150*				1	
23 R&D_SELFFIN_%				0.094*	−0.068	0.235*	1

Note: The magnitude of the correlation coefficients is moderate and the analysis of the tolerance values and VIF indicate that multicollinearity does not seem to be a problem.
For significance levels: * $p<0.01$; print < 0.10. Observations, n = 832.

Table 4.5 Investments vs. R&D: LOGIT model

Independent variable	INV_SELFFIN Logit			R&D_SELFFIN Logit		
	INV_ SELFFIN_A	INV_ SELFFIN_B	INV_ SELFFIN_C	R&D_ SELFFIN_A	R&D_ SELFFIN_B	R&D_ SELFFIN_C
INTERNAL RATIONING	−0.066	−0.179*	−0.316**	−0.147	−0.171	−0.125
	−0.71	−2.22	−3.00	−1.30	−1.83	−1.42
CURRENT RATIO	−0.340*	−0.249*	0.009	0.179	0.033	−0.108
	−2.45	−2.00	0.07	0.75	0.20	−0.83
LEVERAGE	−3.151***	−2.520***	−0.195	0.609	−0.117	−0.865
	−3.94	−3.81	−0.25	0.61	−0.15	−1.23
PUBLIC SUBSIDIES	−0.416*	−0.695***	−1.908***	−0.738**	−1.206***	−2.138***
	−2.05	−4.11	−9.71	−2.71	−5.25	−10.19
TURNOVER	0.208	−0.455	−0.413	−0.356	−0.43	−0.203
	0.43	−1.08	−0.85	−0.62	−0.90	−0.45
ROI	0.056*	0.052**	0.006	0.049	0.031	−0.002
	2.32	2.66	0.3	1.63	1.33	−0.1
ROI SD	−0.032	0.012	0.033	0.03	0.003	0.023
	−0.92	0.37	0.91	0.67	0.08	0.71
TOTAL ASSETS	0.294**	0.318***	0.127	−0.1	−0.108	−0.158
	2.81	3.74	1.33	−0.81	−1.12	−1.76
AGE	0.227	−0.038	−0.258	−0.198	−0.337	−0.302
	1.13	−0.22	−1.19	−0.84	−1.76	−1.69
GROUP	0.108	−0.016	0.029	0.304	−0.001	0.114
	0.50	−0.09	0.13	1.14	0.00	0.58
HI-TECH	1.601*	0.446	0.404	0.355	0.028	−0.133
	2.49	1.23	1.06	0.68	0.07	−0.37
HIGH R&D	−0.747	−0.615	0.81	0.435	0.228	−0.877**
	−1.47	−1.39	1.68	0.90	0.65	−2.71
HIRING	−0.053	−0.238	−0.21	0.970**	0.327	−0.046
	−0.16	−0.85	−0.62	2.96	1.06	−0.15
MULTIPLE BANKING	−0.031	−0.062*	−0.086**	−0.044	−0.042	−0.009
	−1.04	−2.39	−2.6	−1.23	−1.47	−0.33
LOCAL BANK	0.048	0.121	−0.132	−0.129	0.123	0.006
	0.26	0.76	−0.68	−0.57	0.67	0.04
MAIN BANK	−0.004	−0.006	−0.006	−0.007	0.000	−0.006
	−1.08	−1.8	−1.53	−1.55	0.10	−1.67

Continued

Table 4.5 Continued

Independent variable	INV_SELFFIN Logit			R&D_SELFFIN Logit		
	INV_SELFFIN_A	INV_SELFFIN_B	INV_SELFFIN_C	R&D_SELFFIN_A	R&D_SELFFIN_B	R&D_SELFFIN_C
DURATION	0.011	0.007	0.009	0.007	0.005	0.001
	1.15	0.84	0.89	0.68	0.59	0.1
CREDIT RATIONING	−0.325	−0.31	−0.474	0.11	0.161	0.235
	−1.31	−1.29	−1.45	0.34	0.61	0.94
OPACITY	0.802	1.646**	1.800**	0.055	0.654	0.722
	1.24	2.93	2.72	0.07	1.02	1.22
BRANCHES (X 1000)	−0.061	0.019	0.034	−0.011	0.000	−0.066
	−1.13	0.41	0.63	−0.17	0.00	−1.36
HHI LOANS	−4.75	−2.217	−15.31*	−5.504	−5.98	−4.131
	−1.23	−0.63	−2.48	−1.32	−1.60	−1.14
R&D_SELFFIN_%	30.580***	18.75**	5.279			
	3.41	3.14	1.11			
INV_SELFFIN_%				23.560**	23.220***	14.81***
				3.07	4.08	3.68
CONSTANT	1.562	1.075	2.339	2.828	4.545**	6.174***
	1.05	0.88	1.59	1.58	3.18	4.74
chi2 (DF_M)	103.8 (22)	152.5 (22)	188.8 (22)	57.39 (22)	95.54 (22)	208.8 (22)
r2_P	0.118	0.132	0.209	0.09	0.106	0.185
Observations	832	832	832	832	832	832

z statistics reported.
* $p<0.05$, ** $p<0.01$, *** $p<0.001$.

seems weakly related to the internal rationing state. This result can be interpreted from two perspectives. On the one hand, those firms taking advantage of public subsidies are engaged in intensive investment and R&D self-financing. However, the causal relation between the two variables cannot be tested here as a result of firms being engaged in both investments and R&D expenditure. In fact, we cannot ascertain whether it is the presence of the public subsidy that enabled the investments – resulting from a lower self-financing requirement – or the lack of public subsidy that caused this rationing and prevented the investment.[29]

Table 4.6 Investments vs. R&D: OLS model

Independent Variables	INV_SELFFIN_%			R&D_SELFFIN_%		
	Model 1 OLS	Model 2 OLS	Model 3 OLS	Model 4 OLS	Model 5 OLS	Model 6 OLS
INTERNAL RATIONING		−0.031**	−0.028*		0.008	0.000
		−2.60	−2.20		0.74	−0.02
CURRENT RATIO		0.001	−0.028		0.006	0.003
		0.06	−1.49		0.40	0.15
LEVERAGE	−0.451***	−0.302**	−0.364***	−0.130*	−0.062	−0.051
	−7.57	−3.25	−3.53	−2.27	−0.70	−0.51
PUBLIC SUBSIDIES		−0.155***	−0.125***		−0.128***	−0.133***
		−6.04	−4.62		−5.25	−5.11
TURNOVER	0.000	0.001	−0.056	0.000	0.000	−0.047
	1.04	1.08	−0.85	0.28	0.14	−0.73
ROI		0.007*	0.006*		0.006*	0.004
		2.45	2.17		2.34	1.40
ROI SD		0.002	0.001		0.004	0.003
		0.39	0.21		1.01	0.63
TOTAL ASSETS	0.019	0.033**	0.051***	−0.021*	−0.021	−0.026*
	1.94	2.82	3.9	−2.23	−1.9	−2.05
AGE	0.020	0.010	0.000	−0.019	−0.039	−0.043
	1.03	0.44	−0.01	−1.00	−1.83	−1.65
GROUP	0.021	0.001	−0.007	−0.028	−0.010	0.017
	0.82	0.04	−0.24	−1.17	−0.37	0.61
HI-TECH	0.137**	0.114*	0.099	−0.027	−0.001	−0.020
	2.94	2.22	1.85	−0.62	−0.02	−0.38
HIGH R&D		0.114*	0.099*		−0.039	−0.027
		2.47	2.09		−0.90	−0.59
HIRING		−0.0409	−0.0467		0.0672	0.0885*
		−0.96	−1.04		1.67	2.05
MULTIPLE BANKING			−0.012**			−0.001
			−2.85			−0.22

Continued

Table 4.6   Continued

Independent Variables	INV_SELLFIN_%			R&D_SELLFIN_%		
	Model 1 OLS	Model 2 OLS	Model 3 OLS	Model 4 OLS	Model 5 OLS	Model 6 OLS
LOCAL BANK			−0.003			−0.006
			−0.11			−0.26
MAIN BANK			−0.001			0.000
			−1.59			−0.30
DURATION			0.0012			0.0006
			0.99			0.53
CREDIT RATIONING			−0.068			0.014
			−1.82			0.38
OPACITY			0.236**			0.001
			2.71			0.01
BRANCHES (X1000)			0.003			7E-04
			0.38			0.10
HHI LOANS			−0.879			−0.788
			−1.56			−1.45
R&D_SELLFIN_%	0.304***	0.246***	0.247***			
	10.14	7.25	6.98			
INV_SELLFIN_%				0.268***	0.221***	0.230***
				10.14	7.25	6.98
CONSTANT	0.333**	0.305	0.496*	0.997***	1.001***	1.114***
	2.74	1.81	2.51	9.02	6.39	5.96
Observations	1165	928	832	1165	928	832
Adjusted R-squared	0.147	0.187	0.215	0.098	0.129	0.129
r2	0.152	0.199	0.236	0.104	0.142	0.152
aic	977.9	731.3	625.7	828.4	629.9	565.3
bic	1018.4	803.8	734.3	868.9	702.3	673.9
F	29.66	16.24	11.34	19.11	10.77	6.591
df_m	7	14	22	7	14	22
df_r	1157	913	809	1157	913	809

t statistics reported.
* $p<0.05$, ** $p<0.01$,*** $p<0.001$.

We observed that the most important variable to explain self-financing, that is the return on investment (ROI), appears generally relevant with an expected positive impact.[30] Finally, as shown in the LOGIT model, there is a significant positive relation between the self-financed investment and the self-financed R&D percentages. It was thus important to analyse if there was a potential correlation between OLS models on investment self-financing and OLS on R&D self-financing.[31]

Third, to investigate the potential relation between the decision to self-finance investments and R&D we used a seemingly unrelated regression (SUR) specification, which considered a correlation in error terms in Eqs (3) and (4).[32] From the above logit and OLS analyses, some common factors (see for example LEVERAGE, ROI, PUBLIC SUBSIDIES and TOTAL ASSETS) emerged that influence both investment and R&D self-financing. The analysis investigates these relations through a SUR that produces more efficient results.[33] For reasons of robustness the SUR is proposed on two specifications.[34] The results are outlined in the Table 4.7 and some comments are offered hereafter.

First, both investment and R&D self-financing depend on ROI, PUBLIC SUBSIDIES and HHI_LOANS. These results are robust to both SUR specifications (models 1 and 2). Heterogeneous results emerged with reference to INTERNAL RATIONING, TOTAL ASSETS, HIGH_R&D, MULTIPLE BANKING and OPACITY, which are relevant only in traditional investment self-financing. As suggested by the previous OLS analysis, the R&D project is independent of both OPACITY and MULTIPLE BANKING variables. Moreover, contrary to previous studies, CREDIT RATIONING does not appear significant in either investment or self-financing R&D.[35]

In summary, R&D self-financing appears to be driven by three elements: (1) public subsidies, (2) firm performance, i.e. ROI, and (3) leverage and the degree of banking market concentration. The SUR analysis confirms the previous OLS results, i.e. R&D self-financing follows a logic that is less related to firm and banking variables than to public incentives and internal high returns. These results imply that traditional and R&D investment financing decisions appear, at least partially, different.

6. Conclusions

The study analysed the main distinctions between the financing logic of investments and R&D expenditure in a sample of firms engaged in both activities. Descriptive analyses confirmed that R&D expenditure is strongly based on internal financial funding. The econometric

Table 4.7 Investments vs. R&D: SUR model

Dependent Variable	Model 1 SUR		Model 2 SUR	
	INV_ SELFFIN_%	R&D_ SELFFIN_%	INV_ SELFFIN_%	R&D_ SELFFIN_%
INTERNAL RATIONING	−0.028*		−0.030*	−0.007
	−2.29		−2.32	−0.57
CURRENT RATIO	−0.028		−0.029	−0.004
	−1.5		−1.53	−0.22
LEVERAGE	−0.403***	−0.166*	−0.399***	−0.143
	−3.95	−2.35	−3.83	−1.42
PUBLIC SUBSIDIES	−0.168***	−0.176***	−0.168***	−0.172***
	−6.34	−6.99	−6.26	−6.64
TURNOVER	−0.073	−0.061	−0.074	−0.064
	−1.09	−0.95	−1.1	−0.98
ROI	0.008**	0.006*	0.008**	0,006*
	2.69	2.33	2.63	2.01
ROI SD		0.004		0.003
		0.82		0.64
TOTAL ASSETS	0.046***	−0.016	0.047***	−0.015
	3.84	−1.51	3.54	−1.2
AGE		−0.037		−0.043
		−1.66		−1.67
GROUP			−0.001	0.017
			−0.03	0.60
HI-TECH	0.098		0.100	0.003
	1.88		1.83	0.06
HIGH R&D	0.101*		0.099*	−0.004
	2.16		2.05	−0.09
HIRING	−0.028	0.080	−0.028	0.082
	−0.62	1.85	−0.61	1.87
MULTIPLE BANKING	−0.012**		−0.013**	−0.004
	−3.02		−3.13	−0.96

Continued

Table 4.7 Continued

Dependent Variable	Model 1 SUR		Model 2 SUR	
	INV_ SELFFIN_%	R&D_ SELFFIN_%	INV_ SELFFIN_%	R&D_ SELFFIN_%
LOCAL BANK			−0.004	−0.007
			−0.17	−0.3
MAIN BANK	−0.001		−0.001	0.000
	−1.65		−1.78	−0.71
DURATION	0.001		0.001	0.001
	0.97		1.07	0.75
CREDIT RATIONING	−0.067		0.068	0.002
	−1.82		−1.79	−0.05
OPACITY	0.238**		0.251**	0.057
	2.78		2.84	0.67
BRANCHES			0.003	0.001
			0.4	0.19
HHI LOANS	−1.213*	−1.139*	−1.145*	−1.051
	−2.25	−2.2	−2.01	−1.91
CONSTANT	0.803***	1.247***	0.798***	1.298***
	4.8	8.21	4.56	6.95
Obs	834	834	832	832
Parms	16	9	19	21
RMSE	0.353	0.341	0.353	0.340
"R-sq"	0.191	0.098	0.189	0.101
chi2	195.350	90.770	194.430	93.100
P	0.000	0.000	0.000	0.000

Correlation of residuals 0.238 0.238
Breusch-Pagan test of independence: chi2(1) = 47.192 Pr = 0.000 47.255
Pr = 0.000

t statistics reported * p<0.05, ** p<0.01, *** p<0.001.

analysis focused first on the analysis of the decision to self-finance the investment and second on the financial funding mix; once the firm has decided to self-finance its activity, it has to decide how much self-selection to use among all other financial funds.

The empirical evidence demonstrates that firms with a high self-financing investment rate bear out the same behaviour as for R&D expenditure. Both types of self-financing – investment and R&D self-financing – are strongly related from a statistical point of view to the availability of public subsidies and to firms' high returns.

Public subsidies can be interpreted as signals used by firms to increase external financial funds in both traditional and R&D investments. On having have passed "public screening", firms can benefit by decreasing both traditional and R&D self-financing investments and increase their capability to attract external funds.

The empirical evidence shows that internal rationing is crucial to investment self-financing whilst external or credit rationing has a quite irrelevant effect.[36]

Proxies of relationship lending are only partially significant in traditional investments. Firms deciding to engage in R&D self-financing do not exhibit any strong external banking relationship evidence. We can consequently affirm that public subsidy acts as a stimulus of investments and R&D expenditure, and decreases the self-financing component in the financing decisions of profitable firms. Lack of guarantees or collateral, described here as R&D opacity, finds a solution in public subsidy, which also helps the firm to engage in self-financing.

The sample considered, ideal to a *ceteris paribus* comparison of R&D and investment self-financing, rules out by its own definition those firms that have not undertaken entrepreneurial activities, as a result of either credit rationing or their own decision-making. Subsidies, obviously, not only sustain R&D activities but also simultaneously decrease the general self-financing quota of firm financing and reinforce external financing.

At the same time, investments follow a more traditional financing scheme: in smaller firms these are generally self-financed, with lower leverage and a higher ROI. Self-financing is strongly dependent on information opacity. Investment and R&D self-financing increases as information opacity increases.

Traditional investments, less supported by internal capital, have a higher dependency on the "information" environment, as indicated by the banking variables. R&D expenditure is found only in the case of high returns and in the presence of public subsidies to support internal resources.

Notes

1. For a review of the literature supporting the Myers and Majluf theory of hierarchic funding resources, see among others Harris and Raviv (1991), Myers (2003) and Frank and Goyal (2005).
2. Even when possible from a legal point of view, SMEs show a limited interest in the *equity* market, given that it is more expensive when related to *information disclosure*. Generally, SMEs are apparently less prone to sharing control of the firm with third parties, fearing a loss of autonomy and flexibility in the management of their activities.
3. An exclusive relationship with a few banks would guarantee firms investing in R&D against the risk of losing their intellectual property in favour of competitors (cf. infra Bhattacharya and Chiesa, 1995).
4. Similar findings were provided by Herrera and Minetti (2007) on Italian SMEs and by Aghion et al. (2004) on UK quoted firms.
5. The database used for this study is the VIII Survey of Italian Manufacturing Firms conducted by the SME Observatory run by the Medio Credito Centrale in 2001.
6. This evidence suggests that banks are more prone to finance traditional investments occasioned by the introduction of new technologies rather than assisting firms in the R&D of new technology itself.
7. Contrary to the prevailing literature on collateral, Berger and Udell (1990) argue that this is frequently associated with risky debtors, risky loans and risky banks.
8. Capitalia Research Division.
9. It was therefore necessary to identify a homogeneous sample group regarding all the structural variables characterizing firms that carry out both types of investments (R&D > 0 and Investment > 0). Some attention should be paid to the fact that the need to select firms engaged in both activities (investments and R&D) certainly reduces the sample size. Therefore, it excludes firms that are severely rationed to such an extent that it would hamper any form of investments or R&D expense, or firms that, for the given period, deliberately preferred to rule out any investment or R&D expense.
10. Fifty per cent of firms have total assets of less than €12 million and 68 employees; 50 per cent (75 per cent) of firms have total assets below €12 (31) million and employ fewer than 68 (145) persons. Given the size of firms included in our sample, the use of equity is marginal related to the investment financing operations of the Italian SMEs considered.
11. Section C – "Investment, Technological Innovation and Research and Development". In particular, Question C1.5: "How were the investments made during 2001–2003 financed?" (see Capitalia 2005).
12. It should be noted that as we are dealing with a questionnaire the data provided are affected by the compiler's convictions as to how the reported event should be defined.

13. Questions C2.2.1: "In the three-year period 2001–2003, how much did the firm spend on R&D?" and C2.2.2: "How much did it spend?" (cf. Capitalia 2005).
14. Questions C1.1: "In the three-year period 2001–2003, did the firm invest in installations, machinery or equipment?" and C1.2: "How much did it spend?" (cf. Capitalia 2005).
15. The use of external equity appears extremely marginal in both cases.
16. Public funds appear on average more important in financing R&D expenditure compared to other investments. Nevertheless, the literature seems to suggest that public financing does not explain the greatest R&D expenditure. We observe a sort of *ex ante* self-selection of firms: only firms that really intend to undertake an innovative project ask for public funding (cf. Czarnitzki 2006; Meuleman and De Maeseneire 2008).
17. Given that our work enquires into what determines self-financing, identifying available liquid assets or those easily liquidated becomes relevant. On the one hand, direct use of the available cash flow may be preferred in the year to which the survey refers, which in our case is 2003. However, since we are dealing with a three-year survey, we constructed an INTERNAL RATIONING indicator defining the number of periods where the use of internal self-financing resources was difficult as a result of the reduced availability of cash flow in the previous period. Internal rationing, whose map is built via a categorical variable, takes on a higher value if, during the three years considered, a general insufficiency of cash flow to sustain investments and R&D was observed. The previously defined proxy shows an average value equal to 1 in our sample. This means that on average, the firms considered here had insufficient cash flow to cover the investments and R&D expenditure in one out of three years.
18. In our sample, this indicator – as could reasonably be expected – shows a negative correlation with the ratio between debt and total assets, i.e. LEVERAGE. These two explanatory variables simultaneously represent the main indicators used to calculate the financial risk. We expected greater firm risk and potential credit rationing as LEVERAGE increases. A first insight on this point comes from the correlation matrix, which displays an important positive statistical relationship between leverage and credit rationing (cf. Table 4.4).
19. Cf. Hall (2002) Czarnitzki (2006) and Meuleman and De Maeseneire (2008).
20. Section F3, Fiscal subsidies – Question F3.1: "Has the firm used financial and/or fiscal subsidies in the period 2001–2003?"
21. Atzeni and Piga (2007), in order to test the degree of R&D and the self-financing decision, identified firms belonging to the last distribution decile of the ratio between expenditure in R&D and the total assets.
22. This variable was obtained directly from the questionnaire's Section B. LABOUR FORCE. Question B. 2.1: "Did the company recruit in the years 2001–2003?" (see Capitalia 2005). Ninety per cent of firms in our sample reported that they recruited during the period considered.
23. Questionnaire Section F – Question F1.5: "In 2003, would the firm have liked to have obtained more credit at the interest rate agreed with the bank?" (see Capitalia 2005).

24. The dependent variables used as a proxy for self-financing were obtained directly from the questionnaire.
25. This consists of a dichotomy classification of the three self-financing levels stated by firms in the questionnaire and described in the previous sections.
26. Greene (2003).
27. This result is stable and robust to all other models tested (OLS and SUR).
28. We checked the potential correlation among the group of usually associated variables to balance sheet data. OLS analysis is performed by adding blocks of variables to verify the stability of the results. The study based on OLS regressions proceeded by considering three steps in which a sequence of variables was loaded to test the robustness of the specific model. As is known, these components may display significant multicollinearity issues.
29. In this case, the firm is not present in our sample.
30. Only in the more complete model does ROI appear as not significant when compared to the Hiring variable.
31. If this proves to be the case, it would be necessary to perform an eventual SUR evaluation of investments and R&D and to test the potential presence of a correlation in the errors of the two separate OLS regressions.
32. Zellner (1962).
33. The gain in efficiency from using the SUR estimator increases with the correlation between equation errors and decreases with the correlation between equation regressors. The outcomes of the SUR analysis are considered appropriate, referring to how they are explained by the test coefficients in Table 4.7.
34. The first specification is based on a set of statistically significant regressors drawn from the previous OLS regressions. This exercise was aimed at testing whether – given the existence of a "common effect" between investment and R&D self-financing – the previous OLS results could have been erratic. The second specification is based on a larger number of regressors, which were closer to the statistical significance in the previous OLS regressions and could become strongly significant.
35. The choice to finance an investment project is a rational decision made by the firm from a pecking order theory perspective rather than the result of credit rationing.
36. This result may be related to the fact that our sample includes only firms that were engaged in both investments and R&D and were probably not financially constrained.

References

Aghion, P., Bond, S., Klemm, A., and Marinescu, I. (2004) "Technology and Financial Structure: are innovative enterprise different?" *Journal of the European Economic Association*, April-May, 2 (2–3), 277–288.

Atzeni, G., and Piga, C.A. (2007) "R&D Investment, Credit Rationing And Sample Selection" *Bulletin of Economic Research* 59 (2), 149–178.

Berger, A.N., and Udell, G.F. (1990) "Collateral, Loan Quality, and Bank Risk" *Journal of Monetary Economics* 25, 21–42.

Berger, A.N., and Udell, G.F. (1998) "The economics of small business finance: The roles of private equity and debt markets in the financial growth cycle" *Journal of Banking & Finance* 22, 613–673.

Bester, H. (1985) "Screening vs. Rationing in Credit Markets with Imperfect Information" *American Economic Review* 75, 850–855.

Bhattacharya, S., and Chiesa, G. (1995) "Proprietary Information, Financial Intermediation and Research Incentives" *Journal of Financial Intermediation* 4, 328–357.

Capitalia (2005) *Osservatorio sulle Piccole e Medie Imprese, Indagine sulle imprese italiane*, Roma.

Czarnitzki, D. (2002) Research and Development: Financial Constraints and the Role of Public Funding for Small and Medium-sized Enterprises, ZEW Discussion Paper No. 02–74.

Frank, M.Z., and Goyal, V.K. (2005) Trade-off and Pecking Order Theories of Debt, Working Paper, Center for Corporate Governance, Tuck School of Business at Dartmouth.

Gonas, J.S., Highfield, M.J., and Mullineaux, D.J. (2004) "When Are Commercial Loans Secured?" *The Financial Review* 39 79–99

Greene, W.H. (2003) *Econometric Analysis*, 5th edn., Prentice Hall, Inc., London.

Hall, B. H. (2002) "The Financing of Research and Development" *Oxford Review of Economic Policy* 18 (1), 35–51.

Harris, M., and Raviv, A. (1991) "The Theory of Capital Structure" *The Journal of Finance* 46 (1), 297–355.

Hellmann, T., and Stiglitz, J.E. (2000) "Credit and equity rationing in markets with adverse selection" *European Economic Review* 44, 281–304.

Herrera, A.M., and Minetti, R. (2007) "Informed finance and technological change: Evidence from credit relationships" *Journal of Financial Economics* 83, 223–269.

Himmelberg, C.P., and Petersen, B.C. (1994) "R & D and Internal Finance: A Panel Study of Small Firms in High-Tech Industries" *The Review of Economics and Statistics* 76 (1) (Feb), 38–51.

Ozkan, N. (2002) "Effects of financial constraints on research and development investment: an empirical investigation" *Applied Financial Economics* 12, 827–834.

Li, K., and Prabhala, N.R. (2006) Self-Selection Models in Corporate Finance, Working Paper, Center for Corporate Governance, Tuck School of Business at Dartmouth.

Modigliani, F., and Miller, M.H. (1958) "The cost of capital, corporation finance, and the theory of investment" *American Economic Review* 48, 261–297.

Meuleman, M., and De Maeseneire, W. (2008) Do R&D Subsidies Affect SMEs' Access To External Financing?, Vlerick Leuven Gent Working Paper Series 2008/12.

Myers, S.C., and Majluf, N. (1984) "Corporate financing and investment decisions when enterprises have information that investors do not have" *Journal of Financial Economics* 13, 187–221.

Myers, S.C. (2003) "Financing of corporations" in Constantinides, G., Harris, M., and Stulz, R. (eds.) *Handbook of The Economics of Finance: Corporate Finance* 1A, Elsevier, North Holland, Amsterdam.

Zamarian, G.R., and Zaninotto, E. (2006) *Assessing the economic impact of public industrial policies: an empirical investigation on subsidies,* Proceedings of the Convention "EARIE 2006", Amsterdam (NL), 25–28 August 2006.

Zellner, A. (1962) "An Efficient Method of Estimating Seemingly Unrelated Regressions (SUR) and Tests for Aggregation Bias" *Journal of the American Statistical Association* 57, 348–368.

Part 2

Efficiency and Productivity of Financial Intermediaries

5
Incorporating Risk in the Efficiency and Productivity Analysis of Banking Systems

Thomas Weyman-Jones, Miguel Boucinha,
Karligash Kenjegalieva, Geetha Ravishankar,
Nuno Ribeiro and Zhi Shen

1. Introduction

Among the many impacts of the credit crunch will be the necessity for economists to find a reformulation of models for performance measurement in banks. One of the most important issues to address is how to include risk in the measurement of the performance of banking systems. In this contribution, we review three different approaches to the incorporation of risk in measuring the efficiency and productivity performance of banking systems: the use of *equity capital* as an explanatory variable, the role of *scale efficiency change* as an indicator of risky behaviour and, finally, the use of *second moment statistics* to measure risk. The first two approaches can be regarded as indirect measures of risk in contrast to the third, which is a direct measure of it. We illustrate this with empirical work from Boucinha et al. (2009); Kenjegalieva and Weyman-Jones (2009) and Shen et al. (2009). We argue that while the direct approach is theoretically superior it faces very challenging and possibly insurmountable empirical problems.

2. Equity capital and risk in standard models of efficiency and productivity analysis

We begin by analysing the role of equity capital as an explanatory variable in representations of banking technology, as suggested by Bikker and Bos (2008) following the initial suggestion by Mester (1996) – see also Hughes and Mester (2008). Bikker and Bos (2008: 14) – in discussing the standard models of efficiency and productivity analysis in banking, i.e. the intermediation and production models, state that "both models fail to incorporate the management of risk". Hughes and Mester (2008) comment: "Typically in the literature, the cost and profit functions or frontiers are measured without considering the bankís capital structure or bankís choice of risk. This is a serious omission since both are important parts of banking technology." Following Mester (1996), Bikker and Bos argue that including equity capital in a model of banking performance fulfils three tasks: equity may substitute for deposits as a means of funding loans; increased reliance on equity capital may reduce the risk of the bank defaulting on its loans and therefore indicate the risk preferences of its managers and the reliance on equity as a substitute for debt may reflect the relative size of the bank – very small banks may be more reliant on equity financing at the margin.

Hughes and Mester (2008) define the task of a bank as financial intermediary to be the screening and monitoring of borrowers in order to resolve asymmetric information problems between borrowers and lenders. The requirement to repay deposits on demand provides banks with the incentive to do this, and banks have a competitive advantage over other intermediaries in dealing with borrowers with informational advantages. The key effect on efficiency and productivity analysis is that the banks' ability to perform the function efficiently depends on the characteristics of the operating environment, including regulation, property rights and ownership structure. Hughes and Mester argue that in modelling bank behaviour the researcher must consider three aspects of risk: (1) *assessment* – banks' comparative advantage arises from their private information on the deposits of borrowers, (2) *diversification* – pooling loans and deposits reduces liquidity and credit risks and (3) *risk taking* – while banks can monitor loans at lower cost than non-banks, the liquidity of deposits should discipline the banks into limiting the extent of risk taking, and the importance of deposits in the payment system means that banks should always be closely regulated.[1]

In particular, Hughes and Mester (2008) argue for the importance of including equity capital in performance specifications since the cost of equity capital (i.e. the return on equity times the level of equity capital) is an important component of economic profit or economic value added. However, as is well known, the cost of capital and economic value added are not reflected in the published income account reports of banks (Kimball 1998), while Fiordelisi (2007) used the Capital Asset Pricing Model (CAPM) to measure economic value added in banking activity. According to Hughes and Mester (2008), empirical work which uses the cash flow or accounting concept of cost, while it includes the interest cost on deposits (i.e. debt), ignores the cost of equity and there-fore biases the efficiency scores. They recommend including equity as a quasi-fixed input in the cost function so that the shadow price of equity can be estimated. They cite a finding that the mean shadow price of equity for small banks is significantly smaller than for larger banks, implying that small banks over-utilize equity while larger banks under-utilize it possibly as a result of the availability of deposit insurance; this idea is consistent with the stylized fact that small banks tend to be more capitalized than large ones.

It is important to see how the inclusion of equity affects the nature of the model of the bank's technology. Boucinha et al. (2009) argue (on the basis of task 1 from Bikker and Bos 2008) for including it as a fixed input because there are regulatory and rating/reputation objectives which con-strain the optimal choice of equity and there are fixed costs to issuing equity which lead banks to issue capital in relatively large tranches and thus (since there is a bound on the minimum) banks will actually have more capital than the level yielded by the individual static maximiza-tion problem. Consequently, in the short run translog cost model, the negative of the derivative of cost with respect to the fixed level of equity capital should be the shadow return on equity. In some studies, Hughes and Mester (2008) report that the short run cost function incorporates equity capital in the form of a ratio of equity to total assets. In that event, the shadow return on equity can still be inferred from the regression but the equation is fitted subject to the implicit constraint that the return on equity and the return on assets are equal in absolute value and this may therefore bias the estimated shadow return on equity downwards.

Our first review of empirical work on risk in efficiency and productiv-ity analysis of banking systems contrasts the shadow price of equity in two very different contexts. In Boucinha et al. (2009) the variable cost function analysis was applied to a panel dataset of banks in Portugal during the period 1992–2004, while in Shen et al. (2009) the model is applied to ten Asian banking systems over the period 1998–2005. The time periods of the two applications therefore overlap, although the experience and nature of the banking system panels are different in sig-nificant ways. The banking system in Portugal has remained relatively closely monitored by the central bank even during this period of evolv-ing liberalization. It has remained much less affected by the 2007–2008 banking crises associated with sub-prime mortgages than many other Western economy banking systems. In Asian economies, it may have been less easy to insulate the banking systems from the effects of finan-cial crises in those of the US and UK.

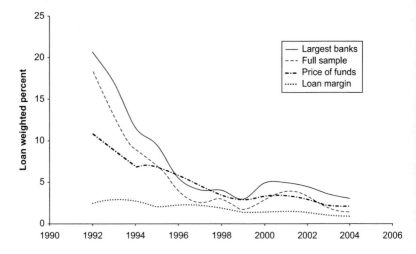

Figure 5.1   Shadow price of equity capital in Portugal (1997–2004)

Figure 5.1 summarizes the results for the case of Portugal. Four time series are plotted: the shadow cost of equity for the full sample derived from fitting the short run variable cost function treating equity capital as a fixed input, the same shadow cost for the largest quintile of banks in terms of loans, the implicit price of funding derived from the reported funding costs and total funds raised and the margin on loans derived as the implicit price on loans minus the marginal cost of loans derived from the fitted translog variable cost function. Each of the aggregated series has been weighted by the individual loan data. The sample period has been characterized by falling interest rates and therefore reduced price of funding and by increased competition amongst the banks, demonstrated by the declining margin on loans. Against this background the shadow price of equity has fallen over the period but with a significant increase during the sub-period 1999–2001. The sub-period increase reflected a rise in money market interest rates and funding costs that followed Portugal's entry into the euro area, and this had a pronounced effect on the shadow cost of equity.[2] A clear finding, in particular, is in confirmation of the Hughes and Mester hypothesis that the shadow price of equity for the largest banks exceeds that for the sample as a whole, with the proportionate difference increasing towards the end of the sample period even as market rates fell and competition increased.

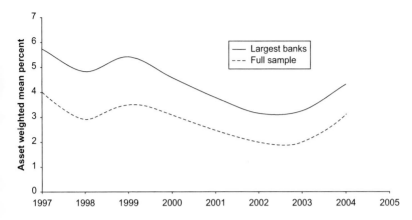

Figure 5.2   Shadow price of equity in ten Asian countries (1997–2004)

In Shen et al. (2009) a similar model is fitted to a panel dataset drawn from banking systems in ten different Asian countries. The results are shown in Figure 5.2.

Once again there is a clear distinction between the shadow cost of equity for the full sample of banks and that for the largest banks, here represented by the largest quartile in terms of total assets. We conclude therefore that making allowance for the capital structure of the different banks in the sample is a critical part of the econometric approach to measuring efficiency; in particular it leads us to focus on the shadow return on capital as a performance indicator derived from the inclusion of equity capital in the estimate of the frontier.

3. Using productivity decompositions to infer risk management behaviour

The previous section examined the problem of incorporating risk into the frontier assessment, although we focused on an indirect measure of risk. This section poses a different question: if it is possible to determine from the dynamic behaviour of banks whether their risk management of loans changes over time or differs in different banking systems. In other words, the purpose is not to measure risk but to infer the presence of risky behaviour from sample data. To complete this task we focus on the decomposition of the total factor productivity change in a banking system. We make use of two primary sources, Bauer (1990) and Orea

(2001), to set up the theory of the approach. The objective is to obtain the decomposition:

Total Factor Productivity (TFP) change = Efficiency change +
Technical change + Scale Efficiency change   (1)

To construct this we took the cost functions estimated for Portugal in Boucinha et al. (2009) and for the sample of Asian countries in Shen et al. (2009) and, in the case of Russia, the results of the estimation of an input distance function (Kenjegalieva and Weyman-Jones 2009). In each case, the discrete index number version of the Bauer (1990) decomposition can be derived by adapting the arguments in Orea (2001), see Boucinha et al. (2009) for details. The output and input price weights may be calibrated using market prices, in which case we require revenue and cost shares for our cases; alternatively an econometric approach using a fully flexible functional form such as the translog function may be adopted, and this is done in the case studies cited here.

The productivity decompositions are shown in Figures 5.3, 5.4 and 5.5 for the cases of Portugal, the Asian sample and Russia respectively. Values of the series exceeding unity indicate a positive contribution to total factor productivity and values below 1 indicate a negative contribution.

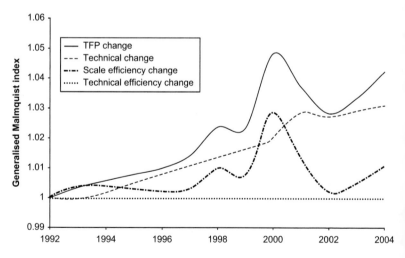

Figure 5.3   Total factor productivity in the banking system in Portugal (1997–2004)

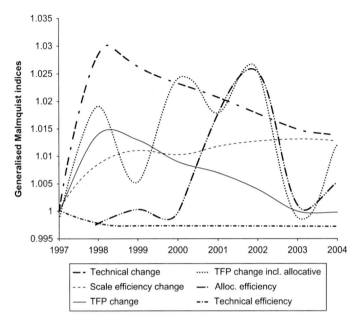

Figure 5.4 Total factor productivity in the banking systems of ten Asian countries (1997–2005)

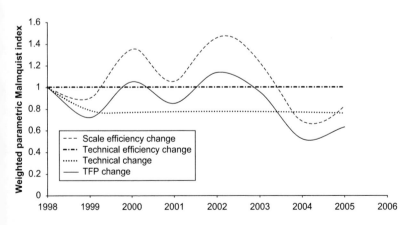

Figure 5.5 Total factor productivity in the banking system of Russia (1998–2005)

In the case of Portugal, there was a steady and accelerating total factor productivity change over the period 1992–2004. Although efficiency change was weak, technical change was very strong and was the major component of total factor productivity change, together with some scale efficiency change reflecting output growth accelerating over input growth. The cost function indicated some scope for scale change in its finding of increasing returns to scale.

In the case of the Asian banking systems, Figure 5.4 extends the productivity decomposition to include an estimate of the allocative component of productivity change. A similar result to Portugal is found, with the sources of total factor productivity change comprising strong technical progress especially at the beginning of the period, and some scale efficiency change.

Both of these samples indicate results for banking systems which have not been major casualties of the recent financial crises. In particular, Portugal is an example of a system which underwent a gradual and smooth liberalization process. Hence, and since loan growth was supported by the regime change brought about by euro area accession, the strong loan expansion was not publicly assessed by the supervisory authorities as a signal of excessive risk taking.

This is not the case for Russia, for which the differences are striking. The central bank became alarmed about excessive loan growth, stating: "growth in banking sector assets has been largely a result of greater lending, with a particularly strong growth in lending to the household sector" (Bank of Russia 2008). The productivity decomposition in Russia is qualitatively different from the other two samples. Here, total factor productivity growth is totally dominated by scale efficiency change, and the other components make only negative or zero contributions. Our conclusions demonstrate a severe decline in productivity after 1998, but recovery from 2000–2005.

Efficiency change is zero, possibly because of the strong presence of state-owned banks; technical change is virtually zero, suggesting low levels of managerial innovation and productivity recovery is all driven by scale efficiency change. However, scale efficiency change is measured by output growth net of input growth, technical change and efficiency change. Hence, while it could reflect actual increasing returns to scale, for which there is some evidence in some of the banks in the sample, a more plausible explanation is that it could reflect an uncontrolled loan expansion strategy with weaker risk management.

We argue that this observation of weak efficiency change suggests that weaker risk management was important in the post-1998 expansion in

Russia. This allows us to draw a modelling inference about the direction from observed productivity components to risk management, rather than the reverse direction of the previous section. We suggest that banking systems where observed scale efficiency change is the dominant component in an otherwise poorly performing system is indicative of weak risk management in general and excessive loan growth in particular. In looking at these three samples we have examples of: (1) an economy where the liberalization process occurred against the background of a solid supervisory framework and without adverse systemic events (Portugal), (2) systems where regulatory oversight has been variable but there has been strong innovation (Asia) and (3) an economy where regulation has been weak, incentives poor and corruption widespread (Russia). The signals from the data correspond to the last case being dominated by scale efficiency change, i.e. excessive loan growth. The fact that productivity change is chiefly driven by output volatility (net of input requirements) is indicative of the highly variable and risky environment in which the Russian banking system was operating in those years. Consequently, we suggest this phenomenon as an indicator of poor risk management.

4. Direct measures of risk in frontiers: banks as portfolio optimizing agents

Above, we considered indirect methods of allowing for risk in empirical models of efficiency and productivity analysis. In this section, we turn to direct methods of including risk, and the risk-return trade-off of utility maximizing agents. Two strands of the literature are useful: the first reflects the non-parametric efficiency methods of evaluating managed investment funds; the second uses econometric models of managerial utility associated with trading return against risk. Applications to the banking system are relatively few, but the seminal work of Tobin (1963) was amongst the earliest studies to hypothesize that in response to interest margins at different times managers of commercial banks would develop different loan strategies according to their perceptions of risk and their risk preferences.

The conventional risk-return trade-off develops a frontier between the variance on a portfolio of loans and the expected return. A number of performance measures related to this portfolio frontier have been developed in the literature on investment fund performance, such as the Treynor, Sharpe and Jensen measures; see Basso and Funari (2001) for a review of these. Basso and Funari and a number of other authors also propose extensions to these using a data envelopment analysis framework. These authors and others working in this field propose a list of outputs and inputs which incorporate a range of measures of portfolio return in the outputs and a range of measures of risk (such as the variance of returns, the half-variance and so on) and operating and set-up cost in the inputs. The measure of efficient performance is then solved from a data envelopment analysis model.

Applying this model to banks would necessitate that the measure of bank outputs included such variables as profit and return on equity, while that of bank inputs included the second, third and, possibly, greater moments of these returns, as well as the operating and capital costs of the different banks. Consequently where data envelopment analysis is used to measure bank performance there is no reason why risk should not be measured directly as an input in the form of the variance of returns. This will give a measure of risk based performance which can be extended to productivity measurement.

One of the few studies to introduce risk directly into an econometric frontier is that of Hughes et al. (2001). The starting point is the idea that maximizing the value of the bank is one of the objectives of management, along with efficient use of inputs and control of costs. The model develops a managerial utility function that depends on profit, π, and input usage, x. At this stage risk does not enter as an explicit variable, but must be assumed to determine the structure of preferences underlying the utility function. The managers are constrained by a budget, essentially the income account, which depends on net after tax marginal profit, p_π; output and input prices, p and w, and the technology which depends on these prices, inputs and outputs, y, as well as the level of equity capital, e. Figure 5.6 presents a diagrammatic analysis of the manager's most preferred production plan. In the figure the combined constraint set is illustrated, together with indifference curves of managerial utility. These indifference curves demonstrate that for cost-concerned managers who also wish to maximize bank value, the indifference curves are upward sloping (increased profit is a *good*, and increased input usage is a *bad*) with an increasing marginal rate of substitution between profit and input usage. At the utility maximizing outcome, the optimal levels of profit and input usage translate into the optimal budget shares. These are to be estimated by specifying the econometric share equation regressions: s_π and s_m, $m = 1, ... , m$ for profit and m inputs.

The shadow return on equity in this model is derived from the fitted profit share equations $\hat{s}_\pi$ and in particular, the standard error of the

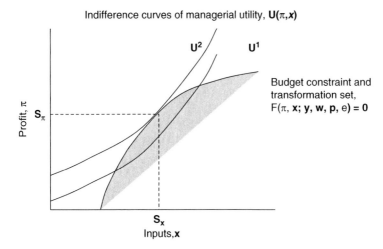

Figure 5.6 Managerial utility maximization

fitted (predicted) return depends on the variance of the fitted profit share adjusted by the gross return on equity:

$$\hat{\sigma}_i = \left[\sqrt{\text{var}\left(\hat{s}_\pi\right)} \right] \left[\mathbf{p}'\mathbf{y}/e \right] \tag{2}$$

This standard error of prediction for the fitted share, $\hat{s}_\pi$ is derived from the variance-covariance matrix and varies across the sample of banks. It is dependent on the explanatory variables ($\mathbf{y}$, $\mathbf{w}$, $\mathbf{p}$, p_π, k), together with the error variances in the system of share equations.

Now Hughes et al. (2001: 2197, Eq. (24)) (see also Hughes and Mester 2008: Eq. (3)), propose the following stochastic frontier for return against risk for different managers:

$$\hat{E}\left(\pi/e\right)_i = a_0 + a_1\hat{\sigma}_i + a_2\hat{\sigma}_i^2 + v_i - u_i \tag{3}$$

Here, the dependent variable is the estimated after tax net return on equity and the composite error term contains both the usual two sided idiosyncratic error, v_i, and the one sided, half normal inefficiency component, u_i. The authors' objective is to measure managerial performance in a relationship which explicitly includes risk. Hughes et al. (2001: 2196) describe the explanatory variable term $\hat{\sigma}_i$ as "an econometric measure of prediction risk, which is a function of the exogenous variables of the production system". An assumption with this model is that the impact of changes in the variance of predicted profit is the same across all banks; however, the potential vulnerability of the bank to the performance variance measure may instead be a more critical variable reflecting some of the network economic models which identify players key to any network and therefore are potentially more vulnerable to changes in the network.

An issue with this model that needs further exploration is the extent to which $\hat{E}(\pi/e)_i$ and $\hat{\sigma}_i$ are jointly determined, or more generally, under what assumptions $\hat{\sigma}_i$ can be considered to be independent of the composite error term in the frontier performance equation. This is the classic problem of generated regressors first identified by Pagan (1984); see also Wooldridge (2002). If $\hat{\sigma}_i$ is not independent of the composed error term in the frontier, the estimators will be biased and inconsistent. The problem is not insurmountable in theory if an instrumental variables (IV) estimator can be found. However, consider the nature of the required instrumental variable: it should be correlated with the variance of profit but uncorrelated with the idiosyncratic error. This is the standard IV assumption; however, we also need an additional requirement: *the instrumental variable for the variance of profit should not be correlated with the measure of profit efficiency.* This would appear to be a very difficult property to find, and therefore we must conclude that this direct approach to modelling risk poses difficult econometric challenges. Generalizing, we would argue that any model that seeks to explain performance y_i by a risk variable which is measured by the variance of performance var(y_i) falls into this category:

$$y_i = f\left(x_i, \mathrm{var}\left(y_i\right); \beta\right) + v_i - u_i \qquad (4)$$

Where u_i measures inefficiency, it is difficult to conceive of an instrumental variable that is correlated with var(y_i) but uncorrelated with u_i. At this time, the direct measure of risk in a bank performance equation therefore appears to raise challenging econometric difficulties.

5. Conclusions

We have reviewed three different approaches to modelling risk in efficiency and productivity analysis of banking systems. The first considers indirect measures of risk; the second tries to determine whether strong or weak risk management can be inferred from data on productivity decomposition and finally, the third considers whether direct measures of risk can be included in the specification of performance measurement regressions.

The approach of using indirect measures of risk stems from the argument of Hughes and Mester (2008) that capital structure, represented by including equity capital in the cost function, and the operating characteristics of the economic environment are important in explaining performance in banking systems. We looked at two empirical studies for Portugal and ten Asian countries where equity capital had been used as an explanatory variable, and we demonstrated how the shadow price of equity could be derived for these samples. We discovered an empirical regularity – that over the period of the 1990s and up to 2005, the shadow price of equity in banking systems had declined, but that it was consistently higher for larger banks than for the full sample, similarly to the findings in Hughes et al. (2001). However, that paper found that most banks over-utilized equity capital relative to the level which would solve their static maximization problem, whereas large banks underutilized capital. In the case of Portugal, evidence of the former but not of the latter result was found. In our second approach we reversed the argument about causation, and tried to infer risk management behaviour from the sample data. We based this inference on the argument that economies where risk management was known to be weak, e.g. as signalled by central bank supervision reports, would show excessive loan growth. Since loan growth in itself shows up in productivity decompositions of the banking system as scale efficiency change, we argued that banking systems with poor risk management would exhibit a total factor productivity decomposition dominated by scale efficiency change. By comparing productivity trends obtained by econometric models of banking system performance for our three empirical samples, we were able to identify that the system known to have weakest loan risk management, i.e. Russia, had a total factor productivity decomposition where scale efficiency change was the only positive component, in contrast to Portugal and Asian economies where technical change was dominant.

The final topic in our review of risk modelling was concerned with direct measures of risk in performance equations. Borrowing from the literature on data envelopment analysis of investment funds, we argued that, along with costs, the measures of the variance of returns, costs or profits could be included as inputs in the data envelopment analysis while the outputs included the returns or profits so that an extended risk-return trade-off could be modelled. Finally we examined a theoretical model of Hughes, Mester and Moon which derived a performance frontier that included an econometric prediction error as an explanatory variable for the performance return. This could potentially be a very

fruitful approach but we argued that there could be difficult econometric challenges arising from possible endogeneity, since the prediction
error may be correlated with the efficiency component of the frontier
error term, and appropriate instrumental variables uncorrelated with
profit/cost efficiency may be difficult to find.

Notes

1. The importance of these points is of course reinforced by the failure to recognize them in the international banking crises of 2007 and 2008.
2. Apart from that, it can be argued that euro area participation after 1999,
   even though with permanently lower and less volatile interest rates, could
   have led to an unsustainable lending boom beyond equilibrium levels. So
   far, this conjecture proved unfounded, as no events involving the failure of
   systemic institutions have occurred, even after the outbursts of the recent
   crisis in 2007.

References

Bank of Russia (2008) *Central Bank of the Russian Federation Supervision Report 2007*, Novosti Press, Moscow.

Basso, A., and Funari, S., (2001) "A data envelopment analysis approach to measure the mutual fund performance" *European Journal of Operational Research*, 135, 477–92.

Bauer, Paul W. (1990) "Decomposing TFP Growth in the Presence of Cost
Inefficiency, Nonconstant Returns to Scale, and Technological Progress"
Journal of Productivity Analysis 1, 287–99.

Bikker, Jacob A., and Bos, Jaap W.B. (2008) *Bank Performance*, Routledge, London.

Boucinha, Miguel, Ribeiro, Nuno, and Weyman-Jones, Thomas (2009) "An
assessment of Portuguese banks' costs and efficiency" *Banco de Portugal Working Paper 22*.

Fiordelisi, Franco (2007) "Shareholder value efficiency in European banking"
Journal of Banking and Finance 31, 2151–71.

Hughes, Joseph P., Mester, Loretta J., and Moon, Choon-Geol (2001) "Are Scale
Economies in Banking Elusive or Illusive: evidence obtained by incorporating
capital structure and risk taking into models of bank production" *Journal of Banking and Finance*, 25, 2169–2208.

Hughes, Joseph P., and Mester, Loretta J. (2008) "Efficiency in Banking: theory,
practice and evidence" *Federal Reserve Bank of Philadelphia Research Working Paper 08/1*, Philadelphia, PA: Federal Reserve Bank of Philadelphia, and in *The Oxford Handbook of Banking*, Edited by Berger, Allen N., Molyneux, Phillip, and Wilson, John (2009) Oxford University Press, Oxford.

Kenjegalieva, Karligash, and Weyman-Jones, Thomas (2009) "Efficiency and productivity of Russian banks: distinguishing heterogeneity and performance" in
Balling, Morten, Gnan, Ernest, Lierman, Frank, and Schoder, Jean-Pierre (eds)

Productivity in the Financial Services Sector, SUERF Studies 2009/4, European Money and Finance Forum, Vienna.

Kimball, Ralph C., (1998) "Economic Profit and Performance Measurement in Banking" *New England Economic Review*, July–August, 35–53.

Mester, L., (1996) "Measuring Efficiency at US Banks: accounting for heterogeneity is important", *Federal Reserve Bank of Philadelphia Research Working Paper 96/11*, Federal Reserve Bank of Philadelphia, Philadelphia, PA.

Orea, Luis (2002) "A Generalised Parametric Malmquist Productivity Index" *Journal of Productivity Analysis*, 18, 5–22.

Shen, Zhi, Liao, Hailin, and Weyman-Jones, Thomas (2009) "Cost Efficiency Analysis in Banking Industries of Ten Asian Countries and Regions" *Journal of Chinese Economic and Business Studies* 7 (2), 199–218.

Pagan, A.R. (1984) "Econometric Issues in the Analysis of Regressions with Generated Regressors" *International Economic Review* 25, 221–47.

Tobin, James (1963) "Commercial Banks as Creators of Money" in Carson, D. (ed.) *Banking and Monetary Studies*, Richard D. Irwin, Homewood, Illinois.

Wooldridge, Jeffrey M. (2002) *Econometric Analysis of Cross Section and Panel Data*, The MIT Press, Cambridge, MA.

6
Efficiency and Environmental Factors in Investment Banking

Nemanja Radić, Claudia Girardone and Franco Fiordelisi

1. Introduction

In the "Great Moderation" era, the investment banking industry in all advanced economies has benefited from the processes of liberalization, internationalization and consolidation activities. An increasing number of financial institutions have been involved in cross-border activities and in providing banking services globally. Investment banks' main business is to intermediate between issuers and investors through the functions of M&A advisory services and underwriting of securities issues. They also provide trading and investment in securities and asset management.

Yet, investment banks' core function lies in the "origination" of large and complex financial instruments that expose them to market risks and imply that their business relies predominantly on the short term.

The recent financial turmoil affected a relatively large number of investment banks. Under pressure for profits, these have contributed to the emergence of an unprecedented system of compensation, a highly leveraged industry and a pervasive risk culture. Post-crisis, surviving banks will have to comply with new constraints, and thus the evaluation of their operating efficiency is likely to gain a new impetus, particularly on the cost side. In this context, the description of modern investment banks' production process should reflect the changes in their business focus. In addition, it should account for risk and other environmental and regulatory factors.

The empirical literature on investment banks' efficiency and environmental variables is fairly scarce. One of the main reasons for this paucity of studies is in the global nature of the industry, which implies that a mere national focus maybe misleading. The objective of this chapter is to assess both cost and profit efficiency for a large sample of investment banks operating in the G7 countries (Canada, France, Germany, Italy, Japan, the UK and the US) and Switzerland over the period 2001–2007. It also aims to introduce a large set of environmental factors (macroeconomic, institutional and regulatory) and to evaluate to what extent they are associated with the estimated efficiency scores. Our results show that with only a few exceptions, cost and profit efficiency scores are generally higher for non-EU countries than for their EU counterparts. Moreover, our evidence clearly indicates that in most cases the relationships between efficiency scores and environmental variables are highly significant.

2. Literature review

Existing literature on bank efficiency reveals that the investment banking sector is surprisingly inadequately explored (e.g. Berger and Humphrey 1997, Berger 2007 and Hughes and Mester, 2008 do not cite any study on investment banks).

The efficiency studies applied to the banking sector focus predominantly on commercial banking (see, e.g. the extensive reviews by Berger and Humphrey 1997; Goddard et al. 2001; Berger 2007; Hughes and Mester 2008). Only a handful of studies (Allen and Rai 1996; Vander Vennet 2002) analyse universal banking (which includes investment banking in its business) and compare it with traditional banking. As far as we are aware, Beccalli (2004) is the only study directly examining the efficiency of investment firms by comparing the cost efficiency of UK and Italian investment firms over the period 1995–1998. The parametric stochastic frontier approach (SFA) is used in order to model cost efficiency.[1] According to the author's findings, controlling for environmental variables is crucial in assessing the investment banking business, since these factors have a significant influence on cost efficiency as well as profitability.

The paucity of efficiency studies for investment banking can be explained by three main factors: first, the lack of good quality data; second, the difficulties in successfully modelling the peculiar nature of investment banks' production process (i.e. a problem of identifying variables) and third, the need to account accurately for different environmental conditions in various countries – investment banking is a global business and efficiency needs to be measured by running an international comparisons of investment banks.

Recent developments in the literature dealing with commercial banks can help to circumvent the last two problems. The identification of the variables to model the production process successfully is a serious problem since the investment banking business is multifaceted. Gardener and Molyneux (1995) categorize the investment banks' business into five main areas: broking (i.e. the broking of securities is a commodity business in which firms appeal to customers mainly on price and integrity), trading (i.e. the trading of securities drives on market volatility), core investment banking (i.e. the underwriting of new issues and advisory work also referred to as Mergers and Acquisitions), fund management (i.e. both retail and wholesale fund management) and interest spreading (i.e. income derivatives from borrowed funds). As such, the accurate measurement of the investment banks' risk taking and risk transferring is a key issue. Recent studies dealing with commercial banks included risk characteristics in cost or profit functions estimation, such as the liquidity risk exposure (Altunbas et al. 2000; Demirgüç-Kunt and Huizinga 2004; Brissimis et al. 2008; Fiordelisi and Molyneux 2009); insolvency risk exposure (Lepetit et al. 2008); credit risk (Athanasoglou et al. 2008; Brissimis et al. 2008; Fiordelisi and Molyneux 2009); capital risk exposure (Dietsch and Lozano-Vivas 2000; Lozano-Vivas et al. 2002; Altunbas et al. 2000; Athanasoglou et al. 2008; Brissimis et al. 2008; Lepetit et al. 2008); market risk exposure (Fiordelisi and Molyneux 2009) and the off-balance risk exposure (Casu and Girardone 2005).

Regarding the need to assess investment banking efficiency on a worldwide base, there is an increasing number of studies dealing with commercial banks which run international comparisons of bank efficiency by including environmental factors to confront environmental differences across countries. By summarizing 100 studies that compare bank efficiencies across different nations, Berger (2007) observe that efficiency has been measured using either the estimation of nation-specific frontiers, or by the estimation of common frontiers including specific variables in the estimation to account for countries' differences. While the first approach guarantees the sample homogeneity, it does not enable the authors to compare banks from different countries directly. In contrast, the second approach allows a direct comparison of efficiency levels and rankings from different countries (Coelli et al. 2005; Bos and Schmiedel 2007) by implicitly assuming that banks in different countries have access to the same technology and effectively compete with each other. However, this approach requires dealing with the sample's heterogeneity by controlling for systematic differences across banks that are not the result of inefficiency;[2] failure to account for heterogeneity is a likely candidate for causing instability of efficiency results, as was recently emphasized by Bos et al. (2008). Various studies focus on country-specific environmental factors in order to avoid this technology problem (see Dietsch and Lozano-Vivas 2000; Lozano-Vivas et al. 2002).

Focusing on recent studies, various factors are used to account for countries' macroeconomic differences: population density (Dietsch and Lozano-Vivas 2000; Lozano-Vivas et al. 2002; Carbo-Valverde et al. 2007; Fiordelisi and Molyneux 2009), the countries' wealth (e.g. the GDP per capita, as in Salas and Saurina 2003; Carbo-Valverde et al. 2007; Fitzpatrick and McQuinn 2007; Brissimis et al. 2008; Fiordelisi and Molyneux 2009), the density of demand and per capita income (Dietsch and Lozano-Vivas 2000; Lozano-Vivas et al. 2002), the FDI inflows and outflows (Beccalli 2004), the short-term interest rate and foreign and public ownership (Brissimis et al. 2008) and inflation and cyclical output (Athanasoglou et al. 2008).

Last it is worth mentioning that investment banks and financial conglomerates, as complex banks, are difficult to monitor and may be so politically and economically powerful to become "too big to discipline". Conflicts of interest may arise when banks engage in such diverse activities as securities underwriting, insurance underwriting and real estate investment, and as a consequence the overall riskiness of the business may increase. Governments may react by restricting banking activity for the sake of stability, but this has a trade-off with performance. Based on these premises, Barth et al. (2004) examine the relationship between bank regulation and supervision, bank development, performance and stability. These authors find that there exists a positive link between regulation and supervisory practices that force accurate information disclosure and limit the moral hazard incentives with greater bank development, overall better performance and increased stability. However, they recognize the need for more research on the topic.

Overall, the vast majority of the literature on bank efficiency focuses on commercial banking. The present study advances the existing literature on investment banks by examining specifically the cost and profit efficiency of these operating in eight large industrialized countries and by investigating the relationship by means of the correlation between efficiency estimates and a set of macroeconomic, institutional and environmental factors.

3. Main methodological issues and data sample

Cost and profit efficiency are measured using the Stochastic Frontier Analysis (SFA), which can be written as follows:[3]

$$ln\ TCi_{,t} = x_{i,t}\ \beta + (V_{i,t} + U_{i,t}) \tag{1}$$

where t denotes the time dimension, $ln\ TC_i$ is the logarithm of the cost of production (pre-tax profits, PT, for the profit function) of the i-th bank, x_i is a $kx1$ vector of input prices and output quantities of the i-th bank, β is a vector of unknown parameters, V_i are random variables which are assumed to be i.i.d $N(0, \sigma_v^2)$ and independent of U_i and U_i are non-negative random variables which are assumed to account for cost inefficiency and to be i.i.d. as truncations at zero of the $N(0, \sigma_U^2)$. Following an approach similar to Altunbas et al. (2000), we use the following translog functional form:[4]

$$\ln TC_{k,t}(\ln TP) = \beta_0 + \sum_{i=1}^{2}\beta_i \ln Y_i + \sum_{j=1}^{2}\alpha_j \ln P_j + \lambda_1 T$$

$$+ \frac{1}{2}\left[\sum_{i=1}^{2}\sum_{j=1}^{2}\delta_{ij} \ln Y_i \ln Y_j + \sum_{i=1}^{2}\sum_{j=1}^{2}\gamma_{ij} \ln P_i \ln P_j + \lambda_{11}T^2\right] + \sum_{i=1}^{2}\sum_{j=1}^{2}\rho_{ij} \ln Y_i \ln P_i + \sum_{i=1}^{2}\beta_{iT}T \ln Y_i +$$

$$\sum_{j=1}^{2}\alpha_{jT}T \ln P_j + \frac{1}{2}\tau_{EE} \ln E \ln E + \tau_E \ln E +$$

$$\sum_{i=1}^{2}\beta_{iE} \ln Y_i \ln E + \sum_{j=1}^{2}\alpha_{jE} \ln P_j \ln E + \epsilon_{kt}$$
$$for\ i \neq j \tag{2}$$

$$\epsilon_{kt} = v_{kt} + u_{kt}$$

where $\ln TC_{kt}$ (ln TP) is the natural logarithm of total cost (total profit) of bank k in period t, Y_i is the vector of output quantities, P_j are the input prices and E represents the bank's equity capital and is included as a fixed input, specifying interaction terms with both output and input prices in line with recent studies (see e.g. Altunbas et al. 2000; Vander

Table 6.1 Sample description: number of banks and average asset size by country

Country/ Year	2001	2002	2003	2004	2005	2006	2007	Total by country	Total assets of the average bank*
Canada	1	1	1	2	3	4	4	16	3,951,175
France	2	2	2	3	5	9	7	30	26,175,525
Germany	6	8	6	8	8	11	8	55	12,182,958
Italy	2	1	2	3	5	6	6	25	1,814,332
Japan	2	6	19	23	23	22	19	114	29,686,104
UK	9	9	10	20	27	32	25	132	36,565,124
USA	15	19	21	18	15	14	9	111	115,358,872
Switzerland	50	44	44	45	45	45	44	317	21,406,169
Total by year	87	90	105	122	131	143	122	800	

Note: * All values are in US$ thousands.

Vennet 2002; Beccalli, 2004. We include the time trend t to capture technological change.[5]

We use banks' balance sheet, income statement and annual report data for the G7 countries and Switzerland from the International Bank Credit Analysis Bankscope Database. Table 6.1 illustrates the breakdown by country of the number and asset size of the banks included in the sample.[6]

The second stage of the methodology implies the analysis of the relationship between the estimated cost and profit efficiency scores for our sample of investment banks and the chosen environmental factors. The main aim is to verify in general the degree of association between the chosen environmental factors and the estimated efficiency scores. In addition, we aim to identify and explain the most significant relationships.

The selection of environmental factors follows the most recent empirical literature in this area.[7] Accordingly, we account for potential differences arising from country-specific aspects of banking technology on the one hand and from the environmental and regulatory conditions on the other. In particular, the economic environment is likely to differ significantly across countries. Three categories of environmental variables are taken into account: (1) those that describe the main macroeconomic conditions, which determine the banking product demand

Table 6.2   Environmental variable definitions and sources

Variable name	Description and source
Macroeconomic conditions[1]	
High-technology exports	Calculated as a % of manufactured exports.
Inflation rate	Rate of inflation, calculated by the log difference of GDP deflator.
Internet users	Internet users per 100 people.
Market capitalization	Total domestic stock market capitalization divided by GDP.
Workers' remittances and compensation of employees	Workers' remittances and compensation of employees received (current US$).
Institutional environment[2]	
Business freedom	Business freedom is about an individual's right to create, operate and close an enterprise without interference from the state. The core for each country is a number between 0 and 100, with 100 equalling the freest business environment.
Investment freedom	This component scrutinizes each country's policies towards the free flow of investment capital (foreign investment as well as internal capital flows). The score for each country is a number between 0 and 100, with 100 equalling no restrictions on transfers or capital.
Financial freedom	Financial freedom is a measure of banking security as well as a measure of independence from government control. The score for each country is a number between 0 and 100, with 100 equalling negligible government influence.
Property rights	An indicator of the protection of private property rights (ranging from 0 to 100). Greater values signify better protection of property rights.
Regulatory restrictions[3]	
Activity restrictions	Measure of the degree to which national regulatory authorities allow banks to engage in the fee-based rather than more traditional interest-spread-based activities (sum of Survey of Bank Regulation and Supervision questions 4.1 through 4.4). Greater values signify more restrictions.

Continued

Table 6.2 Continued

Variable name	Description and source
Official supervisory power	Measure of whether the supervisory authorities have the authority to take specific actions to prevent and correct problems (sum of Survey of Bank Regulation and Supervision questions 5.5, 5.6, 5.7, 6.1, 10.4, 11.2, 11.3.1, 11.3.2, 11.3.3, 11.6, 11.7, 11.9.1, 11.9.2 and 11.9.3).
Supervision	This variable indicates whether there is a single official regulatory body for banks, or whether multiple supervisors share responsibility for supervising the nation's banks. The variable is assigned a value of 1 if there is more than one supervisor and 0 otherwise (based on question 12.1.1 of Survey of Bank Regulation and Supervision).

Sources: [1]World Development Indicators, World Bank; [2]Economic Freedom Index of the Heritage Foundation; [3]Data available from the World Bank – bank regulation and supervision database

characteristics, (2) those that describe the institutional environment and (3) bank regulation and supervision characteristics.

As detailed in Table 6.2, we examine an extensive array of regulatory, supervisory and institutional practices for a broad cross-section of countries at all levels of development and in all parts of the world. The first group of environmental factors is defined as "macroeconomic conditions" and includes high-technology exports, inflation rate, internet users, market capitalization, workers' remittances and compensation of employees. These indicators describe the conditions under which investment banks operate. The second group of environmental variables is defined as "institutional environment" and includes business freedom, financial freedom, investment freedom and property rights. The third and last category is "regulatory restrictions" and includes activity restrictions, official supervisory power and supervision.

4. Efficiency and environmental factors in investment banking

Figure 6.1 displays the mean cost and profit efficiency levels estimated using Eq. (2). In line with the (predominantly commercial) bank

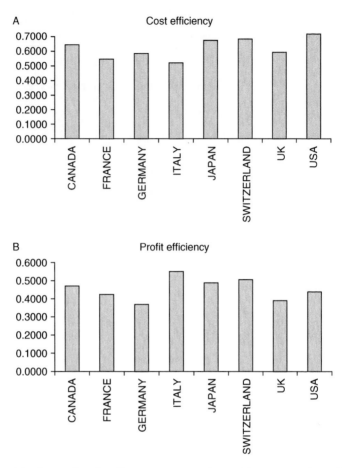

Figure 6.1   Cost and profit efficiency estimates (means) by country (2001–2007)

efficiency literature (see Berger and Mester 1997 for a review; Maudos et al. 2002), the mean cost efficiency scores are on average higher than the profit ones.

Furthermore, our evidence shows that, on average, the estimated cost efficiency scores are generally higher for the non-EU countries in our sample (Canada, Japan, Switzerland and the US), implying better cost management for investment banks operating outside the EU. Similarly, on the profit side, with the exception of Italy, it appears that non-EU countries are on average slightly more profit efficient than their EU counterparts. Moreover, estimated efficiency scores also suggest marked differences over time in the efficiency across the countries included in our sample as illustrated in Figure 6.2.

The figure shows that, with the notable exception of Japan, cost efficiency has clearly improved for most countries over time (panel A). Conversely, a common trend cannot be identified for the profit efficiency (panel B).

Table 6.3 reports the estimated Pearson correlation coefficients, together with their significance levels between the estimated cost and

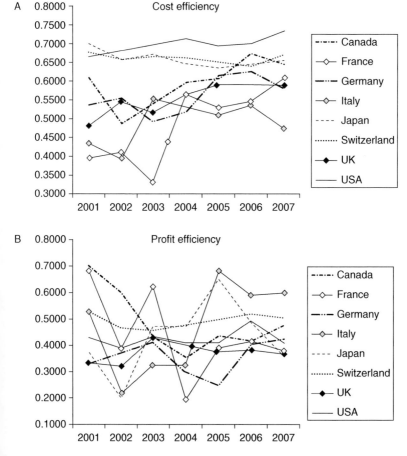

Figure 6.2   Cost and profit efficiency estimates by country over time

Table 6.3   Correlation matrices for the explanatory variables

	Cost efficiency	Profit efficiency	High technology exports	Inflation	Internet users	Market capitalization
Cost efficiency	1.00					
Profit efficiency	−0.23***	1.00				
Macroeconomic conditions						
High technology exports	0.14***	−0.10***	1.00			
Inflation	−0.13***	−0.13***	0.29***	1.00		
Internet users	0.23***	0.06*	0.07*	0.00	1.00	
Market capitalization	0.21***	0.16***	0.06*	0.01	0.43***	1.00
Workers' remittances	−0.28***	−0.19***	0.07*	0.52***	−0.19***	−0.38***
Institutional environment						
Business freedom	−0.01	−0.12***	0.35***	0.50***	0.37***	−0.10**
Investment freedom	−0.10***	−0.16***	0.10***	0.49***	0.21***	0.01
Financial freedom	0.11***	−0.05	0.41***	0.52***	0.14***	0.48***
Property rights	0.13***	−0.08**	0.37***	0.40***	0.32***	0.52***
Regulatory restrictions						
Activity restrictions	0.22***	0.08**	0.08**	−0.35***	−0.02	−0.35***
Official supervisory power	0.15***	0.02	0.52***	0.27***	0.36***	0.68***
Supervision	0.09**	−0.12***	0.28***	0.32***	0.00	−0.39***

*, ** and *** mean statistically significant at 10 %, 5 % and 1 % respectively.

Table 6.3 Continued

Workers' remittances	Business freedom	Investment freedom	Financial freedom	Property rights	Activity restrictions	Official supervisory power	Super-vision
1.00							
0.37***	1.00						
0.42***	0.27***	1.00					
−0.04	0.09**	0.39***	1.00				
−0.01	0.13***	0.53***	0.72***	1.00			
−0.48***	−0.02	−0.49***	−0.39***	−0.48***	1.00		
−0.17***	0.17***	0.14***	0.77***	0.62***	−0.44***	1.00	
0.15***	0.24***	0.30***	0.02	0.25***	0.43***	−0.36***	1.00

profit efficiency scores and our chosen environmental variables explaining macroeconomic, regulatory and institutional conditions. Cost and profit efficiency levels are negatively and significantly correlated, thus suggesting that cost efficient investment banks are not necessarily the most profitable.

The magnitude of the correlation coefficients appears remarkably high for the variables explaining macroeconomic conditions, and particularly so in the case of workers' remittances, compensation of employees and market capitalization. We may also notice that the institutional environment plays an important role in relation to both cost and profit efficiency of investment banks, as shown by the correlation coefficients explaining property rights and investment freedom.

Last, we have found a particularly strong correlation between efficiency and supervision, implying that future research should concentrate on whether there is a single official regulatory of banks, or whether multiple supervisors share responsibility for supervising the investment banks.

5. Conclusions

The recent financial turmoil has uncovered a number of weaknesses in the banking industry and has left the international community with challenging questions about the evolving role of (commercial and) investment banks in the economy and the primary objective of ensuring financial stability. Over the last two decades investment banks' operations, functions and strategies have been increasingly market driven and have contributed to the emergence of an unprecedented system of compensation, a highly leveraged industry and a pervasive risk culture. It is expected that post-crisis investment banks will have to comply with new constraints and thus the evaluation of their operating efficiency is likely to gain a new impetus, particularly on the cost side. Focusing on the efficiency of investment banks prior to the crisis and overall we found that with only a few exceptions, cost and profit efficiency scores were generally higher for non-EU countries (Canada, Japan, Switzerland and the US) than for their EU counterparts. Moreover, our evidence unambiguously shows that in the vast majority of cases the relationships between efficiency scores and environmental variables are highly significant. This gives a preliminary (although rather crude) indication that these factors are important and should be accounted for in the estimation of investment banks' efficiency.

Notes

1. There are two main methods for measuring efficiency: parametric approaches, i.e. stochastic frontier approach (SFA), distribution-free approach (DFA) and thick frontier approach (TFA), and non-parametric approaches, namely Data Envelopment Analysis (DEA) and free disposal hull (FDH). See, among others, Berger and Humphrey (1997).
2. Deprins and Simar (1989) and Kumbhakar and Lovell (2000) observe that it can be difficult to determine if an exogenous variable is a characteristic of production technology or a determinant of productive efficiency.
3. On the SFA, see Aigner, Lovell and Schmidt (1977).
4. The choice of using the translog functional form is motivated by two main reasons. First, Altunbas and Chakravarty (2001) identify some problems associated with more flexible functional forms like the Fourier (Mitchell and Onvural 1996) when dealing with heterogeneous datasets. Second, Berger and Mester (1997) observe that the translog and the Fourier-flexible are substantially equivalent from an economic viewpoint and both rank individual bank efficiency in almost the same order.
5. As usual, symmetry and linear homogeneity restrictions are imposed, thus standardizing total cost TC and input prices P_i by the last input price.
6. We are aware that Bankscope data on investment banks are not as detailed as for commercial banks. One of the main limitations is that the input and output data cannot be disaggregated by investment banking function or activity (e.g. merger and acquisition advisory).
7. We do not follow the approach from Coelli et al. (1999), which proposes two different ways of including environmental conditions or firm-specific factors in the cost/profit function; rather we look for correlation between efficiency results and certain environmental factors.

References

Aigner, D.J, Lovell, C.A.K., Schmidt, P., (1977) "Formulation and estimation of stochastic frontier production functions models". *Journal of Econometrics* 6, 21–37.

Allen, L., and Rai, A. (1996) "Operational efficiency in banking. An international comparison". *Journal of Banking and Finance* 20, 655–72.

Altunbas, Y., and Chakravarty, S.P. (2001) "Frontier cost functions and bank efficiency" *Economics Letters*, 72, 233–240.

Altunbas, Y., Gardener, E.P.M., Molyneux, P., and Moore, B. (2001) "Efficiency in European banking" *European Economic Review* 45, 1931–1955.

Altunbas, Y., Liu, M.H., Molyneux, P., and Seth, R. (2000) "Efficiency and risk in Japanese banking" *Journal of Banking and Finance* 24, 1605–1628.

Athanasoglou, P.P., Brissimis, S.N., Delis, M.D., (2008) "Bank-specific, industry-specific and macroeconomic determinants of bank profitability" *Journal of International Finanancial Markets, Instruments and Money* 18, 121–136.

Barth, J.R., Caprio, G., and Levine, R. (2004) "Bank Regulation and Supervision: What Works Best?" *Journal of Financial Intermediation* 13, 205–248.

Beccalli, E. (2004) "Cross-country comparisons of efficiency: evidence from the UK and Italian investment firms" *Journal of Banking and Finance* 28 1363–1383.

Berger, A.N. (2007) "International comparisons of banking efficiency" *Financial Markets, Institutions & Instruments* 16 (3) 119–144.

Berger, A.N., and Humphrey, D.B. (1997) "Efficiency of financial institutions: international survey and directions for further research" *European Journal of Operational Research* 98, 175–212.

Berger, A.N., and Mester, L.J. (1997) "Inside the black box: what explains differences in the efficiencies of financial institutions?" *Journal of Banking and Finance* 21, 895–947.

Bos, J.W.B., and Schmiedel, H. (2007) "Is there a single frontier in a single European banking market?" *Journal of Banking and Finance* 31, 2081–2102.

Brissimis, S.N., Delis, M.D., and Papanikolaou, N.I. (2008) "Exploring the nexus between banking sector reform and performance" *Journal of Banking and Finance* 32, 2674–2683.

Carbo-Valverde, S., Humphrey, D.B., and Lopez del Paso, R. (2007) "Do cross-country differences in bank efficiency support a policy of "national champions?" *Journal of Banking and Finance* 31, 2173–2188.

Casu, B., and Girardone, C. (2005) "An analysis of the relevance of OBS Items in explaining productivity change in European banking" *Applied Financial Economics* 15, 1053–1061.

Coelli, T., Perelman, S., and Romano, E. (1999) "Accounting for environmental influences in stochastic frontier models: with application to international airlines" *Journal of Productivity Analysis* 11, 251–273.

Demirguç-Kunt, A., and Huizinga, H. (2004) "Market discipline and deposit insurance" *Journal of Monetary Economics* 51, 375–399.

Dietsch, M., and Lozano-Vivas A. (2000) "How the environment determines banking efficiency: a comparison between French and Spanish industries" *Journal of Banking and Finance* 24, 985–1004.

Fitzpatrick, T., and McQuinn, K. (2007) "Measuring bank profit efficiency" *Applied Financial Economics,* 1–8, iFirst.

Gardener, E., and Molyneux P. (1995) *Investment banking: theory and practice,* Euromoney Books, London.

Goddard, J., Molyneux, P., and Wilson, J.O.S. (2001) *European banking: efficiency technology and growth,* John Wiley & Sons, London.

Hicks, J. (1935) "The theory of monopoly" *Econometrica* 3, 1–20.

Hughes, J.P., and Mester, L.J. (2008) "Efficiency in banking: theory, practice and evidence" Working paper, The Wharton School, University of Pennsylvania, Philadelphia, PA.

Kumbhakar, S.C., and Lovell C.A.K. (2000) *Stochastic frontier analysis.* Cambridge University Press, Cambridge.

Lepetit, L., Nys, E., Rous, P., and Tarazi, A. (2008) "Bank income structure and risk – An empirical analysis of European banks" *Journal of Banking and Finance* 32, 1452–1467.

Lozano-Vivas, A., Pastor, J.T., and Pastor, J.M. (2002) "An efficiency comparison of European banking systems operating under different environmental conditions" *Journal of Productivity Analysis* 18, 59–77.

Maudos, J., Pastor, J.M., and Perez, F. (2002) "Competition and efficiency in the Spanish banking sector – the importance of specialization" *Applied Financial Economics* 12, 505–516.

Mitchell, K., and Onvural N.M. (1996) "Economies of scale and scope at large commercial banks: evidence from the Fourier-flexible functional form" *Journal of Money, Credit, and Banking* 28, 178–199.

Salas, V., and Saurina, J. (2003) "Deregulation, market power and risk behavior in Spanish banks" *European Economic Review* 47, 1061–1075.

Vander Vennet, R. (2002) "Cost and profit efficiency of financial conglomerates and universal banks in Europe" *Journal of Money, Credit and Banking* 34 (1), 254–282.

7
Post-merger Bank Efficiency and Stock Market Reaction: the Case of the US versus Europe

Dimitris K. Chronopoulos, Claudia Girardone and John C. Nankervis

1. Introduction

The past two decades have been characterized by a wave of bank mergers that have reshaped both the US and the European financial systems. Specifically, the number of banks fell by almost 40 per cent in Europe and by over 45 per cent in the US between 1985 and 2003. The possibility that these bank mergers will yield efficiency gains for the consolidated banks has long been a subject of debate; yet empirical evidence documented in the literature up to 2000 does not provide an unambiguous answer to this question (see Amel et al. 2004). The consensus view from more recent studies is that bank mergers and acquisitions (M&As) can improve efficiency (see DeYoung et al. 2009). However, a probably more important issue is whether or not stock markets can accurately forecast these efficiency gains upon the announcement of an M&A operation.

The aim of this study is twofold. First, we investigate whether bank mergers have different effects on shareholders' wealth in different markets. For that reason we compare the US and European bank sectors. Second, we examine, using univariate analysis, whether changes in operating efficiency as a result of bank mergers are priced in the stock markets. The hypothesis is that changes in a bank's cost and profit efficiency, following a merger, are likely to affect its cash flows, which in turn should be valued in the stock markets. Specifically, they should be reflected in the market valuation of the acquirer (Aggarwal et al. 2006).

A preview of our results is that European bank mergers enhance the value of the combined entity and that acquiring shareholders in Europe earn significantly greater returns than their US counterparts. Moreover, there is evidence that changes in profit efficiency are positively associated with the abnormal returns.

2. Literature review

Two main approaches used to evaluate potential gains related to M&A activity are typically found in the literature. One examines bank merger performance improvements using accounting data, while the other relies on stock market valuations. The main bulk of existing research adopts one method or the other, and only a handful of recent studies use a combination of the two to investigate the market's ability to forecast post-merger performance changes accurately.

Studies using the accounting approach usually employ financial ratios and/or frontier methods,[1] and have typically found different results in the US compared to Europe. Evidence for the US banking sector shows only slight or no improvement in cost efficiency from M&A activity during the 1980s and early 1990s, which could suggest that the consolidation process might also be fuelled by managerial or other non-profit maximization motives. Specifically, there seems to be no reduction in non-interest expenses or total costs (e.g. Srinivasan 1992; Pilloff 1996) and very little or no significant gain in frontier cost efficiency (e.g. DeYoung 1997; Peristiani 1997).

Evidence from more recent studies paints a different picture. For instance, Cornett et al. (2006) find evidence of revenue efficiency improvements for large mergers and for product and geographically focused mergers. Al-Sharkas et al. (2008) use frontier methods to investigate the efficiency levels of merging banks in the US and show that mergers tend to improve both the cost and profit efficiency of the consolidating banks. Similarly, studies on the European banking sector argue that recent mergers have brought about significant efficiency gains for the consolidating banks. For example, Huizinga et al. (2001) find evidence of an improvement in cost efficiency for consolidating banks and a positive, albeit marginal, gain in their profit efficiency. Consistent with this, Diaz et al. (2004) find that acquisitions generally have a positive effect on the acquiring bank's profitability.

The second approach assumes that the stock market is efficient and therefore that changes in the stock market valuation of the firms involved in the merger reflect the value of the gains resulting from the transaction. Most studies adopting this approach find that the impact of acquisitions on target firms is positive both inside and outside the US market. In contrast, the evidence for the acquirers is mixed. Studies focusing on the US banking industry have repeatedly offered evidence of acquiring shareholders experiencing marginal losses (DeLong 2001, 2003; DeLong and DeYoung 2007). There are some exceptions, however, that document positive gains to the acquiring banks in both the US (James and Wier 1987; Cornett and De 1991) and Europe (Cybo-Ottone and Murgia 2000; Ismail and Davidson 2005). Finally, DeLong (2003) studies the announcement effects of US versus non-US mergers. She finds that non-US acquirers earn more than their US counterparts, but that target shareholders in the US benefit more than target shareholders outside the US. Hagendorff et al. (2008), focusing solely on acquirers' wealth effects from M&As, find similar results.

The majority of the relevant literature tests, either directly or indirectly, for M&A generated gains. However, as already noted, there is a paucity of studies combining both the accounting and the stock market valuation approaches to test whether abnormal market returns are good predictors of post-merger bank performance (no study, to the best of our knowledge, tests this relationship at a cross-country level). This rather limited literature focuses on the US banking sector and seems to offer contradictory findings. In addition, it relies almost entirely on accounting ratios, in spite of the many advantages of using frontier efficiency measures (Berger and Humphrey 1992).

In particular, Cornett and Tehranian (1992) and DeLong and DeYoung (2007) find a positive relationship between stock market reaction to bank merger announcements and post-merger performance, measured as changes in an array of accounting ratios. On the other hand, Pilloff (1996) and Hart and Ipilado (2002) find no evidence of such a relationship. Aggarwal et al. (2006) is the only study to use a parametric frontier method to examine the relationship between profit efficiency and stock market reaction around merger announcements. Using a sample of US bank mergers completed between 1986 and 2001, these authors find that post-merger changes in profit efficiency are positively related to the acquirers' returns, but negatively related to target shareholder's returns.

Our study contributes to the literature by examining the relationship between post-merger performance, measured by efficiency changes derived from the non-parametric DEA method, and the stock market reaction to a sample of European and US bank mergers completed between 1997 and 2003. As far as we are aware, this is the first study to examine this relationship across countries.

3. Data and methodology

3.1. Data used for the empirical analysis

This study employs a large data sample of over 3700 observations from the US and European banking sectors over the period 1996–2006. The event study analysis focuses on M&A deals that took place between 1997 and 2003 and data are drawn from Thomson One Banker. Only transactions that resulted in the acquirer having a stake of at least 50 per cent in a target institution were included in the sample.[2] Our initial dataset is reduced to 100 deals after omitting cases for any one of the following reasons: (1) stock return data for 244 days prior to and 15 days after the deal's announcement are not available in Datastream either for the acquirer or the target; (2) a full calendar year's worth of pre-merger accounting data are not available for either the acquirer or the target; (3) the acquirer has less than three full calendar years of post-merger accounting data available or (4) the merger was between a US and a European banking institution.[3]

Table 7.1 displays some descriptive information for our final bank merger sample. Accounting data for the acquiring and target banks are derived from both the Federal Reserve Y-9 reports and the Bankscope database. It is clear from the table that European merger partners are

Table 7.1   Descriptive statistics for the bank merger sample

Year	Number of mergers			Mean assets of acquirer		Mean assets of target	
	Total	Europe	US	Europe	US	Europe	US
Panel A All mergers							
1997–2003	100	30	70	105,209.5	39,778.1	49,789.6	11,756.2
Panel B By year of merger announcement							
1997	12	5	7	120,303.9	20,226.1	84,228.1	1900.1
1998	8	3	5	49,688.13	63,912.3	13,937.1	10,567.9
1999	17	8	9	136,815	59,405.3	92,491.4	32,811.9
2000	21	8	13	135,124.1	25,769.5	28,059.3	5,699.4
2001	17	3	14	68,810.66	45,846.3	21,322.6	8,271.9
2002	16	3	13	7,918.74	50,448.7	1,787.7	18,806.9
2003	9	–	9	–	17,332.5	–	3,788.6

Note: Asset values are expressed in € millions (2000 prices).

Table 7.2 Time and size distribution of banks included in the estimation of the frontiers

Year	Europe			US		
		Asset size			Asset size	
	Number of obs.	Mean	Median	Number of obs.	Mean	Median
1996	2658	4.467	0.530	1120	4.773	0.363
1997	2084	3.737	0.449	1303	4.656	0.349
1998	3097	4.641	0.463	1467	5.164	0.352
1999	2062	4.564	0.512	1571	5.626	0.352
2000	1962	4.627	0.541	1664	6.073	0.363
2001	1856	4.920	0.563	1763	6.188	0.367
2002	1482	4.236	0.618	1932	6.239	0.369
2003	1661	4.666	0.612	2161	6.282	0.364
2004	1647	5.078	0.661	2276	7.137	0.374
2005	1592	6.952	0.685	2294	7.548	0.402
2006	2090	9.959	0.520	976	13.744	0.962

Note: Asset size values are expressed in € billions (2000 prices).

considerably larger than their US counterparts. More specifically, European acquirers average 2.5 times the size of their US counterparts, and the average discrepancy between the targets in the two regions is even greater.

The same accounting data were used for estimating the US and European cost and profit frontiers over the period 1996–2006. Table 7.2 illustrates the number of banks included in the sample, as well as their total assets, which are expressed in 2000 prices (€ billions).

3.2. Estimation of abnormal returns

To examine whether shareholders experience any change in their wealth when an M&A deal is announced involving their firm as either a target or a bidder, we employ an event study methodology. Following Fuller et al. (2002) and Antoniou et al. (2008), we use a modified market adjusted model, which predicts individual stock returns to be equal to the corresponding benchmark return. As a result, the abnormal return is the difference between the actual return and the benchmark return estimated as:

$$AR_{jt} = R_{jt} - R_{mt} \tag{1}$$

where AR_{jt} is the abnormal return for stock j at time t, R_{jt} is the return on stock j at time t and R_{mt} is the return on the country's benchmark at time t.[4] Cumulative average abnormal returns (CAR) are calculated over the following three different time intervals [–1, +1], [–2, +2] and [–5, +5]. Following Brown and Warner (1985), we calculate the statistical significance as follows:

$$t = \frac{CAR}{\sqrt{T} * S}, \tag{2}$$

where

$$CAR = \sum_{t=t_1}^{t_2} \overline{AR_t} \tag{3}$$

$$\overline{AR_t} = \frac{1}{N_t} \sum_{j=1}^{N_t} AR_{jt} \tag{4}$$

$$S = \sqrt{\left(\sum_{t=-244}^{t=-12} (\overline{AR_t} - A\tilde{R})^2 \right) \Big/ 232} \tag{5}$$

$$A\tilde{R} = \frac{1}{233} \sum_{t=-244}^{t=-12} \overline{AR_t} \tag{6}$$

$$T = t_2 - t_1 + 1, \tag{7}$$

t_1 is the first day of the period for which the CAR is calculated and t_2 is the last.

3.3. Frontier efficiency measurement: non-parametric DEA

To estimate bank efficiency we employ the input-oriented Data Envelopment Analysis (DEA) model with Variable Returns to Scale (VRS) developed by Banker et al. (1984).[5] The relative cost efficiency measure CE_j is obtained as a ratio of the estimated minimum cost bank j could potentially achieve to its realized cost, where $0 < CE_j \leq 1$ and equals unity when the bank is deemed cost efficient.

Although cost efficiency can be seen as a necessary condition for survival under tough competition, it can be argued that profit maximization remains one of banks' primary economic objectives. Another consideration to be mentioned is that cost efficient banks are not necessarily the most efficient on the profit side. Therefore, we also estimate a profit efficiency measure. We follow Maudos and Pastor (2003)'s approach, which allows for estimating an alternative profit measure by non-parametric methods. The alternative profit efficiency measure APE_j is obtained as a ratio between the observed profits of bank j and its estimated potential maximum profits, where $APE_j \leq 1$ and equals unity when the bank is deemed profit efficient.

The input-output definition that we adopt for the estimation of efficiency follows the "intermediation" approach (Berger and Humphrey, 1997). Specifically, the prices of labour, physical capital and other operating expenses are inputs to the production process of banks while total customer loans, other earning assets and non-interest income are outputs. We also include two variables directly in the linear programming problem to account for: (1) differences in bank risk preference (equity over assets) and (2) the economic environment (proxied by per capita income at the state level).

In our analysis we rely on efficiency ranks instead of efficiency values (see e.g. Peristiani 1997; Huizinga et al. 2001). That is, we rank banks based on their efficiency levels, from the smallest to the largest value. Subsequently, the ranks are converted to a uniform scale over [0,1] following Berger et al. (2004). In doing so, we obtain a measure suitable for our analysis, as it is more appropriate than the efficiency levels for comparison purposes across countries and over time (Berger et al. 2004).

4. Empirical results

4.1. Wealth effects of acquirers, targets and combined entities

Cumulative average abnormal returns (CAR) for acquirers, targets and combined entities measured over different event windows are reported in Table 7.3. Panel A reports the results for the entire sample and for the two sub-samples of European and US deals, while panel B illustrates the statistical differences between groups in the stock market reactions to European and US mergers announcements.

Consistent with the literature (e.g. Cybo-Ottone and Murgia 2000; Ismail and Davidson 2005), on average, European bank mergers are found to earn significant abnormal returns for the combined partners, whereas US deals yield returns not statistically different from zero, with the exception of the three-day event window that is marginally significant at the 10 per cent level. As reported in Panel B, this difference in stock market reactions to European and US merger announcements is statistically significant at the 10 per cent level. Focusing on the acquirers, the mean abnormal returns to European acquirers are 0.2 and 0.42 per cent respectively for the three- and five-day intervals, but not statistically different from zero; the only exception is the positive and significant at 1.99 per cent over the 11-day period.

The losses pertaining to US acquirers, on the other hand, range from −2.99 per cent over the three-day interval to −3.98 per cent for the 11-day CAR, all significant at 1 per cent. The difference between the abnormal returns generated by European and US mergers for shareholders of acquirers is again significant at the 5 per cent level. Unlike their counterparts, shareholders of targets everywhere earn significant abnormal returns upon the announcement of a merger deal. In particular US target shareholders appear to earn between 4.7 and 6.3 per cent more than their European counterparts, depending on the time interval over which CAR are estimated. However, as panel B reports, this difference is not statistically significant.

Overall, these results corroborate the findings of e.g. DeLong (2003) and Hagendorff et al. (2008) that market participants in Europe and US are likely to react differently upon announcement of a bank merger.

4.2. Relation between abnormal returns and post-merger performance

This section investigates whether stock markets can identify changes in post-merger operating efficiency. Table 7.4 presents descriptive statistics for the variables used in the univariate analysis. From the table it appears that acquirers, on average, experience a post-merger improvement in their profit efficiency rank (2.8 per cent), but a decline in their cost efficiency (6.1 per cent).

Table 7.5 reports correlation coefficients for Acquirers CAR (A-CAR), Targets CAR (T-CAR), change in profit efficiency rank (ΔPROFITEFF) and change in cost efficiency rank (ΔCOSTEFF). The results show a positive relationship between ΔPROFITEFF and A-CAR that is statistically significant at the 1 per cent level. On the other hand, the relationship between ΔCOSTEFF and A-CAR is negative, but not statistically significant. Moreover, as expected, there appears to be no association between the two measures of efficiency. There is also no evidence of a statistically significant relationship between T-CAR and changes in either profit or the cost efficiency rank of the consolidated entity.

Table 7.3 Cumulative daily abnormal returns to stockholders upon merger announcements

Event Window	No.	Combined entities			Acquirers			Targets		
		CAR (%)	Test of significance		CAR (%)	Test of significance		CAR (%)	Test of significance	
			t-stat.	p-value		t-stat.	p-value		t-stat.	p-value
Panel A Cumulative abnormal returns										
All mergers										
[−1, +1]	100	1.38	4.354	<0.001	−2.09	−5.420	<0.001	18.26	28.212	<0.001
[−2, +2]	100	1.48	3.599	<0.001	−2.40	−4.828	<0.001	20.13	24.096	<0.001
[−5, +5]	100	1.85	3.035	0.003	−2.18	−2.961	0.003	22.14	17.866	<0.001
European mergers										
[−1, +1]	30	2.69	5.121	<0.001	0.02	0.042	0.966	13.85	7.378	<0.001
[−2, +2]	30	3.52	5.185	<0.001	0.42	0.639	0.527	16.84	6.948	<0.001
[−5, +5]	30	5.40	5.369	<0.001	1.99	1.999	0.054	20.6	5.730	<0.001
US mergers										

	N	CAR (%)	t-stat	p	CAR (%)	t-stat	p	CAR (%)	t-stat	p
[-1, +1]	70	0.83	2.091	0.090	-2.99	-5.033	<0.001	20.15	36.114	<0.001
[-2, +2]	70	0.60	1.188	0.239	-3.62	-4.708	<0.001	21.54	29.913	<0.001
[-5, +5]	70	0.33	0.436	0.664	-3.98	-3.490	<0.001	22.80	21.344	<0.001

Panel B Differences between groups

	CAR (%) (t-statistic)		CAR (%) (t-statistic)		CAR (%) (t-statistic)	
Europe vs. US	2.91*	(1.68)	4.04**	(2.36)	-4.70	(-1.17)

Note: The sample consists of 100 US and European bank merger deals. All banks are publicly traded. Panel A reports abnormal returns calculated using the Datastream bank sector index as the benchmark. CARs are averaged for each event window. The statistic is calculates according to Brown and Warner (1985). Panel B reports differences between the mean CARS of the two groups measured over the −2 to +2 day event window. * and ** indicate significance at the 10 % and 5 % levels, respectively.

Table 7.4　Descriptive statistics of the variables used in the univariate analysis

Variable	Mean	Std. dev.
A-CAR$_{(-2,+2)}$	−0.0240	0.0803
T-CAR$_{(-2,+2)}$	0.2013	0.1842
ΔCOSTEFF	−0.0611	0.2449
ΔPROFITEFF	0.0279	0.1058

Note: A-CAR$_{(-2,+2)}$ = the announcement period abnormal return for the acquirer institution; T-CAR$_{(-2,+2)}$ = the announcement period abnormal return for the target institution; ΔCOSTEFF = difference in the 1-year prior and the 3-year average post-merger cost efficiency rankings of the acquiring institutions; ΔPROFITEFF = difference in the 1-year prior and the 3-year average post-merger profit efficiency rankings of the acquiring institutions.

Table 7.5　Pearson correlation coefficients: acquirer banks

	A–CAR$_{(-2,+2)}$	T–CAR$_{(-2,+2)}$	ΔPROFITEFF	ΔCOSTEFF
A-CAR$_{(-2,+2)}$	1.0000			
T-CAR$_{(-2,+2)}$	0.1444	1.0000		
	(0.1518)			
ΔPROFITEFF	0.3358	0.1031	1.0000	
	(0.0006)	(0.3076)		
ΔCOSTEFF	−0.1111	−0.0744	−0.0148	1.0000
	(0.2711)	(0.4619)	(0.8836)	

Notes: p-values are reported in parentheses.
See note to Table 7.4.

To control for heteroscedasticity we also run univariate regressions and report robust standard errors. The results in Table 7.6 indicate the presence of heteroscedasticity in the CARs. When A-CAR and T-CAR are regressed on ΔPROFITEFF (see columns (1) and (3)), the coefficients are statistically significant in both instances. However, the coefficient on ΔCOSTEFF is statistically significant only in regression (2) at the 10 per cent level, and only marginally so.

Overall, findings from the univariate analysis indicate that stock markets can price post-merger efficiency performance, upon announcement

Table 7.6 Abnormal returns and operating efficiency: univariate regressions

	Dependent variable A-CAR$_{(-2, +2)}$		Dependent variable T-CAR$_{(-2, +2)}$	
	(1) Coefficient	(2) Coefficient	(3) Coefficient	(4) Coefficient
INTERCEPT	−0.0311	−0.0262	0.1963	0.1979
	(0.0079)	(0.0083)***	(0.01898)***	(0.0192)***
ΔPROFITEFF	0.2549	–	0.1794	–
	(0.1295)**	–	(0.06807)***	–
ΔCOSTEFF	–	−0.0364	–	−0.0559
	–	(0.0212)*	–	(0.0695)

Notes: *,**,*** indicates significance at the 10 %, 5 % and 1 % levels, respectively. Robust standard errors are reported in parentheses.
See note to Table 7.4.

of a merger. However, in doing so, they seem to rely on forecasts of a performance measure that is more closely related to profit than to cost efficiency.

5. Concluding remarks

It has long been argued in the literature that mergers have the potential to improve the operating efficiencies of the consolidating banks. This study examines whether stock markets can accurately forecast these improvements upon merger announcement. In particular, we investigate 100 US and European bank mergers completed between 1997 and 2003. We use DEA, a non-parametric frontier methodology, to measure changes in cost and profit efficiencies one year prior and three years following the merger and tie these changes back to abnormal returns surrounding the merger announcement.

Results indicate that announcements of European bank mergers enhance the value of the combined entity and that acquiring shareholders in Europe earn significantly greater returns than their US counterparts. Moreover, univariate analysis provides evidence of a positive relationship between stock market reaction and post-merger performance in terms of profit efficiency. It seems that market participants are able to identify efficiency enhancing mergers upon their announcement, using a measure that is closely related to the profit efficiency measure used for our analysis.

Notes

1. Frontier methods allow for the estimation of a bank's efficiency level relative to best practice using accounting measures of inputs, outputs, costs and/or profits (see Section 3).
2. Unlike previous studies involving the European banking industry, we focus our attention on transactions that took place exclusively among banking institutions.
3. For the purpose of this study Europe is defined as the EU-15 (Austria, Belgium, Denmark, Finland, France, Germany, Greece, Ireland, Italy, Luxembourg, the Netherlands, Portugal, Spain, Sweden and the UK) plus Norway and Switzerland.
4. We use the Datastream bank sector index.
5. The input orientation implies input minimization while keeping a given output level; the VRS specification adds a convexity constraint to the original Charnes et al. (1978) model.

References

Aggarwal, R., Akhigbe, A., and McNulty, J.E. (2006) "Are differences in acquiring bank profit efficiency priced in financial markets?" *Journal of Financial Services Research* 30, 265–286.

Al-Sharkas, A.A., Hassan, K.M., and Lawrence, S. (2008) "The impact of mergers and acquisitions on the efficiency of the US banking industry: Further evidence" *Journal of Business, Finance and Accounting* 35, 50–70.

Amel, D., Barnes, C., Panetta, F., and Salleo, C. (2004) "Consolidation and efficiency in the financial sector: a review of the international evidence" *Journal of Banking and Finance* 28, 2493–2519.

Antoniou, A., Arbour, P., and Zhao, H. (2008) "How much is too much: Are merger premiums too high?" *European Financial Management* 14, 268–287.

Banker, R., Charnes, A., and Cooper, W.W. (1984) "Some models for estimating technical and scale efficiencies in Data Envelopment Analysis" *Management Science* 30, 1078–1092.

Berger, A.N., Hassan, I., Klapper, L.F. (2004) "Further evidence on the link between finance and growth: An international analysis of community banking and economic performance" *Journal of Financial Services Research* 25, 169–202.

Berger, A.N., and Humphrey, D.B. (1992) "Megamergers in banking and the use of cost efficiency as an antitrust defence" *Antitrust Bulletin* 33, 541–600.

Berger, A.N., and Humphrey, D.B. (1997) "Efficiency of financial institutions: International survey and directions for future research" *European Journal of Operational Research* 98: 175–212.

Brown, S.J., and Warner, J.B. (1985) "Using daily stock returns. The case of event studies" *Journal of Financial Economics* 14, 3–31.

Charnes, A., Cooper, W.W., and Rhodes, E. (1978) "Measuring the efficiency of decision making units" *European Journal of Operational Research* 2, 429–444.

Cornett, M.M., and De, S. (1991) "Medium of payment in corporate acquisitions: Evidence from interstate bank mergers" *Journal of Money, Credit and Banking* 23, 767–776.

Cornett, M.M., McNutt, J.J., and Tehranian, H. (2006) "Performance changes around bank mergers: revenue announcements versus cost reductions" *Journal of Money, Credit and Banking* 38, 1014–1050.

Cornett, M.M., and Tehranian, H. (1992) "Changes in corporate performance associated with bank acquisitions" *Journal of Financial Economics* 31, 211–234.

Cybo-Ottone, A., and Murgia, M. (2000) "Mergers and shareholder wealth in European banking" *Journal of Banking and Finance* 24, 831–859.

DeLong, G.L. (2001) "Stockholder gains from focusing versus diversifying bank mergers" *Journal of Financial Economics* 59, 221–252.

DeLong, G.L. (2003) "The announcement effects of US versus non-US bank mergers: Do they differ?" *Journal of Financial Research* 26, 487–500.

DeLong, G.L., and DeYoung, R. (2007) "Learning by observing: Information spillovers in the execution and valuation of commercial bank M&As" *Journal of Finance* 62, 181–216.

DeYoung, R. (1997) "Bank mergers, X-efficiency, and the market for corporate control" *Managerial Finance* 23, 32–47.

DeYoung, R., Evanoff, D.D., and Molyneux, P. (2009) "Mergers and acquisitions of financial institutions: A review of the post 2000 literature" *Journal of Financial Services Research* 36, 87–110.

Diaz D.B., Olalla, G.M., and Azofra, S.S. (2004) "Bank acquisitions and performance: Evidence form a panel of European credit entities" *Journal of Economics and Business* 56, 377–404.

Fuller, K., Netter, J., and Stegemoller, M. (2002) "What do returns to acquiring firms tell us? Evidence from firms that make many acquisitions" *Journal of Finance* 57, 1763–1794.

Hagendorff, J., Collins, M., and Keasey, K. (2008) "Investor protection and the value effects of the bank merger announcements in Europe and the US" *Journal of Banking and Finance* 32, 1333–1348.

Hart, J.R., and Ipilado, V.P. (2002) "Inexperienced banks and interstate mergers" *Journal of Economics and Business* 54, 313–330.

Huizinga, H.P., Nelissen, J.H.M., and Vander Vennet, R. (2001) "Efficiency effects of bank mergers and acquisitions in Europe" Tinbergen Institute Discussion Paper 2001–088/3.

Ismail, A., and Davidson, I. (2005) "Further analysis of mergers and shareholder wealth effects in European banking" *Applied Financial Economics* 15, 13–30.

James, C.M., and Weir, P. (1987) "Returns to acquirers and competition in the acquisition market: The case of banking" *Journal of Political Economy* 95, 355–370.

Maudos, J., and Pastor, J.M. (2003) "Cost and profit efficiency in the Spanish banking sector (1985–1996): A non-parametric approach" *Applied Financial Economics* 13, 1–12.

Peristiani, S. (1997) "Do mergers improve the X-efficiency and scale efficiency of U.S. banks? Evidence from the 1980s" *Journal of Money, Credit and Banking* 3, 326–337.

Pilloff, S.J. (1996) "Performance changes and shareholder wealth creation associated with mergers of publicly traded banking institutions" *Journal of Money, Credit and Banking* 28, 294–310.

Srinivasan, A. (1992) "Are there cost savings from bank mergers?" Federal Reserve Bank of Atlanta, *Economic Review* March, 17–28.

Part 3

Consolidation in the Financial Industry

8
The Impact of Corporate Culture, Efficiency and Geographic Distance on M&A Results: the European Case[1]

Franco Fiordelisi and Duccio Martelli

1. Introduction

The volume of merger and acquisition (M&A) transactions has soared over the last few years. According to the Thomson Financial (2007), the volume of worldwide M&As declared during 2007 reached US$ 4.5 trillion in announced deals and US$ 3.8 trillion in completed deals, that is, a 24 per cent increase over the previous record set in 2006. Since 2000, the volume of M&A deals has increased by 32 per cent, despite the fall off during the third quarter of 2007 caused by concerns in the credit markets. The M&A phenomenon concerns all countries worldwide (see Table 8.1); in 2007, M&A deals increased by 25 per cent in North America (reaching a volume of almost US$2 trillion over 2007, that is, 52 per cent of the value of M&A deals worldwide), by 18 per cent in Europe (reaching a volume of almost US$1.3 trillion over 2007, that is, 34 per cent of M&A deals by value worldwide) and also strongly increased in the Asia-Pacific area – by 61 per cent (reaching a volume of almost US$0.4 trillion over 2007, that is, 10 per cent of M&A deals by value worldwide).

Although the growth of the consolidation process concerns almost all industries,[2] most deals take place in the financial, materials and energy supply industries. The consolidation process, which focuses on the banking industry, is particularly important: in 2007, M&A transactions among financial institutions worldwide reached more than 7000 for an overall value of more than US$ 700 billion (see Thomson

Table 8.1   Sample description: large M&A deals in European banking between 2000 and 2007

Year	Number of deals	Value of transactions*				Type of deal	
		Mean	Std. dev.	Minimum	Maximum	Domestic	Cross-border
1997	6.0	4861.0	5052.3	141.1	10,959.0	6.0	0
1998	6.0	6591.9	6180.4	796.1	12,790.6	6.0	0
1999	8.0	7475.6	13088.4	574.9	38,412.9	8.0	0
2000	3.0	4751.8	2780.5	3144.3	7962.5	−2.0	5.0
2001	6.0	1624.5	1449.2	262.5	4169.2	3.0	3.0
2002	7.0	2866.5	5917.6	214.0	16,242.8	7.0	0
2003	3.0	1450.8	749.6	586.6	1925.1	3.0	0
2004	5.0	4989.1	7498.6	511.5	18,256.5	4.0	1.0
2005	5.0	2995.5	2204.6	429.8	5944.1	–	5.0
2006	4.0	17,500.8	18,880.7	200.7	37,624.2	1.0	3.0
2007	3.0	2211.4	1738.6	230.9	3486.5	−2.0	5.0

*Values are in US$ millions.

Financial, 2007: 2). Whereas the growth of M&A operations was primarily observed in North America and the United Kingdom over the 1980s, since the 1990s this phenomenon has been undertaken by all major industrialized nations, with deals often made by banks from different countries – that is, cross-border M&As (see Gugler et al. 2003). The dimension of the M&A phenomenon in European banking during the 2000s resembles that of the US market (Figure 8.1). However, while the number of deals in the US has always been slightly higher than in Europe, in 2007 the value of these deals was higher in the latter than in the former.

A large part of the research undertaken to evaluate the effects produced by M&A transactions has been analysed primarily within US banking and only a small number of studies have focused on European banks. Goddard et al. (2007: 1920) state: "further research is needed in order to identify the types of consolidation activity that yield the highest diversification benefits, and to identify the implications of domestic and cross-border bank mergers for systemic risk." The need for further research in European banking is quite surprising, seeing that there have been a large number of M&A transactions in European banking since

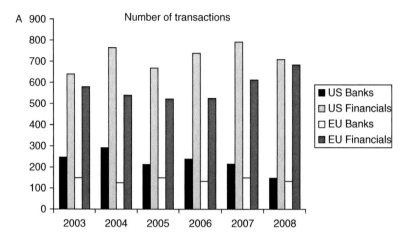

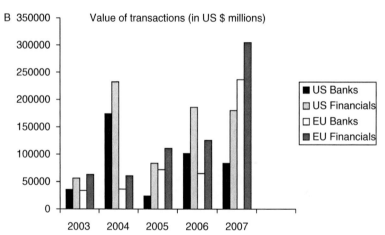

Figure 8.1 Number and value of M&A deals concluded by financial institutions (as acquirers): the US vs. Europe

Source: Thomson *SDC* database.

2000. This paper aims to analyse the effect produced by M&A deals in European banking. The major contribution of our paper is that it provides empirical evidence of the impact of corporate culture on M&A results. Whereas textbooks usually indicate corporate culture as one of the main determinants of successful M&A deals (e.g. Sudarsanam 2003), there is a lack of empirical evidence about the relationship between M&A results and the culture of the banks involved in such deals. This is essentially a result of the difficulty of objectively quantifying corporate culture. We tried to overcome this limitation by assessing official documents (e.g. reports to shareholders and financial statements) using a text analysis approach that has been recently exploited in finance studies (e.g. Tetlock 2007; Tetlock et al. 2008) to evaluate various corporate features. We also considered a large set of factors in order to increase the robustness of our results and to make a comprehensive analysis of the determinants of M&A success (such as cost and revenue efficiency, bank risk taking and financial structure) that are also known to be the rationale of M&A deals. In our analysis, we focus on large M&A deals (over €100 million) among listed banks in the EU-27 between 1 January 1998 and 30 June 2007. We intentionally chose to limit our analysis to the first semester of 2007, since the bank crises (from the second semester) produced a sporadic impact on the M&A trends.

2. Related literature

There is a rich banking literature dealing with M&A results. A large number of studies focus on the short term effects by using the event study method to measure the effects of M&As in banking. The event study evaluates the benefits of M&As by estimating the reaction of the market price of quoted banks involved in the operation at around the time of disclosure of the operation itself (announcement date).

The US banking system has been the main object of these studies (e.g. DeLong and DeYoung 2007; Gupta and Misra 2007). Whereas it was possible to reach overall agreement over event studies in US banking in the 1980s and 1990s (i.e. target shareholders earned substantial positive abnormal returns, bidder stockholders earned marginally negative returns, and the combined abnormal returns were statistically insignificant or economically trivial on average), studies published since 2000 have produced such varied pictures that similar conclusions can no longer be supported. This is probably because of differences in sample selection criteria and the time spans analysed. In the European banking industry, only a small (but increasing) number of studies focus on banking (e.g. Beitel et al. 2004; Campa and Hernando 2006; Schmautzer 2006; Ekkayokkaya et al. 2009). Similarly to the case with the US, the mixed results are probably caused by differences in sample selection criteria and the time spans analysed.

Recently, various studies have attempted to go further than the simple measurement of M&A results, analysing what makes a successful M&A deal by adding a second stage to the analysis. Abnormal returns (hereinafter ARs) estimated by the event study have been regressed in linear models to various factors that are believed to have an impact on the them, as for example geographic and production diversification, the ratio between the target and bidder total assets, the target firm's assets growth, the earnings per share of the target firm, the return on equity (ROE), etc. Although various differences were found, M&As create value for the acquiring firm when the target firm involved is of modest size and with an inferior level of efficiency compared to acquiring firm; target banks create shareholder value especially when there are substantial (production and distribution synergies) with the acquirer and the new bank has great potential to enhance profit efficiency.

The empirical analysis of corporate culture impact on the effects of M&As, focusing on banking, is new since there are no previous studies available. This is quite surprising since management literature sees cultural compatibility between the two companies involved as an essential factor for the success of M&A operations (Kusstatscher and Cooper 2005). For example, Cartwright and Cooper (1993) note that one possible explanation for the high failure rate of company M&As is "culture incompatibility" – the cost of culture conflicts resulting from poor integration made culture fit of equal, if not greater, importance than strategic fit. The cultural conflict between two merging companies may lead to lower commitment and cooperation (Buono et al. 1985), greater turnover among the acquired company's executives (Lubatkin et al. 1999) and a decline in shareholder value for the buying firm (Chatterjee et al. 1992).

Although there is a general agreement in considering corporate culture as one of the main determinants of an M&A deal success (e.g. Larsson et al. 2004), there is a lack of empirical evidence to support this conclusion even in the management literature. This is essentially due to the difficulties in measuring corporate culture. We overcome this limitation by using a text analysis approach that has recently been used in finance studies (e.g. Tetlock 2007; Tetlock et al. 2008) to make a quantitative assessment of corporate features.[3] This approach enables us to estimate corporate culture quantitatively by focusing on the text content of official documents (e.g. reports to shareholders and financial statements) made publicly available by target and bidder banks.

Our chapter brings together two strands of the literature: the first deals with the M&A results assessment using the event study approach and the second focuses on the corporate culture measurement. The main contribution of our paper is to verify if recent large M&A deals (over €100 million) among listed banks in the EU-27 have generated short term value for shareholders of the target and/or acquiring companies and to assess the impact that different corporate cultures have on M&A success. Moreover, we control for the effect on M&A results of a large set of variables considered in previous studies on specific features of the target and bidder companies (as the cost and revenue efficiency, risk taking, etc) and the spatial distance variable.

3. Data and methods

Overall, our sample comprises 56 large M&As involving target banks from 14 European countries and bidder banks from 12 European countries as described previously. We specified a linear model to investigate the relationships between the M&A results and the variables that may influence these results.[4] As dependent variables, we use one expressing the M&A success from the shareholders' standpoint (measured by a dummy variable that is 1 if the bank is in the first quartile of the decreasing cumulative average abnormal returns (CAR) distribution[5] and 0 otherwise), the power oriented corporate (POC) culture, the role oriented corporate (ROC) culture, the task oriented corporate (TOC) culture, the support oriented corporate (SOC) culture, the geographical distance between the target and acquirer companies (D), the scale efficiency (s-eff), the cost efficiency (x-efficiency), the revenue efficiency (τ-eff), the income diversification (ID), the profitability (π), the bank size (S), the credit risk (CR) and the capital risk exposure (CAP). The M&A result (y) is likely to be influenced by these variables with reference to both the acquirer and target banks. Unfortunately, the sample of M&A deals is quite small and thus we cannot double the number of independent variables by considering both acquirers and target companies. For this reason, we calculate the difference between the target and the acquirer banks for each variable (denoted by the subscript (T-A)): in this way, we assume that the M&A result is influenced by each variable gap. The variable definitions are summarized in Table 8.2.

4. Results and conclusions

Our results (Table 8.3) provide evidence that the four corporate culture orientations have a statistically significant link (at the 10 per cent confidence level or less) with the M&A results for the acquirers, bidders, and combined entities: the power oriented corporate culture exhibits a positive statistical link with M&A success for acquirer banks over the longest event window and for the combined entity over the event window

Table 8.2 Variables used to investigate short horizon M&A outcomes and their determinants in European banking

Variables	Symbol	Calculation method
M&A result	y	y is the variable capturing M&A results. This is obtained as a binary variable that is 1 if the bank is in the first quartile of the CAR distribution in a given event window, 0 otherwise. As robustness check, we use a more strict definition of success (i.e. y is a different binary, which is 1 if the bank is in the first decile of the CAR decreasing distribution in a given event window, 0 otherwise) and, second, a less restrictive definition of success (i.e. y is a different binary, which is 1 if the bank CAR is positive and 0 otherwise)
Power oriented culture	POC	POC is obtained using the text analysis
Role oriented culture	ROC	POC is obtained using the text analysis
Task oriented culture	TOC	POC is obtained using the text analysis
Support oriented culture	SOC	SOC is obtained using the text analysis
Distance	D	D refers to the aerial distance between the cities, where the acquirer and target firms' headquarters are located
Scale efficiency	s-eff	s-eff is obtained using Stochastic Frontier analysis
Cost efficiency	x-eff	x-eff is obtained using Stochastic Frontier analysis
Revenue efficiency	τ-eff	τ-eff is obtained using Stochastic Frontier analysis
Profit efficiency	π-eff	π-eff is obtained using Stochastic Frontier analysis
Profitability	π	π is measured as the Return (net income) on Assets (Total assets), i.e. ROA
Size	S	Bank size is measured by the its total assets
Credit risk	CR	CR is obtained as the ratio between the annual provision to loan loss reserves (CRL), i.e. the reserve that covers future unexpected loan losses, and the total loans
Capital risk exposure	CAP	CR is the total amount of liabilities over equity capital
Income diversification	ID	ID is measured by the net non-interest income to net operating income ratio

Table 8.3 The determinants of large successful M&A deals in European banking

Variable	Symbol	D(0;20)		D(0;10)		D(0;3)		D(0;3)	
		Coeff.	Std. Err.	Coeff.	Std. Err.	Coeff.	Std. Err.	Coeff.	Std. Err.
Panel A Acquirer									
Constant		-2.624**	1.107	-2.023***	0.584	-2.048***	0.542	-2.221***	0.644
Power	POC	1.731*	1.028	0.556	0.397	0.538	0.559	0.465	0.445
Role	ROC	-0.784**	0.410	-0.902***	0.318	-0.178	0.325	0.051	0.417
Task	TOC	-0.427	0.374	0.096	0.371	0.506	0.627	0.520	0.890
Support	SOC	0.126	0.463	0.936**	0.445	0.826**	0.411	0.457	0.352
Distance	D	-2.547*	1.500	-1.257*	0.757	-1.419*	0.821	-2.272**	0.991
Scale eff.	S-eff.	1.261*	0.681	0.37	0.465	0.435	0.517	1.456**	0.736
Cost eff.	x-eff.	0.498	0.519	0.241	0.471	0.582	0.522	0.480	0.659
Revenue eff.	τ-eff.	0.054	0.400	0.123	0.443	0.367	0.455	1.040**	0.455
Income div.	ID	0.388	0.589	0.086	0.360	-0.037	0.372	-0.091	0.549
Profitability	π	1.034	0.748	1.469**	0.576	1.024**	0.501	0.175	0.549
Size	S	1.069*	0.638	0.261	0.422	0.506	0.529	1.096**	0.512
Capital risk exp.	CAP	0.171	0.509	0.812	0.582	0.420	0.610	-0.302	0.520
Credit risk	CR	0.823	1.194	0.410	0.363	0.324	0.321	0.042	0.323

Notes: The dependent variable is a dummy variable (D), which is 1 if the bank is in the first quartile of the CAR decreasing distribution in a given event window and 0 otherwise E.g, D(0;20) is the binary variable obtained using the distribution of the CAR referring to the event window (0,20). The symbols *, **, and *** represent significance levels of 10 %, 5 % and 1 % respectively.

Variable	Symbol	D(0;20) Coeff.	D(0;20) Std. Err.	D(0;10) Coeff.	D(0;10) Std. Err.	D(0;3) Coeff.	D(0;3) Std. Err.	D(0;3) Coeff.	D(0;3) Std. Err.
Panel B Target									
Constant		-3.680***	1.292	-4.274	2.722	-2.434***	0.806	-3.808*	2.062
Power	POC	0.626	0.718	1.502	1.199	1.283	0.870	0.149	0.477
Role	ROC	0.160	0.531	-1.359	0.901	-0.403	0.447	-0.227	0.361
Task	TOC	3.818**	1.731	3.304	2.414	1.414	0.992	4.424*	2.422
Support	SOC	-2.663*	1.398	-1.126	1.287	-1.323**	0.643	-1.422*	0.755
Distance	D	0.085	0.780	1.513**	0.865	1.181*	0.695	0.033	0.459
Scale eff.	s–eff	-2.845*	1.588	-5.538	3.730	-1.923**	0.963	-1.744	1.181
Cost eff.	x–eff	-0.089	0.682	-0.654	1.158	0.109	0.817	-0.640	0.613
Revenue eff.	τ–eff	-0.343	0.560	-0.653	1.123	0.993	1.090	-0.052	0.477
Income div.	ID	1.321*	0.595	2.069	1.359	1.348*	0.714	2.185**	1.095
Profitability	π	-0.715	1.38	1.713**	0.665	0.122	0.620	-1.194	1.002
Size	S	-1.115*	0.620	-3.317*	2.017	-1.204***	0.433	-1.531**	0.744
Capital risk exp.	CAP	0.930	0.777	0.972	0.658	-0.625	0.499	0.920	0.927
Credit risk	CR	3.084	2.151	3.996	3.520	1.23	0.840	4.335	3.439

Note: The dependent variable is a dummy variable (D), which is 1 if the bank is in the first quartile of the CAR decreasing distribution in a given event window and 0 otherwise E.g, $D_{(0;20)}$ is the binary variable obtained using the distribution of the CAR referring to the event window (0,20). The symbols *, **, and *** represent significance levels of 10 %, 5 % and 1 % respectively.

Table 8.3 Continued

Variable	Symbol	$D_{(0;20)}$ Coeff.	$D_{(0;20)}$ Std. Err.	$D_{(0;10)}$ Coeff.	$D_{(0;10)}$ Std. Err.	$D_{(0;3)}$ Coeff.	$D_{(0;3)}$ Std. Err.	$D_{(0;3)}$ Coeff.	$D_{(0;3)}$ Std. Err.
Panel C Combined									
Constant		−1.329***	0.354	−2.314***	0.646	−3.290**	1.393	−4.329*	2.257
Power	POC	0.260	0.351	1.141	0.968	1.648	1.231	2.312*	1.221
Role	ROC	−0.466*	0.281	−0.462	0.360	−0.659	0.526	−0.427	0.518
Task	TOC	0.420	0.675	0.876	0.847	2.005*	1.172	2.331*	1.258
Support	SOC	−0.221	0.451	0.303	0.443	−0.202	0.579	−0.538	0.708
Distance	D	0.074	0.466	−1.449*	0.852	−3.069*	1.862	−4.898	3.361
Scale eff.	s-eff	0.143	0.479	0.116	0.528	1.746*	0.957	4.458*	2.631
Cost eff.	x-eff	−0.075	0.439	0.477	0.541	0.677	0.573	1.838	1.484
Revenue eff.	τ-eff	0.362	0.536	0.137	0.496	1.417*	0.848	2.280	1.701
Income div.	ID	0.140	0.459	0.011	0.359	0.733	0.698	0.861	1.125
Profitability	π	−0.009	0.482	1.115	0.586	0.055	0.775	−1.912*	1.043
Size	S	−0.137	0.355	−0.876	0.732	0.507	0.643	1.465	1.284
Capital risk Exp.	CAP	0.259	0.503	0.367	0.565	−0.242	0.543	−1.349**	0.638
Credit risk	CR	0.135	0.233	0.062	0.253	−0.007	0.336	−0.625	0.534

Notes: The dependent variable is a dummy variable (D) that is 1 if the bank is in the first quartile of the CAR decreasing distribution in a given event window, 0 otherwise E.g, $D_{(0,20)}$ is the binary variable obtained using the distribution of the CAR referring to the event window (0,20). The symbols *, **, and *** represent significance levels of 10 %, 5 % and 1 % respectively.

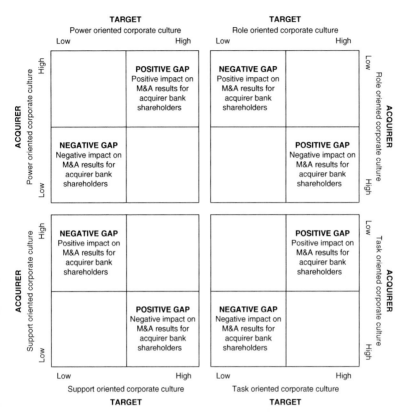

Figure 8.2 Corporate culture and M&A success in EU banking: a summary of estimated empirical relationships

(0,3); the role oriented corporate culture exhibits a negative statistical link with M&A success for the acquirer and combined entity over the event windows (0,10) and (0,20); the task oriented corporate culture exhibits a positive statistical link with M&A success for the target banks over the event windows (0,20) and (0,3); the support oriented corporate culture exhibits a negative statistical link with M&A success for the target banks over the event windows (0,20), (0,5) and (0,3) and for the combined entity over the event window (0,3).

Overall, these results show that if the attitude of the target bank's employees towards cooperating with each other or acting loyally towards the executive is higher than for the acquirer banks (i.e. a positive power oriented culture gap), this situation is positively linked to

M&A effects for acquirer shareholders. Conversely, if the target bank has a less flexible organizational structure (e.g. more bureaucratic or hierarchical) than the acquirer company (i.e. a positive gap in corporate culture role orientation), this has a negative link with the M&A results for acquirer bank's shareholders. Similarly, if the importance attached by the target bank to the achievement of results is greater than for the acquirer bank (i.e. a positive gap in the corporate culture task orientation), this is linked with M&A success for the former's shareholders. In addition, if the target bank views the human resource content as a key part of the corporate culture and the acquirer bank considers it less critical, this has a negative impact on the M&A success from the standpoint of the target bank's shareholders. Figure 8.2 summarizes these findings.

As for the other factors analysed, the geographical distance between the target and acquirer banks' headquarters is found to be negative and statistically significant for the latter (at the 10 per cent confidence level or less) over all event windows. These results are consistent with previous studies, confirming that the proximity of target and acquirer companies confers benefits in the M&A domain. As such, although banking is a global business, our results support the explanation provided by previous studies on the negative link between distance and M&A results (e.g. asymmetric information and adverse selection, in Ragozzino and Reuer 2009; the difficulty of effective communication, in Cummings 2007) and the cost of searching and integration. Our results also support the idea that geographical distance has a positive link with the target bank's shareholders' returns over two event windows: this seems to confirm that the asymmetric information between target and bidder increases in long distance M&A and that target companies' shareholders are able to exploit this.

Notes

1. This chapter is the result of the authors' continuous cooperation. Sections 1 and 3 can be attributed to Franco Fiordelisi and other paragraphs to Duccio Martelli.
2. The number and the value of M&A transactions are substantial in all sectors. For example, the retail sector – that is, the industry least concerned by the M&A phenomenon – registered more than a thousand deals with an overall value of US$ 4.5 billion (see Thomson Financial 2007).
3. For instance, Tetlock (2007) and Tetlock et al. (2008) apply the text analysis to measure the content of press news. In the second step, the authors assess the link between the estimated news content and the company's stock price, profitability indices, and efficiency of market operations.

4. We specific a logit model, estimated by the generalized linear models using the Newton-Raphson (maximum likelihood) optimization; standard error estimates are robust to various kinds of misspecification that allow for intragroup correlation.
5. As such, 1 refers to the highest CAR, indicating a successful M&A deal.

References

Beitel, P., Schiereck, D., and Wahrenburg, M. (2004) "Explaining M&A success in European banks" *European Financial Management* 10, 109–139.
Buono, A.F., Bowditch, J.L., and Lewis, J.W. (1985) "When cultures collide: the anatomy of a merger" *Human Relations* 38, 477–500.
Campa J.M., and Hernando I. (2006) "M&As performance in the European financial industry" *Journal of Banking and Finance* 30, 3367–3392.
Cartwright, S., and Cooper, C.L. (1993) "The Role of Culture Compatibility in Successful Organizational Marriage" *Academy Management Executive* 7, 57–70.
Chatterjee, S., Lubatkin, M., Schweiger, D., and Weber, Y. (1992) "Cultural differences and shareholder value in related mergers: linking equity and human capital" *Strategic Management Journal* 13, 319–334.
Cummings, J. (2007) "Leading groups from a distance: How to mitigate consequences of geographic dispersion", n Weisband, S., and Atwater, L. (eds) *Leadership at a distance*, Lawrence Erlbaum Associates, Taylor and Francis Group, New York, 33–50.
DeLong, G.L., and DeYoung, R. (2007) "Learning by observing: Information spillovers in the execution and valuation of commercial bank M&As" *Journal of Finance* 62, 181–216.
Ekkayokkaya, M., Holmes, P., and Paudyal, K. (2009) "The euro and the changing face of European banking: evidence from mergers and acquisitions" *European Financial Management* 15 (2) 451–476
Goddard, J., Molyneux, P., Wilson, J.O.S., and Tavakoli, M. (2007) "European banking: An overview" *Journal of Banking and Finance* 31, 1911–1935.
Gugler, K., Mueller, D.C., Yurtoglu, B.B., and Zulehner, C. (2003) "The Effects of Mergers: An International Comparison" *International Journal of Industrial Organization* 21, 625–653.
Gupta, A., and Misra, L. (2007) "Deal size, bid premium, and gains in bank mergers: The impact of managerial motivations" *Financial Review* 42, 373–400.
Kusstatscher, V., and Cooper, C.L. (2005) *Managing Emotions in Mergers and Acquisitions*. Edward Elgar Publishing, Cheltenham.
Larsson R., Brousseau K.R., Driver, M.J., and Sweet, P.L. (2004) "The Secrets of Merger and Acquisition Success: A Co-Competence and Motivational Approach to Synergy Realization" in Pablo A.L., and Mansour, J. (eds) *Mergers and Acquisitions. Creating Integrative Knowledge*, Blackwell, Oxford, 3–17.
Lubatkin, M., Schweiger, D., and Weber, Y. (1999) "Top management turnover in related M&As: an additional test of the theory of relative standing" *Journal of Management* 25, 55–73.
Ragozzino, R., and Reuer J.J. (2010) "Geographic Distance and M&A Markets: IPOs as Information Diffusion Mechanisms" *Strategic Management Journal* (forthcoming)

Schmautzer, D. (2006) Cross-border bank mergers: who gains and why? Available at SSRN: http://ssrn.com/abstract=924373 (last access: June 29, 2010).

Sudarsanam, S. (2003) *Creating Value from Mergers and Acquisitions*, FT Prentice Hall, London.

Tetlock, P.C. (2007) "Giving content to investor sentiment: the role of media in the stock market" *Journal of Finance* 62, 1139–1168.

Tetlock, P.C., Saar-Tsechansky, M., and Mackassy, S. (2008) "More Than Words: Quantifying Language to Measure Firms' Fundamentals", *Journal of Finance* 63, 1437–1467.

Thomson Financial (2007) Mergers & Acquisitions Review, Fourth Quarter 2007, available at http://banker.thomsonib.com (last access: June 29, 2010).

9
What does Bank Financial Profile tell Us about Mergers and Acquisitions in Latin American Banking?

Fatima Cardias Williams and Jonathan Williams

1. Introduction

Acts of liberalization feature prominently in the history of Latin American (LatAm) financial sectors. The experience with major structural reforms programmes is mixed: the initial financial liberalization experiments in the 1970s collapsed in the face of the 1980s debt crisis; whereas economic stabilization led to unsustainable credit booms resulting in banking sector crises and government-led banking sector restructuring in the mid-1990s. Across LatAm, bank restructuring is reshaping the industrial structure of banking markets (Gelos and Roldós 2004). Restructuring, and policies such as bank privatization and the repealing of restrictions on foreign bank entry, creates incentives for consolidation via a wave of local and cross-border mergers and acquisitions (M&As), which has raised market concentration. Initially inspired by restructuring, the M&A wave becomes market driven in the 2000s (Carvalho et al. 2009).

The chapter considers efficiency and market power as motives for bank M&As in LatAm. A priori consolidation produces more concentrated markets and increases competition, which impacts on bank efficiency, suggesting a powerful efficiency motive for bank M&As. Under this assumption, efficiently managed banks acquire poorly managed banks and manage assets better in order to generate higher profit and value for their shareholders (Hannan and Rhoades 1987). Consolidation may raise market competition, reducing incentives for banks to exercise market power: for instance, local banks may price competitively to deter new (foreign) entrants, or the latter may do so to secure market share, forcing incumbents to follow suit or exit (see Berger et al. 2000). On the other hand, consolidation can increase market power because banks price less competitively; foreign banks operating in more than one regional market forbear from competitive pricing in one market for fear of retaliation in another. To identify the market power motive we employ social welfare loss, measuring the misallocation of resources attributable to market power as an indicator (Maudos and Fernández de Guevara 2007). A negative, significant coefficient on this variable implies that banks participating in M&As price more competitively and vice-versa.

The empirical evidence finds that LatAm banks operate under monopolistic conditions and increasing consolidation does not weaken competitive conditions, although cross-country differences exist (Yeyati and Micco 2007; Yildirim and Philippatos 2007). This lack of generality in cross-country evidence suggests that competitive gains materialize slowly; rather, consolidation may incentivize banks to exploit market power.[1] Whilst the literature does not accept the notion of collusion between LatAm banks, there are exceptions: banks in some countries possess some degree of market power (Nakane 2001; Nakane et al. 2006), differences in competitive conditions exist across local and national markets and large and foreign owned banks behave competitively in contrast to small and state owned banks (Belaisch 2003).

Employing a discrete choice methodology, we contend that a bank's financial profile informs the probability of its participating in M&As relative to the probability that it does not. Our research uncovers six discrete outcomes associated with consolidation; we classify each bank as belonging to one outcome or to the control group of non-participating banks. The outcomes are: failure, restructured target, domestic buyer, domestic target, foreign buyer and foreign target. A vector of covariates based on the CAMEL taxonomy – often used by bank regulators – is used as proxy for bank financial profile.[2] We apply a multinomial logit model (MLNM) to estimate (1) the importance of each covariate in the financial profile vector across discrete outcomes relative to the control and (2) the importance of every covariate in each outcome relative to the other outcomes. Our model is applied is a sample of 418 banks from four LatAm countries – Argentina, Brazil, Chile and Mexico – yielding a total of 4128 observations from 1985 to 2006.

We address several policy issues. The restructuring process requires decisions on which banks to allow to fail and which to intervene in and keep in operation. We identify if regulators adopt a too-big-to-fail policy, as reported in Asian bank restructurings (Bongini et al. 2001). We compare characteristics of target banks in M&As driven by restructuring and by markets (following Lanine and Vander Vennet 2006; Koetter et al. 2007). In order to recapitalize banks in distress, governments amend laws to allow foreign bank entry, and we investigate if the strategic preferences of foreign and domestic banks are homogeneous (Focarelli et al. 2002; Vander Vennet 1996, 2003). Heterogeneity in the strategic preferences of foreign and domestic banks is required in order to understand evolving market structures under consolidation.

The chapter is structured as follows: Section 2 presents the model and discusses data; Section 3 discusses the results and Section 4 concludes.

2. Methodology and data

Here, we introduce the multinomial logit model, describe the discrete outcomes and discuss the covariates in the vector of CAMEL indicators in this section.

2.1. Multinomial logit model (MNLM)

A bank can experience any of six outcomes or belong to the non-merging control group, with the probability of being in an outcome a function of the vector of bank-specific covariates. Formally, we write the MNLM in Eq. (1).

$$\ln \Omega_{m|b}(x) = \ln \frac{\Pr(y = m \mid x)}{\Pr(y = b \mid x)} = x\beta_{m|b} \qquad \text{for } m = 1 \text{ to } J \qquad (1)$$

where b is the base category or control group and m is the number of alternative outcomes. Since $\ln \Omega_{m|b}(x) = \ln 1 = 0$, it must hold that $\beta_{b/b} = 0$. Thus, the log odds of an outcome compared with itself are always zero, and the effects of any independent variables must also be zero. The J equations may be solved to find the predicted probabilities of an outcome – see Eq. (2).

$$\Pr(Y_i = j) = \frac{\exp(x_i\beta_j)}{\sum_{k=1}^{J} \exp(x_i\beta_k)} \qquad (2)$$

where Y_i is the categorical dependent variable that takes one of the values 1 to J and J is the number of outcomes. The estimated parameters per group, β_j, yield the effect of the covariates, x, on the logged ratio of probabilities relative to the control group, that is, $\ln(\Pr_{ij}/\Pr_{io}) = \beta_j x$.

In Eq> (3), we write the MNLM to illustrate the measurement of the influence of an identical set of covariates, x, for J outcomes with respect the control group.

$$\ln\left(\frac{\mathrm{Pr}_{i_j}}{\mathrm{Pr}_{i_0}}\right) = \beta_{0j} + \beta_{1j}x_{i1} + \beta_{2j}x_{i2} + \beta_{3j}x_{i3} + \dots + \beta_{nj}x_{in} \tag{3}$$

Following Koetter et al. (2007), we report relative risk ratios (RRR) measuring the change of the probability of being in outcome j relative to the probability of being in the control group, for a unit change in the variable x. Eq. (4) shows the calculation of the RRR for a one unit change in covariate x from the value of x to x'.

$$\mathrm{RRR}_i(x, x') = \frac{\mathrm{Pr}(y = j \mid x) / \mathrm{Pr}(y = b \mid x)}{\mathrm{Pr}(y = j \mid x') / \mathrm{Pr}(y = b \mid x')} = e^{\beta j} \tag{4}$$

We interpret the RRR as follows: an RRR of 1 is analogous to a zero coefficient, implying a change in the variable does not affect the probability of being in outcome j relative to the probability of being in the control group. An RRR greater than 1 indicates an increase of the probability ratio as x increases, whilst an RRR less than 1 signifies a decrease in the relative risk to be in outcome j as x increases.

2.2. Outcomes

Sourcing information from central banks, academic papers, newswire services, BankScope and bank websites, we construct six discrete outcomes to identify bank ownership and qualify corporate changes from the consolidation process. Banks may experience more than one outcome, which captures the dynamics of M&A activity:

1. Failed – includes banks liquidated at time *t*, and banks whose ownership, assets and liabilities transfer to another bank during episodes of financial distress, with operations ceasing.
2. Restructured target – banks receiving government support, for instance, injections of capital and/or liquidity, before being sold.
3. Domestic buyer – a locally owned bank acquiring a bank at time *t*.
4. Domestic target – a locally owned bank acquired by another bank at time *t*. In specifying restructured and domestic targets, we differentiate between the mid-1990s restructuring driven acquisitions and later market driven acquisitions.
5. Foreign buyer – foreign owned bank acquiring a bank (local or foreign) at time *t*. We limit the classification to resident foreign owned banks.

6. Foreign target – a bank (locally or foreign owned) acquired by a foreign bank at time *t*. In specifying and domestic and foreign targets, we consider market driven M&A strategies to vary across acquiring bank ownership.

Table 9.1 shows the number of observations in each outcome between 1985 and 2006. There are 4128 observations: Brazil (47 per cent), Argentina (28%), Mexico (13) and Chile (12). In LatAm, 423 observations are in the six discrete outcomes equal to roughly 10 per cent of observations.

The fact that there are more observations on targets than buyers suggests consolidation. The number of observations on domestic buyers hides the fact that some buyers participate in multiple acquisitions. We

Table 9.1 Profile of outcomes: Latin America, 1985–2006

	Outcome	LatAm	Argentina	Brazil	Chile	Mexico
1	Control	3705	1038	1759	447	461
2	Failed	106	28	44	10	24
3	Restructured target	80	20	38	3	19
4	Domestic buyer	92	38	39	6	9
5	Domestic target	34	11	14	7	2
6	Foreign buyer	32	8	16	4	4
7	Foreign target	79	21	23	20	15
	Totals	4128	1164	1933	497	534
% of the number of observations						
1	Control	89.75	89.18	91.00	89.94	86.33
2	Failed	2.57	2.41	2.28	2.01	4.49
3	Restructured target	1.94	1.72	1.97	0.60	3.56
4	Domestic buyer	2.23	3.26	2.02	1.21	1.69
5	Domestic target	0.82	0.95	0.72	1.41	0.37
6	Foreign buyer	0.78	0.69	0.83	0.80	0.75
7	Foreign target	1.91	1.80	1.19	4.02	2.81
	Totals	100	100	100	100	100

Source: Adapted from various sources including central banks, BankScope and bank websites.

find fewer observations on foreign buyers than foreign targets. Whilst several acquisitions, especially of large, locally owned banks constitute direct foreign investment by non-resident parent foreign banks are not included in the sample, there are many cases of subsequent M&As by resident foreign buyers as the ultimate foreign owners seek to consolidate operations.

2.3. Covariates

A voluminous literature exists on the prediction of corporate failure and participation in M&As. As its basic premise Altman (1968) proposes that firms with certain financial profiles have a higher probability of failure than firms with contrasting financial profiles. In constructing discrete outcome models, researchers employ accounting based models like Altman's Z-score, and market based models, although it is ambiguous if one approach dominates (Agarwal and Taffler 2008). In banking, and especially in emerging markets, there is a paucity of listed banks, and this requires the use of accounting based models in discrete choice studies. In brief, underperforming banks have a higher probability of failing and being targets for larger, better performing banks. In crisis episodes, the probability of bank failure increases because of weak capitalization, low earnings and liquidity and poor asset quality (Bongini et al. 2001; Lanine and Vander Vennet 2006).[3]

To provide information relevant to bank regulators, researchers select variables based on the CAMEL approach (West 1985). Our indicator of capitalization is the ratio of equity to assets (ETA). A priori an improving capitalization (an RRR greater than 1) should lower the probabilities of failure (Wheelock and Wilson 2000) and being acquired (Hannan and Rhoades 1987; DeYoung 2003; Koetter et al. 2007). Higher capitalization is expected to raise the probability of a bank being a buyer. We select four asset quality indicators in the financial profile vector. A higher ratio of securities to total assets (STA) implies that a bank is more diversified with a lower overall level of portfolio risk (Koetter et al. 2007). Loan loss reserves to gross loans (LLRL) proxy credit risk: increases in this variable raise the probability of bank failure (Sinkey 1975, 1978) and the probability of being acquired. The third indicator is annual asset growth (TAG). Growth based on imprudent lending should raise the probability of bank failure (DeYoung 2003), although a study of Brazil finds that foreign banks acquire slow growing banks (Cardias Williams and Williams 2008). The final asset quality indicator is the diversification index (DIV): better diversified banks are less likely to fail (Crowley and Loviscek 1990).

Three indicators measure management quality. Estimated operating cost efficiencies (CEFF) and alternative profit efficiencies (PEFF) are derived from stochastic frontier and Fourier flexible functional form methodologies. Efficiency is an important determinant of the internationalization of banking (Berger et al. 2000; Focarelli and Pozzolo 2001); cross-border target banks are less efficient than buyers (Vander Vennet 1996, 2003), with acquiring banks particularly strong in terms of profit efficiency (Akhavein et al. 1997). The probability of bank failure is associated with poor cost control (DeYoung 2003), with domestic targets exhibiting weaker efficiencies (O'Keefe 1996; Koetter et al. 2007). We expect the RRR on CEFF and PEFF to exceed unity for buyers and fall below unity for failed, restructured and domestic target banks. The Z-score is the third management quality variable, indicating how management controls overall risk (Hannan and Hanweck 1988). We expect increases in Z to lower the probability of failure and being a target.

Earnings are measured by return on assets (ROA). Increasing ROA should lower the probabilities of failure (Wheelock and Wilson 2000) and being acquired (O'Keefe 1996; Focarelli et al. 2002; Lanine and Vander Vennet 2006). The liquidity indicator is the ratio of liquid assets to customer and short term funding (LIQ). An increase in liquidity should lessen the probabilities of failure (West 1985) and being acquired (O'Keefe 1996; Worthington 2004). We estimate market power (WLTA) as social welfare loss caused by market power (Maudos and Fernández de Guevara 2007). A priori an RRR exceeding unity suggests market power motivates M&As whereas an RRR of less than unity implies that banks characterized by competitive pricing are more likely to participate in M&As. We use the logarithm of total assets to control for bank size (lnTA). Increasing size lowers the probability of being a target, but not always significantly (Hannan and Rhoades 1987).

Finally, four variables control for cross-country differences: the logarithm of real GDP per capita (lnGDPpc) controls for wealth; the rate of annual change in GDP (GDPgro) controls for business cycle fluctuations which affect bank failure rates (DeYoung 2003); deposit bank assets to central bank and deposit bank assets is a measure of the importance of the private sector in allocating resources (DBACBA) and liquid liabilities to GDP is an indicator of financial depth.

Table 9.2a summarizes the covariates and expected relationships; Table 9.2b provides descriptive statistics on each covariate by outcome. We sourced bank data from BankScope and the IBCA databases converting data into US$ millions at 2000 prices. Control data are from

Table 9.2a   Covariates used in MNLM

Covariate	Proxy	Expected relationships
ETA	Capitalization	Poor capitalization raises probability of bank failure, increases probability of a bank being a target (Hannan and Rhoades 1987; Wheelock and Wilson 2000; Lanine and Vander Vennet, 2006).
STA	Asset quality	Higher ratio implies bank is more diversified with lower overall level of asset risk (Koetter et al. 2007).
LLRL	Asset quality	Banks with poor credit risk profile are more likely to be targets (Koetter et al. 2007).
TAG	Asset quality	Captures risk of expanding too quickly or too slowly. Slower growth expected to raise probability of being a target.
DIV	Diversification index	Calculated as $\sum_{i=1}^{3}\left(X_i / Q\right)^2$, where the X's are customer loans, interbank loans, and securities, and Q is the sum of X (total earning assets) (see Acharya et al. 2006). Increase in loan intensity lowers probability of foreign involvement in M&As.
PEFF[1] CEFF[1] Z	Management quality and risk	Less efficient banks expected to be targets (O'Keefe 1996; Vander Vennet 1996, 2003; Koetter et al. 2007). On average, there are no cost efficiency gains from M&A activity (Berger and Humphrey 1997), but large profit efficiency gains are found (Akhavein et al. 1997). Following Hannan and Hanweck (1988) Z = ROA + ETA / σ_{ROA}. The denominator is a three year rolling average.
ROA	Earnings	Mixed results in literature.
LIQ	Liquidity	More liquid banks expected in M&As as buyer or target.
WLTA	Market power	Calculated following Maudos and de Guevara (2007).
lnTA	Size	Small banks expected to be targets (O'Keefe, 1997; Wheelock and Wilson 2000; Worthington 2004; Koetter et al. 2007).
lnGDPpc	GDP per capita	Captures economic wealth of country across time.
GDPgr	GDP growth rate	Measures rate of economic growth annually.
DBACBA	Deposit banks assets/central bank + deposit bank assets	Measures relative development of private banking sector in share of banking sector assets. A higher ratio implies a more developed financial system.
LLDGP	Liquid liabilities-GDP	Measures financial depth.

Table 9.2b Descriptive statistics, by outcome

Indicator	1 Control		2 Failed		3 Res-Target		4 D-buyer		5 D-Target		6 F-buyer		7 F-target	
	Avg	Std	Avg	Std	Avg	Std	Avg	Std	Avg	Std	Avg	Std	Avg	Std
TA, US$ millions	3408	10,533	4717	10,623	3573	6329	10,505	15,751	1929	2742	3708	5849	3910	6158
STA	18.92	18.72	22.06	20.39	20.67	18.83	18.55	13.11	14.07	11.69	20.18	16.17	16.99	19.72
ETA	19.14	19.32	16.88	20.98	6.95	19.33	12.74	11.59	19.15	15.27	12.54	10.95	13.36	15.00
LLR	8.98	70.07	13.41	29.08	14.30	19.08	7.30	9.51	13.56	18.63	4.93	7.45	7.19	12.62
TAG	23.00	135.73	0.79	41.85	39.21	194.93	15.10	37.84	17.15	84.70	99.02	222.38	22.69	60.97
DIV	58.74	16.83	59.25	17.58	58.04	15.27	55.78	13.96	59.02	15.13	57.68	17.16	65.04	16.69
PEFF	49.73	25.54	44.15	28.60	41.20	30.14	56.60	24.07	43.26	25.53	46.85	29.61	49.82	28.54
CEFF	65.08	20.95	67.72	18.06	62.09	22.57	66.22	18.60	66.18	18.93	55.18	26.78	67.45	22.95
Z score	24.23	56.76	20.39	27.97	8.16	15.86	26.12	30.54	14.41	15.87	17.59	25.50	25.44	40.34
ROA	1.45	8.21	0.43	9.71	-3.70	14.94	0.90	4.68	-2.15	12.77	0.45	4.26	0.47	6.42
LIQ	71.95	837.41	41.38	103.08	25.94	48.34	36.04	142.65	23.46	28.56	33.40	54.91	32.88	100.07
WLTA	5.10	12.33	3.22	9.26	1.66	9.52	2.43	6.91	3.86	7.99	1.61	5.66	1.54	6.08
InTA	6.40	1.88	6.44	2.27	7.01	1.64	7.87	2.00	6.35	1.83	7.26	1.69	7.05	1.84
lnGDPpc	7.43	2.15	7.61	1.64	7.88	1.05	7.88	1.83	6.94	2.83	7.50	1.95	6.62	2.76
GDPgro	3.17	4.07	2.33	3.67	2.90	3.03	3.11	3.60	1.45	4.48	3.73	3.22	3.48	3.69
DBACBA	82.61	10.99	84.98	14.12	86.66	9.46	87.18	7.72	83.26	8.32	87.89	9.03	86.41	9.58
LLGDP	32.02	11.19	31.80	6.67	26.96	7.43	31.30	9.68	37.57	10.32	33.30	7.05	33.63	8.92

Note: All variables are expressed as percentages except where noted.

the World Bank Financial Structure and World Economic Outlook databases.

We can rewrite Eq. (3) as Eq. (5) to show the MNLM to be estimated:

$$\ln\left(\Pr_{ij}/\Pr_{i0}\right) = \beta_{0j} + \beta_{1j}ETA_{i1} + \beta_{2j}STA_{i2} + \beta_{3j}LLRL_{i3} + \beta_{4j}TAG_{i4} +$$
$$\beta_{5j}DIV_{i5} + \beta_{6j}PEFF_{i6} + \beta_{7j}CEFF_{i7} + \beta_{j8}Z_{i8} + \beta_{9j}ROA_{i9}$$
$$+ \beta_{10j}LIQ_{i10} + \beta_{11j}WLTA_{i11} + \beta_{j12}LNTA_{i12}$$
$$+ \beta_{j13}LNGDPPC_{i13} + \beta_{j14}GDPGRO_{i14} + \beta_{j15}DBACBA_{i15}$$
$$+ \beta_{j16}LLGDP_{i16} \tag{5}$$

where J = number of outcomes (1 to 7), ETA = equity-to-assets, STA = securities-to-assets, LLRL = loan loss reserves-to-gross loans, TAG = annual asset growth, DIV = diversification index, PEFF = estimated alternative profit efficiency, CEFF = estimated operating cost efficiency, Z = Z-score, ROA = profit before tax-to-assets, LIQ = liquid assets to deposits and money market funding, WLTA = welfare loss-to-total assets, LNTA = natural log of total assets, LNGDPPC = natural log of GDP per capita in country k at time t, GDPGRO = annual percentage change in GDP in country k at time t, DBACBA = deposit bank assets-to-deposit bank assets plus central bank assets in country k at time t and LLGDP = liquid liabilities to GDP in country k at time t. A set of year dummy variables is specified (omitting 1985 and 1986) but not reported. All data are in percentages (except where noted) and each covariate is specified with a lag of one year.

3. Results

The results are given in two subsections: 3.1., the specification analysis of the MNLM, and 3.2, the discussion of the relative risk ratios.

3.1. Specification analysis

We specify six discrete outcomes associated with consolidation. A Wald test verifies if the data support the choice of outcomes. The null hypothesis is $H_0 = \beta_{1,m|n} = \ldots = \beta_{K,m|n} = 0$ with the test statistic drawn from the $\chi 2$ distribution. If none of the independent variables significantly affects the odds of alternative m versus alternative n, this implies that m and n are indistinguishable with respect to the variables in the model (Long and Freese 2006). Table 9.3 presents the test statistics showing that the null hypothesis cannot be accepted for any combination of the six discrete outcomes.

Table 9.3 Wald tests for combining alternatives outcomes

Odds comparing		LatAm	Argentina	Brazil	Chile	Mexico
Alt. 1	Alt. 2	χ^2	χ^2	χ^2	χ^2	χ^2
Fail	Res-Target	19,861.36	50,895.91	11,651.40	29,388.48	36,667.92
Fail	D-Buyer	4471.70	15,658.32	8399.63	16,742.20	8654.45
Fail	D-Target	4754.61	11,874.84	22,534.76	20,246.05	11,754.15
Fail	F-Buyer	7952.08	8628.82	6044.86	461,000.00	18,212.10
Fail	F-Target	6729.31	25,382.62	11,092.23	27,767.09	12,075.40
Fail	Control	147.92	52,616.18	97,950.16	21,903.09	14,338.06
Res-Target	D-Buyer	21,766.96	19,831.56	29,988.37	7981.63	26,473.96
Res-Target	D-Target	15,621.46	25,493.34	54,562.48	8715.23	6057.42
Res-Target	F-Buyer	7166.31	22,698.75	15,935.52	54,000.94	15,432.88
Res-Target	F-Target	8954.27	23,198.60	16,065.84	12,927.30	27,789.43
Res-Target	Control	74,097.14	29,812.16	141,000.00	38,286.40	17,959.53
D-Buyer	D-Target	3172.07	12,915.50	33,404.18	7924.60	4476.06
D-Buyer	F-Buyer	5810.61	22,011.72	28,265.89	17,344.38	11,385.03
D-Buyer	F-Target	3353.31	22,834.92	19,682.07	25,746.11	14,714.06
D-Buyer	Control	170.97	41,109.97	42,597.53	7806.67	13,440.12
D-Target	F-Buyer	1875.62	15,619.88	19,693.36	20,006.31	3935.22
D-Target	F-Target	971.87	20,400.19	21,885.10	13,577.54	6760.38
D-Target	Control	14,486.49	31,530.66	72,497.25	9252.64	382.60
F-Buyer	F-Target	2984.79	16,486.84	6606.59	15,554.31	16,925.34
F-Buyer	Control	21,206.88	11,433.36	37,692.17	13,888.48	9209.16
F-Target	Control	27,766.24	55,885.74	95,437.84	22,218.41	15,061.37

Note: All χ^2 test statistics are statistically significant at the 1 % level.

A second Wald procedure tests the effect of multiple independent variables; that is, $H_0 = \beta_{k,1/b} = ... \beta_{k,J/b} = \beta_{l,1/b} = ... = \beta_{l,J/b} = 0$. Table 9.4 shows test statistics and significance levels. The test allows the null to be tested for each covariate. For the LatAm sample, bank asset size (lnTA), market power (WLTA) and asset growth (TAG) are significant at the 1 per cent level, with cost efficiency (CEFF), profit efficiency (PEFF) and securities to assets (STA) significant at 5 per cent. Further tests at the country level for Argentina and Brazil reveal cross-border differences in the importance of individual indicators of financial profile: for

Table 9.4   Wald tests for independent variables

Variable	LatAm χ2 (d.f. = 6)	Argentina χ2 (d.f. = 6)	Brazil χ2 (d.f. = 6)
ETA	5.996	3.612	11.557*
STA	14.887**	5.245	11.467*
LLR	2.045	16.532**	4.752
TAG	21.261***	10.921*	19.687***
DIV	9.939	4.854	9.896
PEFF	14.720**	11.141*	21.018***
CEFF	16.287**	14.54**	39.178***
ZSCO	7.307	2.696	6.277
RoA	10.518	5.264	7.604
LIQ	3.841	6.969	11.159*
WLTA	27.264***	9.838	14.295**
lnTA	57.757***	13.501**	51.086***
ln GDP pc	26.070***		
GDPgro	13.389**		
DBACBA	14.187**		
LLGDP	26.787***		

***, **, *Significant at 1, 5 and 10 per cent respectively.

instance, the asset quality indicator – loan loss reserves (LLRL) is significant for Argentina but not for Brazil, whereas the capitalization indictor (ETA) shows the opposite. Both market power and efficiencies are very strongly significant for Brazil but only the efficiencies are significant for Argentina. Whilst the findings suggest statistical grounds for deselecting some indicators we maintain the CAMEL.

Finally, a likelihood ratio test compares the estimated model (4) with a restricted one specifying only the intercept as a covariate; that is, $H_0 = \beta_{k,1/b} = \ldots = \beta_{k,J/b} = 0$. That the test statistic is –1675.51 with 183 degrees of freedom shows that the null is overwhelmingly rejected by the data. Generally, the MNLM is well specified.

3.2. Relative Risk Ratios

The RRR (see Eq. (4)) measures the change in the probability of a bank being in outcome j relative to the probability of being in the control group, for a unit change in a covariate. Since the covariates are expressed as percentages (except where noted), an RRR of 0.9914 on the profit efficiency of failed banks implies that a one percentage point increase in profit efficiency leads to a 0.086 per cent lower probability of becoming a failed bank relative to the probability of being in the control group for the one unit change (Koetter et al. 2007). The RRRs are shown by each outcome in Table 9.5.

Let us consider the efficiency and market power motives for M&A. Efficiency motives for consolidation appear to be well supported by the empirical evidence at least for domestically owned banks. The importance of profit efficiency as a predictor of corporate change, reported elsewhere, is confirmed in LatAm. A unit increase in profit efficiency lowers the probability of a bank failing and being restructured, whilst raising the probability of it being a domestic buyer. The RRR on profit efficiency for foreign targets implies that efficient banks are selected for

Table 9.5   Relative Risk Ratios, by outcome, LatAm

Variable	2 Failed	3 Res-target	4 D-buyer	5 D-target	6 F-buyer	7 F-target
ETA	0.9950	0.9870**	1.0070	1.0068	0.9933	0.9898
STA	1.0147***	1.0079	1.0081	0.9756**	1.0004	0.9980
LLR	0.9999	1.0002	0.9962	1.0002	0.9539	0.9984
TAG	0.9913***	1.0004	0.9984	0.9998	1.0018***	0.9999
DIV	0.9984	0.9992	0.9979	0.9902	0.9830	1.0202***
PEFF	0.9914*	0.9909*	1.0151***	0.9927	0.9981	1.0014
CEFF	1.0145**	0.9903	1.0027	0.9995	0.9737***	0.9934
Z	0.9984	0.9716*	1.0006	0.9815*	0.9978	0.9992
RoA	1.0022	0.9701***	0.9857	0.9722*	0.9694	0.9949
Liq	0.9999	0.9999	1.0000	0.9920	0.9997	0.9998
WLTA	0.9787	0.9750*	0.9536***	0.9876	0.9274***	0.9552***
lnTA	0.9211	1.1572*	1.5914***	1.0379	1.3566**	1.2606***
LnGDPpc	1.2463***	1.5443**	1.2440**	0.9374	1.0330	0.8536**
GDP growth	0.8787***	1.0348	1.0172	1.0148	1.1453*	1.0508
DBACBA	1.0527***	1.0361**	0.9997	1.0167	1.0257	0.9943
LLGDP	1.1220***	1.1087**	1.0049	1.0570	1.0490	0.9713

Notes: Observations: 3739; pseudo log likelihood: -1675.5066; pseudo R^2: 0.1791. ***, **, *: significant at 1, 5 and 10 % respectively; robust standard errors.

acquisition – evidence of cherry picking – although the relationship is insignificant.

We find significant evidence of a market power motive in consolidation. For each outcome (except failed and domestic target), the RRRs are negative and significant. That is, a unit increase in welfare loss lowers the probability of a bank being restructured, a domestic buyer, a foreign buyer or a foreign target relative to the probability of being in the control group. Furthermore, the probabilities associated with unit changes in market power are larger than for any other covariate: a unit increase in welfare loss reduces the probability of a bank being a buyer by 7.26 per cent (foreign) and 4.64 per cent (domestic), a foreign target by 4.48 per cent and a restructured target by 2.5 per cent. In short, if increasing concentration allows banks some degree of market power, there is a lower probability that banks with less competitive pricing strategies will either buy another bank or be acquired. There are possible explanations for the observed relationships. Both domestic and foreign buyers – generally larger institutions – appear to be more competitive, at least in terms of pricing, confirming previous findings of different bank types facing different competitive conditions in national markets. Although we cannot be certain from the estimates, our findings may reflect increasing competition between large domestically and foreign owned banks, both looking to expand market share. The evidence implies that foreign banks use a cherry picking strategy to acquire more competitive banks.

In terms of decisions taken to close some troubled banks whilst restructuring others, our evidence confirms previous findings that failed banks that grow slowly (TAG) lose a larger proportion of potential profit to inefficiencies. Restructured banks are significantly larger than the control group, providing tentative evidence of a too-big-to-fail policy (especially when we observe failed banks to be smaller, albeit only insignificantly so compared to those in the control group). The LatAm finding is consistent with evidence from Asia; the restructured targets include former state owned banks, on which it is notoriously difficult to foreclose irrespective of financial underperformance. Surprisingly, banks with a higher proportion of securities in their portfolio (STA), indicating a lower portfolio risk, are more likely to fail than belong to the control group. Restructured and domestic targets share the characteristics of being more risky (Z) with lower earnings (ROA) compared to the control group. However, restructured targets are undercapitalized and less profit efficient than the control group, suggesting differences between restructuring driven and market driven M&As.

In contrast to failed banks and restructured targets, a unit change in profit efficiency raises the probability of a bank being a domestic buyer, over being in the control group, by 1.51 per cent. Domestic buyers are considerably larger in size relative to the control group than banks belonging to any of the other outcomes. This is expected given the strategic expansion of large, domestically owned banks and increasing foreign bank penetration. Foreign buyers, like their domestically owned counterparts, are significantly larger than the control group, but unlike domestic buyers foreign ones achieve significantly faster asset growth than the control group. Unsurprisingly, foreign buyers exhibit a lower level of cost efficiency, consistent with findings in other studies that note foreign banks' willingness to expend costs in order to improve asset quality at LatAm subsidiaries.

The relationships on the covariates of domestic targets are as expected. Target banks are less profitable and more risky, with fewer securities in their portfolios. Foreign targets, however, show a different set of characteristics – holding a less diversified portfolio (DIV) and significantly larger than the control group. The findings suggest bank strategies vary by ownership: domestic banks acquire underperforming banks in an attempt to realize improvements, as implied by the efficiency motive of M&A, while foreign banks tend to buy better performing banks to complement their own business.

4. Conclusions

We contend that bank financial profile can predict participation in M&As. We used a multinomial logit model to examine the dynamics of bank consolidation in LatAm and tests justified our model specification. Our empirical evidence supports the efficiency and market power motives for M&As. The importance of efficiency is noted in the literature. Efficient, large, domestic banks buy underperforming and weakly efficient ones, attempting to realize performance gains in acquisitions. Our study is amongst the earliest to report a market power motive underlying bank M&As: banks characterized by more competitive pricing (not exercising market power) are more likely to participate in M&As, particularly as buyers, irrespective of ownership (domestic or foreign).

We observe some similarities between domestic and foreign buyers; both are large and price more competitively. Whereas domestic buyers are profit efficient, foreign buyers are fast growing. However, we observe heterogeneity in their acquisition strategies: our results imply that foreign banks cherry pick large, competitive and more specialized targets whereas domestic banks buy underperforming ones. Our other evidence concurs with the literature. Failed banks are small, less efficient and slow growing. Consistent with that for the 1988 Asian bank restructurings, our evidence suggests that a too-big-to-fail policy is adopted for larger banks. The evidence should satisfy policy makers who are expecting higher market concentration to produce a more competitive outcome. As such, one can make inferences concerning the evolving consolidation process in LatAm.

Notes

1. Non-competitive market structures can produce oligopolistic behaviour by banks, as greater consolidation incentivises banks to exploit market power rather than improve efficiency. Highly concentrated market structures may limit the deepening of intermediation and development of more efficient banking sectors (Rojas Suarez, 2007).
2. CAMEL stands for capital adequacy, asset quality, management ability, earnings performance and liquidity.
3. Failed banks often exit the market via their acquisition by other banks.

References

Agarwal, V., and Taffler, R. (2008) "Comparing the performance of market-based and accounting-based bankruptcy prediction models" *Journal of Banking and Finance* 32, 1541–1151.

Akhavein, J.D., Berger, A.N., and Humphrey, D.B. (1997) "The effects of mega-amergers on efficiency and prices: Evidence from a bank profit function" *Review of Industrial Organisation* 12, 95–130.

Altman, E.I. (1968) "Financial ratios, discriminant analysis and the prediction of corporate bankruptcy" *Journal of Finance* 23, 589–609.

Belaisch, A. (2003) Do Brazilian banks compete? IMF Working Paper No. 113.

Berger, A.N., and Humphrey, D.B. (1997) "Efficiency of financial institutions: International survey and directions for future research" *European Journal of Operational Research* 98, 175–212.

Berger, A.N., DeYoung, R., Genay, H., and Udell, G.F. (2000) "Globalization of Financial Institutions: Evidence from Cross-Border Banking Performance" *Brookings-Wharton Papers on Financial Services* 3, 23–157.

Bongini, P., Claessens, S., and Ferri, G. (2001) "The political economy of distress in East Asian financial institutions" *Journal of Financial Services Research* 19, 5–25.

Cardias Williams, F., and Williams, J. (2008) "Does ownership explain bank M&A? The case of domestic banks and foreign banks in Brazil" in Arestis, P., and de Paula, L.F. (eds), *Financial Liberalization and Economic Performance in Emerging Countries*, Palgrave Macmillan, Basingstoke, 194–216.

Carvalho, F.J.C., Paula, L.F., and Williams, J., (2009) "Banking in Latin America" in Berger, A., Molyneux. P., and Wilson, J. (eds) *The Oxford Handbook of Banking*, Oxford University Press, Oxford, 868–902.

Crowley, F.D., and Loviscek, A.L. (1990) "New directions in predicting bank failures: The case of small banks" *North American Review of Economics and Finance* 1 (1), 145–162.

DeYoung, R. (2003) "De novo bank exit" *Journal of Money, Credit and Banking* 35 (5), 711–728.

Focarelli, D., Panetta, F., and Salleo, C. (2002) "Why do banks merge?" *Journal of Money, Credit and Banking* 34 (4), 1047–1066.

Focarelli, D., and Pozzolo, A.F. (2001) "The patterns of cross-border bank mergers and shareholdings in OECD countries" *Journal of Banking and Finance* 25, 2305–2337.

Gelos, R.G., and Roldós, J. (2004) "Consolidation and market structure in emerging market banking systems" *Emerging Markets Review* 5, 39–59.

Hannan, T.H., and Hanweck, G.A. (1988) "Bank insolvency risk and the market for large certificates of deposits" *Journal of Money, Credit and Banking* 20 (2) 203–211.

Hannan, T.H., and Rhodes, S.A. (1987) "Acquisition targets and motives: The case of the banking industry" *The Review of Economics and Statistics* 69 (1) 67–74.

Koetter, M., Bos, J.W.B., Heid, F., Kool, C.J.M., Kolari, J.W., and Porath, D. (2007) "Accounting for distress in bank mergers" *Journal of Banking and Finance* 31, 3200–3217.

Lanine, G., and Vander Vennet, R. (2006) "Failure prediction in the Russian bank sector with logit and trait recognition models" *Expert Systems with Applications* 30, 463–478.

Long, J.S., and Freese, J., (2006) *Regression Models for Categorical Dependent Variables Using Stata*, Stata Press, College Station, TX.

Maudos, J., and Fernández de Guevara, J. (2007) "The cost of market power in banking: social welfare loss vs. cost inefficiency" *Journal of Banking and Finance* 31, 2103–2125.

Nakane, M.I. (2001) A test of competition in Brazilian banking. Banco Central do Brasil Working Paper Series No. 12, March.

Nakane, M.I., Alencar, L.S., and Kanczuk, F. (2006) Demand for bank services and market power in Brazilian banking. Banco Central do Brasil Working Paper Series 107, June.

O'Keefe, J.P. (1996) "Banking industry consolidation: Financial attributes of merging banks" *FDIC Banking Review* 9, 18–38.

Rojas-Suarez, L. (2007) The provision of banking services in Latin America: Obstacles and recommendations. Center for Global Development Working Paper No. 124, June.

Sinkey, J.F. (1975) "A multivariate statistical analysis of the characteristics of problem banks" The *Journal of Finance* **20**, 21–36.

Sinkey, J.F. (1978) "Identifying 'Problem' Banks: How Do the Banking Authorities Measure A Bank's Risk Exposure" *Journal of Money, Credit, and Banking* 10 (2),184–193.

Vander Vennet, R. (1996) "The effect of mergers and acquisitions on the efficiency and profitability of EC credit institutions" *Journal of Banking and Finance* 20, 1531–1558.

Vander Vennet, R. (2003) "Cross-border mergers in European banking and bank efficiency" in Herrmann, H., and Lipsey, R. (eds) *Foreign direct investment in the real and financial sector of industrial countries*, Springer Verlag, Wiesbaden, 295–315.

West, R.C. (1985) "A factor-analytic approach to bank condition" *Journal of Banking and Finance* **9**, 253–266.

Wheelock, D.C., and Wilson, P.W. (2000) "Why do banks disappear? The determinants of US bank failures and acquisitions" *The Review of Economics and Statistics* 82 (1), 127–138.

Worthington, A.C. (2004) "Determinants of merger and acquisition activity in Australian cooperative deposit-taking institutions" *Journal of Business Research* 57, 47–57.

Yeyati, E.L., and Micco, A. (2007) "Concentration and foreign penetration in Latin American banking sectors: Impact on competition and risk" *Journal of Banking and Finance* 31, 1633–1647.

Yildirim, H.S., and Philippatos, G.C. (2007) "Restructuring, consolidation and competition in Latin American banking markets" *Journal of Banking and Finance* 31, 629–639.

10
What are the Determinants of Mergers and Acquisitions in Banking?[1]

Elena Beccalli and Pascal Frantz

1. Introduction

This study investigates the determinants of the likelihood of being involved in mergers and acquisitions (M&As) in banking. Given that the M&A market has been especially active in banking, the main aim here is to test whether it is possible to predict *ex ante* potential acquirers and targets on the basis of a set of bank specific and regulatory/institutional characteristics. We suggest that significant implications follow. Professional investors in the secondary markets would have at their disposal a method of identifying firms more likely to be targets and acquirers, and hence to select the stocks to be included in their portfolios. Managers in the banking industry would have a way to identify the probability of running into an M&A operation, and therefore to put in place mechanisms to favour or to block it.

A large body of literature is devoted to the *ex-post* measurement of realized performance gains (we counted six studies for the US and 17 for the EU in DeYoung et al. 2009),[2] whereas less attention was devoted to the *ex ante* examination of the features of acquired banks that potentially determine the *ex post* gains (one study only on US banking – Hannan and Pilloff 2006 – was referred to in this regard in DeYoung et al., 2009). Our chapter seeks to build upon this latter literature on the *ex ante* prediction of M&A deals, by examining the determinants of the likelihood of being involved in an M&A (either as targets or acquirers) during a recent "normal" sample period before the financial crisis that began in 2007 affected takeover activity.

The distinctive contribution of our chapter is to extend the existing literature by testing the multinomial logistic model specified by using two approaches for the identification of the relevant determinants (the more traditional hypotheses development and factor analysis), by considering a larger set of variables (both the more traditional bank specific variables and the regulatory/institutional ones) and by predicting the likelihood of becoming either a target or an acquirer.

The results obtained from the multinomial logistic regression indicate that a higher likelihood to be acquirers is found for larger banks, banks with a history of high growth, banks with higher cost X-efficiency and banks with lower capital strength, whereas a higher likelihood to be targets is found for banks with lower free cash flow, lower management efficiency, lower capitalization and lower liquidity. Moreover, the two approaches for the selection of variables (hypotheses development and factor analysis) provide different results for variables (such as regulatory/institutional and specialization) with a high correlation with others; hence they suggest the importance of using a different approach for the selection of variables (factor analysis in addition to hypotheses development).

Section 2 presents the motivation for this study in light of the literature on the *ex ante* likelihood of begin involved in M&As. Section 3 considers the methodological issues concerning the multinominal logit. Section 4 discusses the two approaches (hypotheses development and factor analysis) for the identification of the determinants. It also presents the sample and data. Section 5 describes the empirical results. Section 6 concludes.

2. Literature and motivations

In banking literature, most of the empirical evidence on the prediction of M&As relates to bank specific characteristics associated with becoming targets (Hannan and Rhoades 1987; Moore 1996, 1997; Hadlock et al. 1999; Wheelock and Wilson 2000; Hannan and Pillof 2006; Goddard et al. 2009; Hernando et al. 2009), with only one exception that also considers the likelihood of becoming acquirers (Focarelli et al., 2002). The methodology traditionally used is the logit model (Moore 1996, 1997; Hadlock et al. 1999; Focarelli et al. 2002; Hernando et al. 2009),[3] but fewer attempts have been made to test the more sophisticated proportional hazard model (Wheelock and Wilson 2000; Hannan and Pillof 2006; Goddard et al. 2009).[4]

Based on the logit methodology, few studies refer to bank specific characteristics for the US industry (Moore 1996, 1997; Hadlock et al.

1999), and only one for the EU industry (Hernando et al., 2009), by investigating only the features of acquired banks.[5] Moore (1997) analyses the financial determinants of becoming a target in relation to whether or not the acquiring bank is located within the market in which the target bank operated between 1993 and 1996. He reports that bank's shares, profitability and capital-asset ratio are all negatively related to the likelihood of it being acquired; the effect of market concentration is negative for in-market acquisitions and positive for out-of-market acquisitions. Hadlock et al. (1999) investigate the effect of management incentives, corporate governance and performance on the likelihood of a US bank being acquired over the period 1982–1992. They find that banks with higher levels of management ownership are less likely to be acquired, and that high rates of management turnover follow bank acquisitions. However no relationship between earnings and the probability of acquisition is documented. Hernando et al. (2009) analyse the probability of being acquired by another bank in the EU over the period 1997–2004. Their results suggest that poorly managed banks (high cost to income) and larger banks are more likely to be acquired by other banks in the same country. Moreover, banks operating in more concentrated markets are less likely to be acquired by other banks in the same country but are more likely to be acquired by foreign banks.

The only study that includes regulatory and environmental factors (e.g. differences in the regulatory and supervision framework, market environment and economic conditions), in addition to bank specific characteristics, as determinants of commercial bank acquisitions refers to EU banking over the period 1997–2002 (Pasiouras et al. 2007b). By employing a multinomial logit, they find that: (1) targets and acquirers were significantly larger, less well capitalized and less efficient in terms of expense management; (2) targets were less profitable with lower growth prospects, and acquirers more profitable with higher growth prospects and (3) external factors have affected targets and acquirers differently, and their effects have not been consistent or robust to sample size changes.

3. Methodology

A multinomial logistic regression explains the likelihood of an event taking place as a function of a vector of independent variables X and parameters B, with the function taking a particular form. Let us denote the multinomial response variable indicating the occurrence of an event in a distinct time interval ranging from 0 to T by Y_t and the constant defining the risk in the case of X=0 by α. It then follows that:

$$p(Y_t = i \big| t - 1, X) = \frac{e^{a + B.X}}{1 + e^{a + B.X}} \tag{1}$$

where: i=1 represents the event of becoming an acquirer, i=2 represents the event of becoming a target and i=0 represents the event of being uninvolved in M&A; $p(Y_t = i|t - 1, X)$ represents the probability that $Y_t = i$ at date t conditional on the information set available at date t-1. The parameters α and β are estimated by the logistic regression.

4. Independent variables

We use two approaches for the identification of the determinants to be used in the multinomial logit regression: hypotheses development and factor analysis.

4.1. Hypotheses development

Following the approach of Palepu (1986), the selection of the variables to be included in the acquisition likelihood model is first done on the basis of hypotheses on the types of banks that are likely to become acquirers or targets in M&As.[6] Table 10.1 shows the set of six pre-specified hypotheses used in this study,[7] and the relevant bank specific and regulatory/institutional variables, as well as the expected sign in an acquisition likelihood prediction model. Each hypothesis is discussed below.

4.1.1. Size hypothesis

As regards the likelihood of being targets, the size hypothesis relates to either the synergies or the transaction costs associated with the acquisition of a firm. Synergies materialize in economies of scale, economies of scope and market power; these synergies imply that the larger the bank, the higher the likelihood of being a target (Pasiouras et al. 2007a; Hernando et al. 2008). Transaction costs include costs associated with the post-deal integration of the target into the acquiror's organization, as well as the cost of fighting a longer battle for the acquisition; these costs are likely to increase with the target size and hence the larger the bank, the lower the likelihood of being a target (Palepu 1986). With regard to the likelihood to be acquirers, the synergies size hypothesis dominates; hence large banks are more likely to be acquirers (Hannan and Pilloff 2006).

Table 10.1 Acquisition likelihood hypotheses and independent variables

Hypothesis	Variable	Name	Variable proxy	Expected sign acquirers	Expected sign targets
Hp 1. Bank size hypothesis	Size	LNTA	Ln (Total assets)	+	+/–
Hp 2. Free cash flow hypothesis	Free cash flow return	FCFR	[Operating income – (Earning assets – Earning assets$_{LV1}$) + (Deposits – Deposits$_{LV1}$)] / Operating income	+/–	–
Hp 3. Inefficient management hypothesis	Cost X-efficiency	COST_EFF	Stochastic cost X-efficiency	+	–
	Profit X-efficiency	PROF_EFF	Stochastic profit X-efficiency	+	–
Hp 4. Specialization of the business hypothesis	Specialization	LOANS	Total loans / Total assets	–	+/–
	Net interest margin	NIM	[Interest income – Interest expense]/Loans	–	+/–
Hp 5. Growth-resource hypothesis	Liquidity	LIQ	Liquid assets / Total assets	+/–	+/–
	Capital strength	EQAS	Equity / Total assets	–	+/–
	Growth	GROWTH	[Total assets – Total assets$_{LV1}$]/ Total assets$_{LV1}$	+	+/–
Hp 6. Regulatory/ institutional variable hypothesis	Economic freedom	EC_FREE	Includes business/ trade/monetary/fiscal freedom, freedom from government, property rights, investment/ financial freedom, freedom from corruption and labour freedom [Heritage Foundation]	+/–	+/–
	Regulatory quality	REG_Q	Ability of the government to formulate and implement sound policies and regulations that permit and promote private sector development [World Bank]	+/–	+/–
	Banking industry size	CLAIMS	Bank claims on the private sector/GDP [Euromonitor]	+/–	+/–

The empirical evidence on size (usually measured with total assets, as in our study) and target prediction in banking is mixed: some studies show that larger banks are more likely to be acquired (Hannan and Pilloff 2007; Pasiouras et al. 2007a, 2007b; Hernando et al 2008) and some others that smaller banks are more likely to be acquired (Focarelli et al. 2002; Hannan and Pilloff 2007), whereas others find that the effect of size is insignificant (Hannan and Rhoades 1987; Moore 1996). The few studies on the prediction of acquirers all confirm that larger banks are in contrast proven to be more likely acquirers (Focarelli et al. 2002; Pasiouras et al. 2007b).

4.1.2. Free cash flow hypothesis

Firms that over-invest are likely to be targets of acquiring firms which can make better investment decisions (Jensen, 1986). Firms that tend to over-invest, tend to invest in negative NPV and therefore are more likely to be taken over. In banking, the free cash flow hypothesis has not been tested in prior studies. We define free cash flow as operating income less the change in earning assets plus the change in deposits, scaled by operating income.

4.1.3. Inefficient management hypothesis

The inefficient management hypothesis derives from the finance theory argument that if the managers of a firm fail to maximize its value, they will be replaced by the acquisition mechanism (Palepu 1986). The rationale is that the acquiring firms can improve the management of the resources of the acquired firm by transferring superior skills.

In prior studies, inefficient management is proxied by accounting profitability and/or accounting cost management (Focarelli et al. 1999; Hannan and Pilloff 2007; Pasiouras et al. 2007a, 2007b; Hernando et al. 2008). The substantial evidence on the prediction of targets tends to show that less efficient banks are more likely to be acquired (among others, Moore 1996; Focarelli et al. 2002; Hannan and Pilloff 2007; Pasiouras et al. 2007a, 2007b; Hernando et al. 2008),[8] and coherently the handful of studies on the prediction of acquirers show that more efficient banks are more likely to be acquirers (Focarelli et al. 1999; Pasiouras et al. 2007b).

This paper is the first study to use a more advanced measure of operational inefficiency at the global level – the so-called X-inefficiency. It is a measure of managerial best practice, and represents the distance of the position of equilibrium of each bank from the optimal operative frontier. X-inefficiency was framed as in Beccalli and Frantz (2009), or rather: (1) cost efficiency, which provides a measure of how close a bank is to the cost sustained by the best practice bank to produce a given mix of outputs (assuming that the banks are operating under the same conditions), and (2) profit efficiency, which provides a measure of how close a bank is to the realisation of the maximum level of profit given its level of outputs.

4.1.4. Specialization of the business hypothesis

The specialization of the business hypothesis refers to the relevance of loan activity. In the identification of targets, the likely direction effect is not clear, as it can be: (1) positive – banks with high loan activity have aggressive behaviour and a strong market penetration with important, established customer relationships (Hannan and Rhoades 1987) – or (2) negative – banks with low loan activity lack lending opportunities, and they tend to be acquired by another bank with better lending opportunities (Moore 1996). In the prediction of acquirers, a higher specialization (high loan activity) determines higher integration costs after the deal and more difficulties in exploiting the benefits of business diversification on the revenue side (Beccalli and Frantz 2009), and therefore impacts negatively on the likelihood of being an acquirer.

The extensive evidence on the prediction of targets in banking, where the loan activity is proxied by the loan to asset ratio, tends to find a negative effect (Hannan and Rhoades, 1987; Moor 1996; Pasiouras et al. 2007b), even if this is not significant in all cases. The only study on the prediction of acquirers (Pasiouras et al. 2007b) finds instead a positive effect, even if it is not statistically significant in all the specifications of the model. In this study, in addition to the traditional loan to asset ratio, we employ a specialization ratio based on profit and loss measures: net interest margin, measured as [(net interest income – interest expense)/loans].

4.1.5. Growth-resource hypothesis

The growth-resource hypothesis requires the investigation of two dimensions: resources (measured by capital strength and liquidity) and growth.

The capital strength of a bank, proxied by equity over total assets, can be either negatively or positively related with its prospects for being acquired. Among the explanations on a negative relationship are that: (1) if capitalization is an index of managerial efficiency, acquirers prefer less capitalized banks as they would generate larger gains from the presumed better management generated by the acquirers (Hannan and Pilloff 2006); (2) acquirers prefer lower capitalization because they require a lower payment (Hannan and Rhoades 1987) and (3) acquirers prefer a high levels of leverage because it enables them to maximize the magnitude of the post-merger performance relative to the cost of achieving those gains (Hannan and Pilloff 2006). Among the explanations for a positive relationship are that: (1) acquirers prefer more capitalized banks if they face regulatory pressures to increase capitalization (Hannan and Pilloff 2006) and (2) if capitalization is an index of the inability of a bank to diversify assets, then the assets of more capitalized banks would be worth more to better diversified acquirers than to the current owner, and thus this increases the likelihood of being acquired (Hannan and Pilloff 2006). No expectation is provided in previous studies for the relationship between capital strength and the likelihood of being an acquirer. We offer here two explanations, both for a negative relationship: (1) if capitalization is an index of managerial efficiency, banks with skilful managers who are able to operate successfully with a high leverage tend to become more likely acquirers; (2) if acquirers face regulatory pressures to increase capitalization above current levels, the less capitalized banks will tend to become more likely acquirers. Most of the previous studies document a negative relationship between capital strength and the likelihood of being a target (Hannan and Rhoades 1987; Moore 1996, Hannan and Pilloff 2006; Pasiouras et al. 2007b); the only study on the likelihood of being acquirers shows a negative relationship, too (Pasiouras et al. 2007b).

On the resources sides, the other variable to be considered is liquidity, because without the necessary liquidity a bank may fail. Once again the effect of liquidity on acquisition is unclear (Pasiouras et al. 2007a). It can be: (1) either positive – banks may acquire banks because of their good liquidity position and thus to avoid the risk of liquidity shocks – or (2) negative – banks may be acquired as they have run into liquidity problems that are difficult to resolve. The study in the banking literature that considered liquidity found it had a negative relationship with the likelihood of becoming targets and acquirers (Pasiouras et al. 2007b). In the present study we measure liquidity as the ratio between liquid assets and total assets.

Another variable is included to account for growth, which may be indicative of: (1) the prospects of rapid expansion in the target market after the acquisition, which would imply a higher likelihood of being targets in presence of high growth (Hannan and Rhoades 1987), and/or (2) a history of slow expansion, which would imply a higher likelihood of being targets in the presence of low growth since this may attract acquirers who would seek to increase the value of the targets by accelerating the latter's growth rate (Moore 1996). Here we advance the hypothesis that a history of high growth would increase the likelihood of being acquirers since on the one hand high historical growth contributes to making banks bigger and thus to their having the resources/ size that make an acquisition more likely, and on the other high historical growth provides incentives to banks to become even bigger. Previous studies in banking on the prediction of being targets find either a positive relationship (Hannan and Rhoades 1987), a negative relationship (Moore 1996; Pasiouras et al. 2007b) or a non-significant relationship (Hernando et al. 2008). The only study on the likelihood of being acquirers shows a positive relationship (Pasiouras et al. 2007b). In the present study we proxy growth in terms of total assets growth during the three years preceding the deal.

4.1.6. *Regulatory/institutional hypothesis*

With respect to the regulatory/institutional hypothesis – proxied by economic freedom, regulatory quality and the size of the banking industry where a bank is located – we have no *ex ante* expectations about its effect on the likelihood of being involved in an M&A deal. A positive effect could result because a bank is more likely to be involved in M&A activity if it is located in a country better able to formulate and implement sound policies and regulations or with higher freedom in economic activities. In contrast, a negative effect could be justified when regulatory quality, economic freedom and the size of the banking industry are considered as proxies for the maturity of the financial system. Higher regulatory quality, higher economic freedom and a bigger banking industry all contribute to a higher level of maturity for the financial system, which implies lower benefits from M&As.

Regulatory/institutional variables have not been tested in prior studies, with one exception (Pasiouras et al. 2007b). External factors (capital requirements, disciplinary powers of the authorities, economic freedom, regulatory restrictions on bank activities, liquidity requirements and deposit insurer power) have affected targets and acquirers differently, and these effects have not been consistent or robust to sample size changes.

4.2. Factor analysis and independent variables

Factor analysis extracts common factors explaining much of the variation in a set of variables using the principal components and varimax methods in order to facilitate the interpretation of these factors:

$$F_i = \sum_{i=1}^{m} \lambda_i x_i \qquad (2)$$

with cov(Fi, Fj) = 0 whenever i ≠ j. This implies that factors are orthogonal and therefore no multicollinearity problem.

4.3. Dataset and sample

The dataset is obtained by combining three sources: Thomson One Banker M&A for data on the M&A operations; Thomson Financial Datastream for the prices of listed banks, benchmark and economic indices and Bankscope for balance sheet and profit and loss data of the banks involved in M&A operations (M&A sample) and of banks not involved (control sample).

The sample is limited to credit institutions as defined in the Second Banking Directive. It comprises M&A deals announced between 1/1/1991 and 30/9/2006 in which the acquirer is an EU bank and the target is a bank operating in any country of the world. The M&A sample refers to 777 deals – involving acquirers and 312 deals involving targets – for which full financial information about the participating banks is available. It is a unique sample – bigger than any other sample used for the analysis of M&A operations in the EU banking industry. Table 10.2 shows the total number of deals in which a bank is involved either as an acquirer or as a target in each country and year, and the total panel under observation.

The control sample consists of all banks – never engaged in any merger or acquisition over the life span of this study – that match the nationalities of the acquirers and targets during a specific year. The control sample consists of 6268 observations over the period 1991–2005.

5. Empirical results

We first examine bank specific characteristics and regulatory/institutional variables for acquirers and targets in the year prior to the deal. The values highlighted in Table 10.3 show that the size of acquirers in comparison with targets is larger (the difference is statistically significant at 1 per cent). The levels of cost efficiency and profit efficiency are higher for acquirers than for targets in the year before the deal (with statistically significant differences). Interestingly, the level of specialization in traditional banking activity is lower for acquirers than for targets (the

Table 10.2 Number of M&A deals involving acquirers and targets (by country and by year)

Country	1991	1992	1993	1994	1995	1996	1997	1998	1999	2000	2001	2002	2003	2004	2005	2006	Total
Panel A Number of deals involving acquirers																	
Austria				4	2	1	5	1	5	2				1			21
Belgium				3	4	4	5	6	1	2	3		1	1	1	1	32
Denmark	1		1	2		1	2	2	2	3		2		2			18
Estonia					1	1											2
Finland			1	1		1											3
France	11	6	9	17	7	10	7	7	6	4	9	5	4	10	3		115
Germany	2	5	2	10	7	4	14	7	7	4	1	2	1	1			67
Greece									6	4		3	2		2	1	18
Hungary											1		1	3	1		6
Iceland													2	4			6
Ireland					2												2
Italy	5	1	3	15	21	8	14	13	22	27	20	17	11	6	16		199
Luxembourg								1					2		1	1	5
Netherlands			2	1	2	3	1	4	3	3		2	1	1			23
Norway				1	1	2							3	3			10
Poland							2	1	6	2	4		1	1			17
Portugal		2	1	1	2	2	1	2	3	11			1		1		27
Spain	6	6	6	3	4	10	8	12	14	12	6	7	5	3		2	104
Sweden	2	1	1	1				3	12	4	3	1	1	1			30
Switzerland	1	1	4	7	1	5	5	1	2	1		1	2				31

Continued

Table 10.2 Continued

Country	1991	1992	1993	1994	1995	1996	1997	1998	1999	2000	2001	2002	2003	2004	2005	2006	Total
Turkey															1		1
UK	1	5	1	3	3	5	5	2	8	2	1	1	1	2			40
Total	29	27	30	69	57	57	69	62	97	81	48	41	34	41	29	6	777

Panel B Number of deals involving targets

Country	1991	1992	1993	1994	1995	1996	1997	1998	1999	2000	2001	2002	2003	2004	2005	2006	Total
Argentina						1	4	2		2	1		1				11
Australia					1								1				2
Austria				1			3	1	2	2							9
Belgium	1	1		1	2			3			2			2			12
Brazil								1		2					1		4
Canada							1			1							2
Chile						1	1		2								4
Colombia								1	1	1	2						5
Denmark				1					4	1	1	2		1			10
Estonia								2									2
Finland									1								1
France	3	4	5	5	3	1	3	3	7	2	1	2	2	5			46
Germany		1	3			1	3		1	1	1	1					12
Greece								3	7	2	1		1	2			16
Hungary						1		1	1								3
Iceland													2				2
India																	2

	1	2	3	4	5	6	7	8	9	10	11	12	13	14	15	16	Total
Ireland													1	1	1		3
Italy		1	1	2		1		2	5	8	5	5	2	2	4	1	41
Lebanon	1																1
Luxembourg						1								1			2
Mexico					1			2		1		1		1			5
Morocco																	
Netherlands			1				2						1	1			4
New Zealand	2																2
Norway			1	1		1	2	1	2		4	1		4	1		13
Poland		1						5	6	4							17
Portugal					1	1	1	2	3		2	2					12
Romania													1	1			1
South Africa			1										1	1			2
South Korea						1	1	1	1	1							4
Spain	1	3	1	4	1	2	2	5	7	1	1			1			33
Sweden														2			2
Switzerland		1				1	1		1			1					3
Thailand							1										1
Turkey																2	2
UK	1	1	1	3	3	1	2	1	2	1				2		1	18
US						2		1	1	1				1	1		5
Venezuela																	
Total	6	11	11	19	12	12	26	33	53	39	22	15	15	28	6	4	312

Table 10.3 Descriptive statistics

Bank type		LNTA	FCFR	COST_EFF	PROF_EFF	LOANS
Acquirers	Mean	17.5686	−3.9288	0.8002	0.7976	0.5219
	N	382	271	382	382	382
	Std. dev.	1.8943	22.5448	0.11744	0.0894	0.1438
	Min	0.0000	−230.3079	0.0000	0.0000	0.0000
	Max	20.5312	102.3117	0.9483	0.9262	0.8923
	Median	17.7483	−1.2380	0.8401	0.82189	0.5252
Targets	Mean	15.8186	−22.7631	0.7731	0.7518	0.5382
	N	243	142	243	243	243
	Std. dev.	3.1226	294.3067	0.1716	0.1801	0.2064
	Min	0.0000	−3352.6011	0.0000	0.0000	0.0000
	Max	19.8921	587.0000	0.9561	0.9418	0.9564
	Median	16.0717	0.0000	0.8218	0.8095	0.5429
Control	Mean	15.7050	−1.2096	0.7815	0.7526	0.5461
	N	3473	2092	3473	3473	3473
	Std. dev.	1.8466	112.8055	0.1306	0.1402	0.2125
	Min	0.0000	−1891.2455	0.0000	0.0000	0.0000
	Max	20.5235	3947.1280	0.9676	1.0000	0.9648
	Median	15.6112	−0.0839	0.8205	0.7886	0.5570
Total	Mean	15.8855	−2.7255	0.7828	0.7568	0.5433
	N	4098	2505	4098	4098	4098
	Std. dev.	2.0227	124.8330	0.1323	0.1396	0.2068
	Min	0.0000	−3352.6011	0.0000	0.0000	0.0000
	Max	20.5312	3947.1281	0.9677	1.0000	0.9648
	Median	15.7859	−0.1922	0.8227	0.79289	0.5478
	Tolerance test	0.621	0.994	0.689	0.780	0.525
	VIF	1.609	1.006	1.450	1.281	1.904
Acquirers – Targets	t-test for differences in means	1.7500***	18.8344	0.0271**	0.4579***	−0.0163
M&A – Control	t-test for differences in means	1.1832***	−9.1949	0.0082	0.0272***	−0.0178*

NIM	LIQ	LEV	GROWTH	EC_FREE	REG_Q	CLAIMS
0.0427	0.2004	0.0555	1.5017	6.4526	1.1208	0.8256
382	181	0382	349	270	249	382
0.0354	0.1482	0.0281	12.2662	0.6680	0.3385	0.3042
0.0000	0.0000	0.0000	−0.9800	0.0000	0.0000	0.0000
0.5587	0.87	0.2750	184.97	7.93	1.9450	1.6800
0.0359	0.1637	0.0514	0.1068	6.3650	1.0500	0.8017
0.0522	0.1516	0.0706	0.1548	6.3508	1.0261	0.7390
243	102	243	221	203	195	243
0.0657	0.1289	0.0563	0.5707	1.2718	0.4687	0.34096
0.0000	0.0000	0.0000	−0.9900	0.0000	−1.0600	0.0000
0.9412	0.78	0.5189	6.32	8.09	1.9400	1.6600
0.0425	0.1285	0.0579	0.0776	6.4500	1.0200	0.7733
0.2070	0.2258	0.0833	0.1823	6.6623	1.0498	0.8120
3473	2198	3473	3053	2728	2538	3468
7.0310	0.1881	0.0731	1.0277	0.7508	0.6129	0.3604
−1.0000	0.0000	0.0000	−1.0000	0.0000	−1.1300	0.0000
412.5180	1.09	0.8279	31.90	8.12	2.0100	1.6800
0.0437	0.1727	0.0640	0.0861	6.5800	1.1600	0.8036
0.1825	0.2209	0.0799	0.3077	6.6248	1.0542	0.8089
4098	2481	4098	3623	3201	2982	4093
6.4728	0.1840	0.0697	3.9393	0.7928	0.5865	0.3548
−1.0000	0.0000	0.0000	−1.0000	0.0000	−1.1300	0.0000
412.5180	1.09	0.8279	184.97	8.12	2.0100	1.6800
0.0426	0.1707	0.0622	0.0883	6.5400	1.1000	0.8017
0.930	0.709	0.593	0.973	0.378	0.430	0.426
1.075	1.411	1.687	1.027	2.648	2.480	2.347
−0.0095**	0.0488**	0.0151***	1.3470*	0.10172***	0.0948**	0.0867***
−0.1606	−0.0429***	0.0218***	.7972***	−0.2534***	0.0294	0.0154

Note: Variables (as defined in Table 10.1) refer the year prior to the deal. ***, **, * T-test respectively statistically significant at 1 %, 5 % and 10 %.

difference is statistically significant only when specialization is proxied by net interest margin). With respect to resources, acquirers show better capital strength and a higher liquidity in comparison to targets in the year prior to the deal (the differences are statistically significant at 1 per cent). Furthermore, acquirers show higher growth over the recent past in comparison to targets. Finally, as for regulatory/institutional variables, acquirers seem to be located in countries with higher regulatory quality, higher economic freedom and a bigger banking industry (all of the differences are statically significant).

We then move to the comparison of bank specific characteristics and regulatory/institutional variables for M&A banks and for the control sample of banks not involved in any deal. As reported in Table 10.3, the size of M&A banks is larger than the one for banks not involved (the difference is statistically significant at 1 per cent). The level of profit efficiency is higher for M&A banks than for non-M&A banks (with the differences statistically significant at 1 per cent). As regards the specialization of the business, the level of traditional banking activity is lower for M&A banks than for non-M&A banks (the difference is statistically significant at 5 per cent only when specialization is proxied by loans over total assets). With respect to resources, M&A banks show a higher capital strength and a lower liquidity in comparison with non-M&A banks in the year prior to the deal (with the differences statistically significant at 1 per cent). Furthermore, M&A banks show higher growth over the recent past in comparison with non-M&A banks. Finally, as for regulatory/institutional variables, M&A banks are located in countries with lower economic freedom (all the differences are statically significant at 1 per cent).

The correlations between the above independent variables have been tested in order to investigate the existence of multicollinearity problems. On average, correlation values are low, providing a preliminary indication of low/absent multicollinearity problems. However, for regulatory/environmental variables, the higher correlation requires us to measure multicollinearity diagnostic statistics. The tolerance index and variance inflation factor confirm that no multicollinearity problem affects the variables assumed to be determinants of the likelihood of being acquirers and targets, although higher values of the indices are observed for the regulatory/institutional variables.

5.1. Logit analysis based on hypothesis development

The evidence on the likelihood of becoming an acquirer (Table 10.4, panel A) shows that larger banks are more likely to be acquirers, which

Table 10.4 Multinomial logit with hypotheses' variables

Variables (lagged values by 1 year)*	Hp 1	Hp 2	Hp 3	Hp 4	Hp 5	Hp 6
Panel A Acquirer likelihood models						
Intercept	−11.752*** (388.503)	−12.206*** (256.960)	−16.021*** (171.641)	−15.035*** (146.410)	−14.682*** (60.734)	−6.535*** (7.371)
Size	0.572*** (279.506)	0.600*** (193.380)	0.592*** (182.681)	0.543*** (155.411)	0.407*** (36.608)	0.526*** (42.647)
Free cash flow		0.000 (.118)	0.000 (.045)	0.000 (.119)	0.000 (.090)	0.000 (.002)
Cost X–efficiency			1.085* (2.001)	2.590*** (9.489)	5.899*** (20.244)	4.376*** (7.560)
Profit X–efficiency			3.923*** (23.520)	4.034*** (23.278)	4.893*** (19.522)	4.644*** (13.702)
Specialization				−2.321*** (24.466)	−4.176*** (38.694)	−3.475*** (15.422)
Net interest margin				−4.120** (5.733)	−4.744*** (6.901)	−5.168* (7.139)
Liquidity					−1.211* (3.011)	−1.068 (1.509)
Capital strength					−7.695** (5.919)	−4.940 (1.816)
Growth					0.892*** (10.780)	1.082*** (12.280)
Economic freedom						−0.157*** (35.280)
Regulatory quality						1.355*** (13.186)
Industry size						−0.642 (1.915)
Panel B Target likelihood models						
Intercept	−3.129*** (32.733)	−3.542*** (24.297)	−1.992*** (7.165)	−1.716** (5.769)	−0.925 (0.647)	0.180 (0.028)
Size	0.030 (.751)	0.053 (1.413)	0.092** (4.632)	0.087** (4.244)	0.098 (2.048)	0.277*** (10.725)
FCFR		−0.001** (3.796)	−0.001** (3.451)	−0.001* (3.477)	−0.002* (3.248)	−0.002* (2.893)
Cost X-eff			−1.999*** (9.212)	−1.606** (4.383)	−0.446 (0.118)	−1.662 (1.399)
Profit X-eff			−0.813 (1.984)	−1.039* (2.883)	−0.540 (0.398)	−0.120 (0.015)

Continued

Table 10.4   Continued

Variables (lagged values by 1 year)*	Hp 1	Hp 2	Hp 3	Hp 4	Hp 5	Hp 6
Specialization				−0.453 (0.743)	−2.525*** (10.806)	−1.888** (4.243)
Net interest margin				−1.781* (2.663)	−0.025 (0..009)	−0.003 (0.000)
Liquidity					−4.551*** (17.867)	−4.920*** (17.615)
Capital strength					−11.024*** (6.625)	−8.567*** (3.134)
Growth					−0.234 (0.112)	0.058 (0.007)
Economic freedom						−0.045* (3.782)
Regulatory quality						0.674* (3.736)
Industry size						−2.123*** (13.680)
N. acquirers	382	271	271	271	153	130
N. targets	243	142	142	142	66	61
N. non involved	3473	2092	2092	2092	1507	1368
Nagelkerke R^2	0.122	0.142	0.164	0.179	0.238	0.307

Notes: Variables (as defined in Table 10.1) refer the year prior to the deal. Wald test in parentheses; ***, **, * T–test respectively statistically significant at 1 %, 5 % and 10 %. N: number of observations.

provides support for the synergies hypothesis. With respect to the inefficient management hypothesis, as expected, banks with higher X-efficiency (on the cost and profit side) are likely acquirers. There is, furthermore, evidence that banks that specialize more in loan activities are less likely to be acquirers: this suggests that higher specialization determines higher integration costs after the deal and more difficulties in exploiting the benefits of business diversification on the revenue side. With regard to the growth-resources hypothesis, in some of the specifications of the model banks with a lower capitalization are more likely to be acquirers: if capitalization is an index of managerial efficiency, banks with skilful managers who are able to operate successfully with a high leverage tend to become more likely acquirers. Moreover, a history of high growth increases the likelihood of being acquirers: on the one hand past growth contributes to making banks bigger and thus to their having the resources/size that make an acquisition more likely; on the other growth provides incentives to banks to become even bigger. Finally, with regard to regulatory/institutional variables, banks in a country with higher regulatory quality and less economic freedom are more likely to be acquirers. This last finding must, however, be treated with caution because of the relatively high correlation between these variables, which forces us to move to the factor analysis.

The evidence on the likelihood of becoming a target (Table 10.4, panel B) shows that larger banks tend to be more likely targets, but not in all the specifications of the model, which would suggest that transaction costs associated with large deals possibly balance out the synergies coming from the deal itself. Interestingly, banks with negative free cash flow are more likely to be targets: this suggests that banks that tend to over-invest, tend to invest in negative NPV and therefore are more likely to be taken over. Furthermore, as expected, banks with inefficient management (i.e. lower cost X-efficiency) are likely targets. With respect to the growth-resources hypothesis, the evidence shows that banks with less liquidity are more likely targets: they may be acquired as they have run into liquidity problems they find difficult to resolve. In addition, banks with lower capitalization are more likely targets. It is of note that banks located in bigger banking industries are less likely targets. Finally, similarly to the finding for acquirers, banks in a country with higher regulatory quality and less economic freedom are more likely to be acquirers; once again, caution should be taken in the interpretation of this result.

We finally distinguish between recurrent acquirers (leading the M&A market) and occasional acquirers (involved in one deal only over the sample period).[9] The likelihood of being an acquirer in multiple deals in comparison to a single deal depends on several bank specific characteristics. More precisely, it increases with size, decreases with specialization, increases with growth, decreases with capital strength and increases with the size of the banking industry.

5.2. Factor analysis

Using the original set of variables consisting of nine bank specific variables and three regulatory/institutional variables (as described in Table 10.1), factors with eigenvalues exceeding 0.8 are extracted and rotated using the varimax method in order to facilitate their interpretation. As shown in Table 10.5, panel A, a first factor, accounting for 21.2 per cent

Table 10.5 Factor analysis – rotated component matrix

	Panel A							Panel B								
	Factors derived from the original set of variables							Factors derived from the extended set of variables								
Variables	F1	F2	F3	F4	F5	F6	F7	F1	F2	F3	F4	F5	F6	F7	F8	F9
Size	0.236	-0.111	0.828	0.31	0.14	0.016	-0.041	-0.535	0.098	0.288	-0.473	-0.235	0.012	0.235	-0.013	-0.053
Free cash flow	-0.009	-0.007	-0.004	0.002	0.002	0.028	0.996	0.014	-0.001	-0.042	-0.020	-0.035	-0.004	0.013	0.078	0.979
Cost X-efficiency	-0.027	0.278	0.033	0.909	-0.054	0.009	0.004	0.150	0.086	0.039	0.167	0.014	0.850	0.061	-0.075	0.058
Profit X-efficiency	0.459	0.239	0.21	-0.172	0.017	0.365	-0.075	-0.075	0.133	0.065	-0.099	0.745	-0.165	0.260	0.116	-0.113
Specialization	0.119	0.832	0.088	0.19	-0.158	0.009	-0.007	0.024	0.018	0.053	0.872	-0.123	0.117	0.026	-0.020	-0.054
Net interest margin	0.013	0.011	-0.062	-0.046	0.966	0.005	0.002	0.792	0.042	-0.157	-0.134	-0.175	0.063	-0.036	-0.095	0.025
Liquidity	-0.065	-0.817	-0.003	-0.077	-0.135	0.015	0.001	0.084	0.045	-0.236	-0.714	0.061	-0.176	-0.357	0.096	-0.041
Capital strength	0.074	-0.234	-0.81	0.243	0.265	0.033	-0.037	0.921	-0.021	-0.068	0.114	0.061	0.092	-0.007	0.041	0.006
Growth	0.019	-0.046	-0.044	0.036	0.002	0.955	0.043	0.003	-0.010	0.062	-0.060	-0.011	0.034	-0.028	0.941	0.085
Economic freedom	0.876	-0.007	0.059	0.163	0.026	-0.003	0.008	-0.039	0.119	0.850	0.135	-0.131	-0.004	-0.218	0.085	-0.015
Regulatory quality	0.854	0.137	0.078	0.003	0.015	0.008	0.016	-0.144	0.090	0.785	0.108	0.099	0.220	0.053	0.032	0.024

Industry size	0.87	0.027	−0.035	−0.116	−0.015	0.03	−0.019	0.032	−0.058	0.735	−0.066	0.153	−0.284	0.015	−0.022	−0.066
Average cost efficiency								−0.024	0.285	−0.085	0.075	0.023	0.784	−0.080	0.130	−0.072
Average profit efficiency								0.003	−0.111	0.055	−0.058	0.881	0.161	−0.012	−0.119	0.048
Average ROE								−0.197	0.632	0.000	0.175	0.306	0.028	−0.357	0.055	0.081
Average ROA								0.152	0.867	0.053	−0.025	−0.016	0.113	−0.076	−0.009	−0.067
ROE								0.146	0.772	0.114	−0.117	−0.131	0.280	0.247	−0.022	0.037
ROA								0.725	0.475	0.037	−0.076	−0.166	0.223	0.195	0.024	0.005
Asset undervaluation								0.655	0.103	0.082	−0.108	−0.071	0.020	0.142	0.328	−0.078
Tier 1 capital								0.760	0.001	−0.035	0.212	0.157	−0.004	−0.012	−0.031	0.029
Total capital ratio								0.777	0.027	0.036	−0.117	−0.093	−0.080	−0.199	−0.100	0.001
Net interbank ratio								−0.096	−0.026	−0.164	0.234	0.245	−0.023	0.752	−0.009	0.025
Proportion of variance explained																
By factor	21.2%	13.2%	11.8%	9.1%	8.9%	8.7%	8.4%	18.4%	9.7%	8.1%	7.8%	7.8%	5.3%	5.0%	4.7%	
Cumulative Proportion	21.2%	34.4%	46.2%	55.3%	64.2%	73.0%	81.3%	18.4%	28.1%	37.8%	45.9%	53.8%	61.6%	66.9%	71.9%	76.6%

of the variance in this set of variables, has loadings exceeding 0.8 on economic freedom, regulatory quality and industry size, and a loading exceeding 0.45 on profit efficiency. This first factor will be referred to as the regulatory/institutional factor. A second factor, accounting for 13.2 per cent of the variance, has a loading exceeding 0.8 on the ratio of loans over total assets and a loading lower than -0.8 on liquidity. This second factor will be referred to as the specialization/liquidity factor. A third factor, accounting for 11.8 per cent of the variance, has a loading exceeding 0.8 on size and a loading lower than -0.8 on the ratio of equity over total assets. This third factor will be referred to as the size/capital strength factor. A fourth factor, accounting for 9.1 per cent of the variance, has a loading exceeding 0.9 on cost efficiency and will be referred to as the cost efficiency factor. A fifth factor, accounting for 8.9 per cent of the variance, has a loading exceeding 0.9 on net interest margin and will be referred to as the net interest margin factor. A sixth factor, accounting for 8.7 per cent of the variance, which has a loading exceeding 0.9 on past growth will be referred to as the growth factor. A seventh factor, accounting for 8.4 per cent of the variance, will be referred to as the free cash flow factor.

We then use an extended set of variables, where in addition to the variables listed in Table 10.1, we include: average performance measures for the overall banking industry in each country (average cost efficiency, average profit efficiency, average ROE and average ROA), straight accounting ratios for each bank (i.e. ROE and ROA), asset undervaluation for each bank (proxied by market to book value), measures of capital adequacy (i.e. tier 1 capital and total capital ratio for individual banks) and a bank specific measure of liquidity on the interbank market (i.e. net interbank ratio). Using the extended set of variables, factors with eigenvalues exceeding 0.8 are again extracted and rotated using the varimax method in order to facilitate their interpretation. As shown in Table 10.5, panel B, a first factor, accounting for 18.4 per cent of the variance, has a loading exceeding 0.9 on the ratio of equity over total assets; loadings exceeding 0.7 on the net interest margin, the tier 1 capital ratio, the total capital ratio and the return on assets; loadings exceeding 0.6 on undervaluation and loadings lower than –0.5 on size. This first factor will be referred to as the capital adequacy/capital strength/net interest margin. A second factor, accounting for 9.7 per cent of the variance, has a loading exceeding 0.8 on the average return on assets in the industry, a loading exceeding 0.7 on the return on equity, a loading exceeding 0.6 on the average return on equity in the industry and a loading close to 0.5 on the return on assets. This factor will be referred to as the accounting performance factor. A third factor, accounting for 9.7 per cent of the variance, has a loading exceeding 0.8 on economic freedom and loading exceeding 0.7 on the quality of regulation and the ratio of bank claims in the industry over GDP. This factor will be referred to as the regulatory/institutional factor. A fourth factor, accounting for 8.1 per cent of the variance, has a loading exceeding 0.8 on the ratio of loans over total assets and a loading lower than −0.7 on the liquid asset ratio. This factor will be referred to as the specialization/liquidity factor. A fifth factor, accounting for 7.8% of the variance, with a loading exceeding 0.7 on profit efficiency and a loading exceeding 0.8 on average profit efficiency in the industry, will be referred to as the profit efficiency factor. A sixth factor, accounting for 7.8 per cent of the variance, with a loading exceeding 0.8 on cost efficiency and a loading exceeding 0.7 on average cost efficiency in the industry will be referred to as the cost efficiency factor. A seventh factor, accounting for 5.3 per cent of the variance, with a loading above 0.7 on net interbank balance deflated by assets will be referred to as the net interbank factor. An eighth factor, accounting for 5.0% of the variance, with a loading exceeding 0.9 on past growth will be referred to as the growth factor. A ninth factor, accounting for 4.6 per cent of the variance, with a loading exceeding 0.9 on free cash flows will be referred to as the free cash flow factor.

5.3. Logit analysis based on factor analysis

Let us first consider the set of factors derived from the original set of variables. As shown in Table 10.6, panel A, the logistic regression suggests that the regulatory/institutional factor has a negative influence on a bank being involved in M&As either as an acquirer or as a target. Hence, the higher the economic freedom and regulatory quality, and the larger the industry, the lower the likelihood of a bank becoming an acquirer or a target. This finding derived from a logistic regression based on factor analysis differs from the one obtained from a logistic regression based on hypotheses development. Specifically, under the factor analysis the overall set of regulatory/institutional variables has a negative effect on the likelihood of being involved in an M&A deal. This suggests that the overall set of regulatory/institutional variables can be seen as a proxy for the maturity of the financial system: higher regulatory quality and economic freedom, combined with a bigger size of the banking industry, contribute to a higher level of maturity of the financial system, which implies lower benefits from M&A deals. This finding based on factor analysis appears to be stronger than the one based on

Table 10.6   Multinomial logit with common factors

	Panel A				Panel B		
Factors	Description	Acquirers	Targets	Factors	Description	Acquirers	Targets
Λ	Intercept	−3.345*** (350.167)	−3.492*** (365.446)	λ	Intercept	−2.915*** (187.840)	−3.311*** (177.411)
F1	Regulatory/ institutional	−0.369*** (9.226)	−0.528*** (11.855)	F1	Capital adequacy/ interest margin	−1.917*** (30.375)	−1.188*** (7.497)
F2	Specialization/ liquidity	0.256* (3.444)	0.379** (4.668)	F2	Accounting performance	0.299 (2.308)	0.429 (2.135)
F3	Size/capital strength	2.043*** (103.731)	1.031*** (22.116)	F3	Regulatory/ institutional	−0.238* (3.410)	−0.105 (0.344)
F4	Cost efficiency	0.143 (1.116)	−0.325*** (8.096)	F4	Specialization/ liquidity	−0.750*** (19.863)	−0.417* (3.454)
F5	Net interest margin	0.125 (1.729)	0.063 (0.482)	F5	Efficiency	0.209 (1.587)	0.232 (1.060)
F6	Growth	0.392*** (21.395)	−0.077 (0.139)	F6	Efficiency	0.282** (4.952)	0.553** (4.943)
F7	Free cash flow	−0.086 (0.544)	−0.189* (2.800)	F7	Net interbank	0.809*** (29.105)	0.637*** (9.017)
				F8	Growth	0.282** (4.962)	−0.233 (0.802)
				F9	Free cash flow	0.010 (0.002)	−0.229** (4.011)
N. acquirers	130			N. acquirers	93		
N. targets	61			N. targets	39		
N. non involved	1368			N. non involved	644		
Nagelkerke R^2	0.219			Nagelkerke R^2	0.302		

hypothesis development: factor analysis eliminates multicollinearity problems, and hence shows a marked advantage over the hypotheses development approach in presence of variables with high correlation, as it is in the case of the set of regulatory/institutional variables.

With respect to bank specific variables, the specialization/liquidity factor is shown to have a positive influence on a bank becoming involved in M&As as an acquirer or a target. Hence, the higher a bank's specialization and the lower its liquidity, the higher the likelihood of it becoming involved in M&As as an acquirer or a target. The positive effect attributed to specialization under the factor analysis approach differs from the negative effect found under the hypotheses development approach. This difference once again may be explained by the relatively high correlation of this variable with some other bank specific variables. The size/capital strength factor has a positive influence on a bank becoming involved in M&As as an acquirer and a target. Hence, the larger a bank's size and the weaker its capital strength, the higher the likelihood of it becoming involved in M&As either as an acquirer or as a target. The cost efficiency factor has a negative influence on a bank becoming involved in M&As as a target, but the net interest margin factor has no influence on the likelihood of a bank becoming either an acquirer or a target. The growth factor has a positive effect on a bank becoming involved in M&A as an acquirer, while the free cash flow factor has a negative effect on a bank becoming involved in M&A as a target.

Overall, the above results derived from a logistic analysis based on common factors are qualitatively similar to those generated by a logistic regression based on hypotheses development, with the exception of the variables (regulatory/institutional and specialization) with a high correlation with other variables; hence they suggest the importance of using a different approach for the selection of variables (i.e. factor analysis in addition to the more traditional hypotheses development).

Let us now consider the set of factors derived from the extended set of variables. As shown in Table 10.6, panel B, the logistic regression suggests that the capital adequacy/capital strength/net interest margin factor has a negative influence on a bank being involved in M&As either as an acquirer or as a target. Hence, the higher a bank's capital strength, net interest margin and capital adequacy, the lower the likelihood of it becoming involved in M&As as an acquirer or a target. The accounting performance factor has no influence on the likelihood of a bank becoming involved in M&As either as an acquirer or as a target. This supports our choice not to include an accounting performance measure in the original set of variables. The regulatory/institutional factor has a negative effect on the likelihood of a bank becoming involved in M&A either as an acquirer or as a target, as was found for the original set of variables. The specialization/liquidity factor is shown to have a negative influence on a bank becoming involved in M&As as an acquirer. Hence, the higher a bank's specialization and the lower its liquidity, the higher the likelihood of it becoming involved in M&As as an acquirer, as was found for the original set of variables. The profit efficiency factor has no influence on the likelihood of a bank becoming involved in M&As either as an acquirer or as a target. The cost efficiency factor has a positive effect on the likelihood of a bank becoming involved in M&As either as an acquirer (or as a target, but here the statistical significance is only 10 per cent). The net interbank factor has a positive effect on the likelihood of a bank becoming involved in M&As either as an acquirer or as a target. The growth factor has a positive influence on a bank becoming involved in M&As as an acquirer, while the free cash flow factor has a negative influence on a bank becoming involved in M&As as a target.

6. Conclusions

This paper investigates the determinants of the likelihood of being involved in an M&A in banking. Using a sample of 777 deals involving EU acquirers and 312 deals involving targets located throughout the world over the period 1991–2006, we extend and integrate the literature on the *ex ante* features of acquired banks that potentially determine the *ex post* gains. Specifically we investigate a set of possible determinants of M&A operations that include both traditional bank specific characteristics and regulatory/institutional indicators by measuring their influence on a bank being involved in an M&A either as an acquirer or as a target. Furthermore, a methodological advancement is proposed by testing simultaneously two approaches for the selection of variables (the more traditional hypotheses development and factor analysis).

The two approaches for selection of variables tend to provide common results with respect to bank specific variables. The weaker a bank's capital strength, the higher the likelihood of it becoming involved in M&A either as an acquirer or as a target. On the one hand, banks with skilful managers able to operate successfully with a high leverage tend to become more likely acquirers. On the other hand, banks with lower capitalization may be acquired because they require lower payments in the case of an acquisition and may produce larger gains from the presumed better management generated by the acquirers. The lower a bank's liquidity, the higher the likelihood of this bank becoming involved in an M&A as a target: banks may be acquired if they have run into liquidity problems difficult to resolve. The larger a bank's size, the higher the likelihood of it becoming an acquirer because of the synergies associated with the deal; the effect of the bank's size on the likelihood of becoming a target tends to be positive but not in all the specifications, which would suggest that transaction costs associated with large deals may balance out the possible synergies. A history of growth contributes positively to the likelihood of a bank becoming an acquirer. Cost X-efficiency has a negative influence on a bank being involved in an M&A as a target, suggesting that inefficient management increases the likelihood of acquisition. Similarly, free cash flow has a negative effect on a bank becoming involved in an M&A as a target: banks with over-investments, and negative NPV projects, are more likely to be taken over. For one determinant (a bank's specialization in traditional loan activity), the two approaches produce different results: the effect is positive for acquirers and targets under the factor approach, whereas it is negative under that of hypotheses development.

The two approaches for selection of variables provide different results for regulatory/institutional variables: a negative effect on the likelihood of being involved in an M&A under factor analysis approach, and a mixed effect under that of hypotheses development. The finding based on factor analysis appears to be stronger than the one based on the hypothesis development approach: factor analysis eliminates multicollinearity problems, and thus has a marked advantage over the hypotheses development approach in cases of variables with high correlation, as is the case for the set of regulatory/institutional variables. Hence, the overall set of regulatory/institutional variables can be seen as a proxy for the maturity of the financial system, which implies lower benefits from M&A deals and thus a negative effect on the likelihood of being involved in an M&A.

In short, the findings based on common factors show some differences in comparison to the ones based on hypotheses development, specifically for variables (such as the regulatory/institutional and specialization ones) with a high correlation with others: this suggests the importance of using a different approach for the selection of variables (factor analysis in addition to hypotheses development).

Notes

1. The authors wish to acknowledge the constructive comments offered by Francesco Cesarini, Mario Anolli and participants at the Wolpertinger Conference 2009.
2. Overall M&A operations appear to have resulted in financial gains (measured by straight ratio analysis or efficiency frontiers) for the EU and US banking industries (for an extensive review see DeYoung et al. 2009).
3. Other interesting studies not on the banking industry concern methodological issues in the logit regression (Palepu 1986) and misclassification errors in binomial takeover prediction models (Powell and Yawson 2007).
4. A third methodology used in one study (Pasiouras et al. 2007a) is based on three multicriteria approaches, namely MHDIS, PAIRCLAS and UTADIS, with all models developed and tested using a tenfold cross validation approach.
5. The only exception is a study that specifically refers to Italian banks (Focarelli et al. 2002) over the period 1984–1996, by considering the probability of their becoming either a target or an acquirer.

6. Palepu (1986) criticizes the practice of starting with a large number of popular financial ratios and using a step-wise procedure to select the variables to retain.
7. We have also tested the market to book hypothesis (firms with a low market to book are "cheap" buys, and thus are more likely to be targets) and the price-earnings hypothesis (firms with high price-earnings ratios seek to acquire firms with low price-earnings ratios to realize an instantaneous capital gain). Although these hypotheses are popular in the press, their economic validity is suspect (Palepu 1986). In our study, none of these hypotheses has been proven to be statistically significant.
8. Two studies on US banking (Hannan and Rhoades 1987; Hadlock et al. 1999) and one study on Western European banking (Lanine and Vander Vennet 2007) provide evidence against the inefficient management hypothesis.
9. Results available on request from the authors.

References

Beccalli, E., and Frantz, P. (2009) "M&A Operations and Performance in Banking" *Journal of Financial Services Research* 36, 203–226.

DeYoung, R., Evanoff, D.D., and Molyneux, P. (2009) "Mergers and Acquisitions of Financial Institutions: A Review of the Post-2000 Literature" *Journal of Financial Services Research* 36, 87–110.

Focarelli, D., Panetta, F., and Salleo, C. (2002) "Why Do Banks Merge?" *Journal of Money, Credit, and Banking* 34, 1047–1066.

Goddard, J., McKillop, D., and Wilson, J.O.S. (2009) "Which credit unions are acquired?" *Journal of Financial Services Research* 36, 231–252

Hadlock, C., Houston, J., and Ryngaert, M. (1999) "The role of managerial incentives in bank acquisitions" *Journal of Banking and Finance* 23, 221–249.

Hannan T., and Pilloff, S. (2006) Acquisition targets and motives in the banking industry, Finance and Economics Discussion Series Divisions of Research & Statistics and Monetary Affairs, Federal Reserve Board, Working paper n. 40, Washington.

Hannan T., and Rhoades, S.A. (1987) "Acquisition targets and motives: the case of the banking industry" *The Review of Economics and Statistics* 69, 67–74.

Hernando, I., Nieto, M.J., and Wall, L.D. (2009) "Determinants of domestic and cross-border bank acquisitions in the European Union" *Journal of Banking and Finance* 33, 1022–1032.

Jensen, M. (1986) "Agency Costs of Free Cash Flow, Corporate Finance and Takeovers" *American Economic Review* 76, 323–29.

Lanine, G., and Vander Vennet, R. (2007) "Microeconomic determinants of acquisitions of Eastern European banks by Western European banks" *Economics of Transition* 15, 285–308.

Moore, R. (1996) "Banking's merger fervor: Survival of the fittest?" *Federal Reserve Bank of Dallas Financial Industry Studies*, December, 9–15.

Moore, R. (1997) "Bank Acquisition Determinants: Implications for Small Business Credit, Working Paper, Federal Reserve Bank of Dallas, April.

Palepu, K.G. (1986) "Predicting Takeover Targets. A Methodological and Empirical Analysis" *Journal of Accounting and Economics* 8, 3–35.

Pasiouras, F., Tanna, S., and Zopounidis, C. (2007a) "The identification of acquisition targets in the EU banking industry: An application of multicriteria approaches" *International Review of Financial Analysis* 16, 262–281.

Pasiouras F., Tanna, S., and Gaganis, C. (2007b) What Drives Acquisitions in the EU Banking Industry? The Role of Bank Regulation and Supervision Framework, Bank Specific and Market Specific Factors, Working Paper Series, No. 2007-3, Coventry University.

Powell, R., and Yawson, A. (2007) "Are Corporate Restructuring Events Driven by Common Factors? Implications for Takeover Prediction" *Journal of Business Finance & Accounting* 34, 1169–1192.

Wheelock, D.C., and Wilson, P.W. (2000) "Why do banks disappear? The determinants of U.S. bank failures and acquisitions" *The Review of Economics and Statistics* 82, 127–138.

Part 4
Corporate Governance Issues

11
An Assessment of Compliance with the Italian Code of Corporate Governance[1]

Marcello Bianchi, Angela Ciavarella, Valerio Novembre and Rossella Signoretti

1. Introduction

Over the past decade, close attention has been paid to the role that corporate governance plays in capital markets and more generally in the economic system. As a matter of fact, it has been hypothesized and, in some cases, empirically demonstrated that good corporate governance improves firms' performance, guarantees a higher degree of transparency in the market and increases shareholders' protection.

In order to improve corporate governance, several self-regulatory codes have been issued across countries. Such codes are sets of recommendations on the different items that characterize a proper system of governance. They set standards on the board of directors' role and composition, on the structure and functioning of internal committees, on directors' remuneration and on related party transactions. Such codes are usually based on voluntary compliance and adopt the "comply or explain" principle[2] whereby firms are required to state clearly the reasons behind non-compliance.

Self-regulatory initiatives on corporate governance have received close attention from academia as well as from markets and regulators.

A key issue that has been debated in the academic literature is whether these codes are really effective in prompting better governance by favouring the actual adoption of best practices. Different streams of literature have found mixed evidence on this issue. For example, with reference to the UK, Dahya et al. (2002) analyse the effects of the Cadbury Code's[3] recommendation requiring greater independence of the board of directors,[4] which relies on the assumption that greater independence improves board oversight. The authors use as a proxy for board oversight the top management turnover and find that it effectively increased after the adoption of the code, thus proving an improvement in the functioning of the board. In contrast, De Jong et al. (2005), looking at the Netherlands, analyse the effect of the private sector self-regulation initiatives on corporate governance practices and find that the introduction of the Peters Committee's code did not affect corporate governance characteristics and their relationships with firms' value.

As regards the markets and the regulators, close attention has been paid to the assessment of compliance with codes of self-discipline. As argued by RiskMetrics (2009), "monitoring encompasses a variety of activities involving the observance and analysis of the practical application of code provisions by companies". These activities are normally performed with a box-ticking approach by market-wide monitors[5] that generally find high degrees of compliance. For example, the Dutch Monitoring Committee (Corporate Governance Code Monitoring Committee 2007) finds a 95 per cent level of adherence to the Dutch code's prescriptions, the German report (Werder and Talaulicar 2008) shows that companies implement 84 per cent of the German code's recommendations and the Belgian report (Belgian Governance Institute and FEB-VBO 2006) estimates a level of adherence of nearly 80 per cent to its national code. Other bodies perform a more in-depth analysis and present findings at both market-wide and company levels. Among those, the Portuguese CMVM (Comisão do Mercado de Valores Mobiliários 2008) reports a 58 per cent degree of compliance to its code while the Spanish CNMV (Comisión Nacional del Mercado de Valores 2007) finds nearly 75 per cent.

With respect to the Italian case, every year Assonime releases a report reviewing the level of compliance of Italian listed companies.[6] The results have generally been extremely satisfactory, showing a high degree of compliance with the national code (Codice di Autodisciplina). In particular, the results of the 2008 report show that more than 95 per cent (94 in 2007) of the Italian listed companies declare that they are compliant with the code.[7] However, while the high level of compliance found by Assonime is in line with the results of formal evaluations of compliance as performed in other European countries, it is in contrast with most of the literature on Italian corporate governance, which has often been very sceptical about the quality of the Italian system (cf. Zingales 1994; Volpin 2002; Nevona 2003; Dyck and Zingales 2004; Bigelli et al. 2007). These inconsistencies are not even the result of possible intrinsic weakness of the code's provisions, which instead are in line with international standards. In contrast, we hypothesize that the inconsistency between the expected level of compliance and its assessed level might be caused by the fact that the actual degree of compliance differs from what is formally stated.

In order to test the research question empirically, we try to build up a more analytically grounded assessment of compliance, looking at one of the most important features of corporate governance codes, namely how companies manage transactions for which the interests of insiders and outsiders are most likely to be in conflict (i.e. related party transactions, hereafter RPTs). This is particularly relevant in the Italian market where, as a result of the high degree of ownership concentration, conflicts of interest arise especially between controlling shareholders and minorities. We thus build a compliance indicator (called the Compliance on Related party transactions indicator, *breviter CoRe*). It measures the quality of RPTs' internal procedures and is based on the analysis of the 2007 Reports on Corporate Governance, in which issuers are asked not only to state whether but also to explain how they actually put the suggested provisions into practice. We examine all the 262 companies listed on the Italian MTA at the end of 2007.

Our results confirm the stated hypothesis, and show that the adoption of the best practices suggested by the national code for dealing with potential conflicts of interest arising from RPTs is markedly weaker and much more differentiated than is formally declared in the reports. In spite of a declaration of high compliance, listed companies show poor results in terms of actual compliance with the code's best practices. In particular, we find that whereas 85.9 per cent of the market is formally compliant, only 32.6 per cent of our sample has implemented the code's recommendations in a sufficiently satisfactory way. The gap between formal and actual compliance is higher for non-financial firms and smaller companies. Moreover, our investigation suggests that actual compliance is higher in companies where board structure is more aligned with best practices and where foreign institutional investors participate in GMs.

The rest of the paper is organized as follows: Section 2 introduces the Italian Corporate Governance Code, Section 3 describes the methodology used for developing the *CoRe* indicator, Section 4 presents our results on the relation between formal and actual compliance while Section 5 focuses on the determinants of actual compliance and Section 6 concludes.

2. The Italian Corporate Governance Code

The Italian Corporate Governance Code was first published in 1999 by the Corporate Governance Committee and promoted by the Italian Stock Exchange (Borsa Italiana) in order to strengthen the competitiveness of the Italian financial market. The code was then revised in 2006 in order to update its provisions according to both the evolution of international best practices and the amended domestic legislation regarding company law and investor protection.[8] The code as a whole is based on the application of a "comply or explain" principle: its adoption is voluntary and, in cases of non-compliance, companies are required to explain why they have not complied. The code's provisions are set in terms of Principles, Criteria and Comment. Compliance is required only for Principles and Criteria; however "issuers are urged to take into account the indications and suggestions found in the comment included at the bottom of each article".

Although there is a disclosure and explanation "obligation" in cases of non-compliance, the Corporate Governance Code's implementation does not rely on enforcement mechanisms or independent monitoring.[9] The main mechanism that should favour its adoption is therefore based on reputational sanctions that the market is supposed to impose on issuers that do not (or do not sufficiently) comply with the provisions that the code suggests. The effectiveness of market discipline depends at least on two key aspects. On the one hand, issuers should ensure a proper disclosure to the market as regards the concrete adoption of the code's recommendations and their observance. On the other hand, market participants should be able to evaluate the actual extent to which issuers have implemented the recommended practices and to turn an evaluation of weak compliance into a reputational sanction.

In order to evaluate issuers' compliance with the code, we build an indicator which focuses on a key topic of corporate governance in Italy whereby the Corporate Governance Code is the primary (self-)regulatory reference:[10] the substantial and procedural fairness of RPTs. We choose to evaluate the quality of corporate governance practices by focusing on this particular aspect because we recognize that RPTs represent the main channel for diverting value from the firm, especially in companies which show a high degree of ownership concentration. As Bebchuk and Hamdani (2009: 40) point out: "assessing the governance of CS companies [companies with a controlling shareholder] requires close attention to the arrangements governing freezeouts, related-party transactions with the controller or entities affiliated with it, and taking corporate opportunities".

The way Italian companies handle this particular aspect of the code in their governance practices is relevant from two main points of view. First, exploitation of minority shareholders through transactions with controlling or significant shareholders or managers is a primary risk, as suggested by several studies on the private benefits of control in Italy (cf. Nevona 2003: Dyck and Zingales 2004). This is because of the high ownership concentration and the diffusion of control enhancing mechanisms (CEMs) such as pyramids, non-voting shares and coalitions (cf. Barca and Becht 2001; Bianchi et al. 2001, 2008; Faccio and Lang 2002; Bianchi and Bianco 2007). Second, the code itself sets particular disclosure obligations on the handling of RPTs: not only on whether companies comply or not with the relevant recommendations but also on the explanation of the procedures adopted according to them.

3. The *CoRe* indicator: methodology

Our firm-level indicator is based on the analysis of 2007 Reports on Corporate Governance, in which issuers are asked to declare and explain the extent to which they are compliant with the code's recommendations concerning RPTs.

The relevant provisions are those set forth in Principle 1 ("Role of the Board of Directors"), and in Principle 9 ("Directors' Interests and Transactions with Related Parties"). In short, they recommend that:

- the board, after requiring a pre-emptive opinion from the internal audit committee,[11] adopt a procedure for the approval of RPTs;
- the evaluation and the approval of significant transactions (among which RPTs), as defined by companies, lie with the board;
- the board define criteria to identify transactions for which board approval should be accompanied by an opinion from the internal audit committee and/or by the assistance of independent experts;
- the board set solutions for the handling of situations in which a director has an interest in a transaction.

Other and more specific best practices are suggested in the Comment to Principle 9: "the provision of a prior opinion of the internal control committee, entrusting negotiations to one or more independent directors (or directors having no ties with the related party), the recourse to independent experts (possibly selected by independent directors)".

Table 11.1 The methodology for the assignment of the scores with respect to the two components of the *CoRe* indicator (i.e. the identification of significant RPTs and the procedures adopted for their approval)

The methodology for the *CoRe* indicator

A Identification of significant RPTs

		Width of the area of RPTs subject to the *ad hoc* procedures	
		All transactions	Atypical transactions only
Transparency of the significance test	Quantitative criteria	2	1
	Undisclosed or not objective criteria	0.5	0

B Procedures for significant RPT approval

Adoption of the suggested best practices	Prior opinion by the internal audit committee	Binding	1
		Non-binding	0.5
		Not envisaged	0
	Recourse to independent advisors	Selected by independent directors	1
		Selected by the board	0.5
		Not envisaged	0
	Abstention or duty to leave for interested directors	Binding	1
		Unanimous vote	0.75
		Non-binding	0.5
		Not envisaged	0

With regard to the handling of directors' interests, and in consideration of the recent amendments to domestic legislation,[12] the code does not recommend that an interested director leave or abstain from duty. However such move, even though there is no obligation in law for it, is recognized by the code as being a not infrequent practice within Italian companies and as an effective solution that "may contribute to avoiding or reducing the risk of an alteration of the correct formation of the will of the board of directors".

The *CoRe* indicator is aimed at evaluating substantial compliance, which in our methodology implies compliance not only with the Principles and Criteria, but also with the best practices suggested in the Comment.

In particular, the indicator measures two main aspects of the code's implementation.

First, it evaluates the transparency and breadth of the criteria that issuers set to identify significant transactions (RPTs among them) subject to specific approval procedures, and assigns a score to these that ranges from 0 to 2. The rationale is that the wider the area of transactions subject to strengthened procedures and the more objective the criteria set to identify those transactions, the higher the quality of the company's procedures with reference to the identification of RPTs (see Table 11.1, section a).

Second, it looks at the quality of compliance with the principles regarding the approval of RPTs by verifying whether companies adopt three best practices suggested by the code, namely the provision of a prior opinion of the internal control committee, the recourse to independent experts (who could be appointed by independent directors) and the abstention or duty to leave for interested directors. We assign a score, ranging from 0 to 3, which reflects the actual implementation of those practices and evaluates cases in which a certain standard is required to, or simply can, be adopted. The criterion for the assignment is that the more effective the standards that companies set, and the less discretionary their application, the higher the level of substantial and procedural fairness they ensure (see Table 11.1, section b).

The *CoRe* indicator is calculated as the simple sum of the two scores.

4. Formal versus actual compliance

Our analysis addresses 262 companies, namely the total number of those listed on the Italian MTA at the end of 2007. However, we exclude 26 firms for which neither the Annual Report nor the specific procedure for RPTs is available. This is mainly a result of the fact that most of those issuers were no longer listed at the time when our data were collected, and are not therefore subject anymore to listed companies' disclosure provisions. Hence, our final dataset is composed of 236 companies.

Table 11.2 summarizes the main results of the *CoRe* indicator and distinguishes its two components as described above. At first glance, the results seem to confirm our hypothesis: the degree of compliance with the code of self-discipline is far lower than Assonime's figures would

Table 11.2   Descriptive statistics for the *CoRe* indicator

	RPTs identification	RPTs approval	*CoRe* indicator
Mean	0.72	1.04	1.76
Median	0.50	1.00	1.50
Min	0.00	0.00	0.00
Max	2.00	3.00	5.00
Std. dev.	0.82	0.75	1.21

suggest. In particular, the average *CoRe* indicator scores only 1.76 on a scale of 5. Scoring 0.72 (out of 2) and 1.05 (out of 3) respectively, both the RPT Identification and RPT Approval sub-indexes confirm a level of actual compliance which is only one-third of the possible top level. As regards variance, RPT procedures seem fairly variable across companies, with a standard deviation of 1.21.

In contrast, formal compliance with the code appears to be very high and quite widespread across listed companies: Assonime's figures (see Assonime and Emittenti Titoli (2009) show that a very high proportion of listed companies (85.9 per cent) have adopted a procedure for RPTs in line with the code's provisions (see Table 11.3).

In order to compare Assonime's assessment on formal compliance with our results, we consider as "actually compliant" firms for which our *CoRe* indicator is higher than 2. In fact, this threshold allows us to identify firms that are either highly compliant in at least one of the two observed aspects or sufficiently compliant in both aspects.

Consequently, we are able to compare formal and substantial compliance both on an aggregated and a disaggregated basis. Overall, while 85.9 per cent of the market (250 out of 291 companies) is formally compliant, only 32.6 per cent of our sample (77 out of 236 companies) has implemented the code's recommendations in a proper way according to our evaluation. At a more disaggregated level, Table 11.3 compares formal and actual compliance for financial and non-financial firms. Financial firms appear to be more compliant with the code's provisions, but the gap between formal and actual compliance is quite high. Finally, Table 11.4 shows the levels of formal and actual compliance for firms in the S&P Mib, Midex and All Star indices. Substantial compliance is notably lower than formal compliance for firms in all of the mentioned

Table 11.3 Comparison between actual and formal compliance by sector

	Actual compliance				Formal compliance		
Sector	Total N. of firms	Average *CoRe* indicator	N. actually compliant firms	% actually compliant firms	Total N. of firms	N. formally compliant firms	% formally compliant firms
Financial	30	2.27	14	46.7	35	31	88.6
Non-financial	206	1.69	63	30.6	256	219	85.5
Total	236	1.76	77	32.6	291	250	85.9

Table 11.4 Comparison between actual and formal compliance by market index

	Actual compliance				Formal compliance		
Market index	Total N. of firms	Average *CoRe* indicator	N. actually compliant firms	% actually compliant firms	Total N. of firms	N. formally compliant firms	% formally compliant firms
S&P Mib	36	2.33	16	44.4	37	35	94.6
Midex	38	2.13	17	44.7	43	41	95.3
All Star	69	1.69	22	31.9	79	75	94.9
Other	93	1.44	22	23.7	100	75	75.0

market indices. However, it appears that the gap between formal and actual compliance is lower for larger caps – firms in the S&P Mib and Midex indices – than for smaller companies.

A possible explanation for this finding is that there might be a misperception on what a code is really meant for. If we assume, as most of the market participants do, that a code is a collection of best practices, then it should be clear that a best practice can no longer be defined as such when it is followed by the whole market. Consequently, not only is it legitimate for a company not to follow a self-discipline regulation thoroughly, but it is in actual fact natural that only a part of the market does so. However, if the market is satisfied with a mere formal statement of compliance, companies will inevitably tend to go along with it, and will not feel the need to actually pursue the code's principles. In contrast, if it is assumed that the code sets only minimum standards, then the high level of compliance formally stated reveals the need for appropriate monitoring and enforcement mechanisms.

5. Determinants of actual compliance: some preliminary evidence

In order to understand the evidence mentioned, we further analyse the link between the *CoRe* indicator and some of the companies' key features (Table 11.5).

Data confirm what was found in the previous comparison of formal and actual compliance, i.e. that the *CoRe* is positively and significantly correlated with corporate size[13] and financial sector. In particular, the first finding indicates that bigger companies are more subject to market scrutiny and thus have more incentives to comply with the code. In contrast, the second finding implies that the public regulation to which financial firms are subject might have a positive influence on the adoption of an effective system of corporate governance.

Further work has been done on the relationship between the *CoRe* indicator and some key variables that characterize a company's ownership and control structure and its internal mechanisms of corporate governance as well as the presence and activism of institutional investors.

With reference to the nature of the controlling agent, data demonstrate that, consistently with the literature on self-dealing transactions, family owned firms are less compliant with the code's indications. Concerning CEMs,[14] such as non-voting shares and voting caps (normative CEMs) as well as pyramidal groups, evidence from the *CoRe* indicator shows that the companies adopting one of the mentioned CEMs are also more in line with the code's recommendations on RPTs. However, a more in-depth analysis indicates that only the adoption of normative CEMs is positively correlated with actual compliance, while pyramids seem negatively correlated (although this result is not significant). It might be that firms adopting CEMs are interested in showing good governance standards, but within pyramidal groups this interest could be outweighed by the higher incentive to exploit minorities by reason of the higher leverage effect.

Regarding the relationship between the level of compliance and the internal governance characteristics, data show that companies whose boards are most in line with some key, widely acknowledged, best practices and with legislation that protects minorities are better able to implement the code. In particular, the *CoRe* is significantly higher in companies where the board includes a sufficient percentage of independent direc-

Table 11.5   *CoRe* indicator and firms' characteristics: test of difference between means

Area	Variable		N. of firms	Average *CoRe*	t statistics	p-value
Sector						
	Financial		30	2.27**	−2.45	0.015
	Non-financial		206	1.69**		
Ownership and control structure						
	Family controlled firms	Yes	174	1.64**	2.54	0.012
		No	62	2.09**		
	State owned enterprises	Yes	28	2.24**	−2.23	0.026
		No	208	1.70**		
	Control Enhancing Mechanisms (CEMs)	Yes	65	2.00*		
		No	171	1.67*	−1.87	0.061
	Pyramids	Yes	31	1.62		
		No	205	1.78	0.66	0.504
	Normative CEMs	Yes	42	2.27***	−3.02	0.002
		No	194	1.66***		
Internal governance						
	Weight of independent directors in the board	<20 %	31	1.20***	2.82	0.005
		>=20 %	205	1.85***		
	Internal audit committee with a majority of independent directors	Yes	184	1.94***	−4.45	0.000
		No	52	1.13***		
	Presence of director appointed by minority shareholders	Yes	26	2.42***	−2.97	0.003
		No	208	1.68***		
Institutional investors						
	Major holdings by institutional investors					
	Total	Yes	134	1.84	−1.11	0.266
		No	102	1.66		
	Italian	Yes	36	1.50	1.42	0.154
		No	200	1.81		

Continued

Table 11.5   Continued

Area	Variable			N. of firms	Average *CoRe*	t statistics	p-value
		Italian	Yes	36	1.50	1.42	0.154
			No	200	1.81		
		Foreign	Yes	121	1.89*	−1.69	0.091
			No	115	1.63*		
	Ownership by Italian funds > 0.5%	Yes		174	1.91***	−3.22	0.001
		No		62	1.34***		
	Participation in GMs						
		Total	Yes	155	1.95***	−4.33	0.000
			No	55	1.16***		
		Italian	Yes	46	2.28***	−3.56	0.000
			No	164	1.58***		
		Foreign	Yes	154	1.96***	−4.56	0.000
			No	56	1.14***		

*, ** and *** indicate statistical significance at 90 %, 95 % and 99 % respectively.

tors (at least 20 per cent) and at least one minority director, and where the internal audit committee has a majority independent directors.

The relation between the *CoRe* indicator and the presence and activism of institutional investors has been tested. Such investors are supposed to play a beneficial role in improving firms' governance, either by monitoring managers and voicing their disappointment or by selling their shares. Consistently with these indications, the holding of a major stake (higher than 2 per cent) by an institutional investor appears to positively (but not significantly) influence compliance. However, data show that the nationality of institutional major shareholders is crucial, since only foreign major investors positively and significantly affect compliance.

Below the 2 per cent threshold, we find that companies in which Italian mutual funds hold a sufficient stake (more than 0.5 per cent) have on average a higher *CoRe*. In contrast to the evidence on major shareholdings, this result indicates that Italian institutional investors also exert a positive influence on corporate governance. However, the higher *CoRe* indicator found for these companies might be more the effect of funds' asset allocation than the result of their monitoring of companies. Indeed, recent studies have found that Italian funds tend to invest in companies characterized by a sound governance system (Barucci and Falini 2005).

Last, institutional investors' activism, proxied by their attendance at the GM,[15] is also significantly associated with better compliance with the code. This result is confirmed for both Italian and foreign institutional investors.

6. Conclusion

In this chapter we have tried to assess the effectiveness of soft law in prompting the adoption of best practices. We thus built a compliance indicator (the *CoRe* indicator) aimed at measuring the degree of compliance with the Italian code's provisions on RPTs. Our results suggest that the adoption of best practices suggested by the code for dealing with potential conflicts of interest arising from RPTs is markedly weaker and much more differentiated than what formally declared in company reports. In spite of a declaration of high compliance, listed companies show poor results in terms of actual compliance with the code's best practices. With reference to the potential factors driving actual compliance, our analysis suggests that the *CoRe* indicator is systematically higher in firms which have good internal governance mechanisms, are actively monitored by institutional investors or are subject to micro prudential supervision.

Notes

1. Opinions expressed in this chapter are exclusively the authors' and do not necessarily reflect those of CONSOB.
2. The European Commission, after having performed a comparative study on corporate governance codes in Member States (Weil, Gothshal & Manges LLP 2002), mandated the comply or explain principle through 2006/46/EC.
3. The Cadbury Code was replaced by the so-called Combined Code in 2002.
4. In particular, the Cadbury Code required that the board include at least three outside directors and that the same individual could not occupy the position of chairman and CEO at the same time.
5. Market-wide monitors, as defined by RiskMetrics (2009), are either public (i.e. financial markets authorities and securities exchanges) or private (such as trade bodies, professional organizations, analysts and academics).
6. More in-depth focuses on single items of the regulation are also sometimes provided. For example, in 2008 Assonime assessed the level of actual compliance with the provisions regarding independent directors, while in 2009 it focused on the internal control systems.
7. Cf. the Assonime and Emittenti Titoli (2007) and (2008) reports on the implementation of the code for 2006 and 2007 respectively.

8. Company law was substantially reformed by Legislative Decree n. 310/2004; Law n. 262/2005 introduced several provisions regarding listed companies' governance systems.
9. As mentioned earlier, an assessment of the code's adoption is annually provided by Assonime. Disclosure on each company's compliance is left to self-reporting in the Annual Report on Corporate Governance or in the Annual Directors' Report.
10. Actually, article 2391-*bis* of the Italian Civil Law, introduced in 2004's reform, entrusts CONSOB with defining general principles in order to ensure the substantial and procedural fairness of RPTs. Two draft regulations were issued by CONSOB in April 2008 and in August 2009; the final regulation is still to be adopted.
11. A committee composed of non-executive directors, the majority of whom it is recommended should be independent.
12. If a director has an interest in a transaction which conflicts with the company's interest, he/she is not required to abstain from voting on the transaction (article 2391 of the Italian Civil Law, amended by the company law reform).
13. The correlation between the *CoRe* and capitalization is 0.173, significant at the 99 per cent level.
14. These mechanisms allow the controlling shareholders to minimize the capital they risk in the company and/or to reduce the risk of a takeover, and thus give higher incentives to insiders to extract value from the company.
15. Information available for 210 companies.

References

Assonime and Emittenti Titoli (2007) "Analisi dello stato di attuazione del Codice di Autodisciplina delle società quotate (anno 2007)" *Assonime Note e Studi* 112/2007.
Assonime and Emittenti Titoli (2009) "Analisi dello stato di attuazione del Codice di Autodisciplina delle società quotate (anno 2008)" *Assonime Note e Studi* 1/2009.
Barca, F., and Becht, M. (2001) *The Control of Corporate Europe*, Oxford University Press, Oxford.
Barucci, E., and Falini, J. (2005) Institutional Investors and Corporate Governance in Italy: an analysis of their stockholdings, http://www1.mate.polimi.it/ing-fin/document/inst.pdf (last access July 15, 2010).
Bebchuk, L.A., and Hamdani, A. (2009) The elusive quest for global governance standards, Discussion Paper n. 633, Harvard Law School, http://papers.ssrn.com/sol3/papers.cfm?abstract_id=1374331 (last access July 15, 2010).
Belgian Governance Institute and FEB – VBO (2006) *Le Respect du Code Belge de Gouvernance d'Entreprise: un état de la question*, http://www.vbo-feb.be/index.html?file=2409 (last access July 15, 2010).
Bianchi, M., Bianco, M., and Enriques, L. (2001) "Pyramidal groups and the separation between ownership and control in Italy" in Barca, F., and Becht, M. (2001), *The Control of Corporate Europe*, Oxford University Press, Oxford.
Bianchi, M., and Bianco, M. (2007) "La corporate governance in Italia negli ultimi 15 anni: dalle piramidi alle coalizioni?", in Gnesutta C., Rey G.M., and

Romagnoli, G.C. (eds) *Capitale industriale e capitale finanziario nell'economia globale*, il Mulino, Bologna.

Bianchi, M., and Bianco, M. (2008) "The evolution of ownership and control structure in Italy in the last 15 years", paper presented at the Conference "Corporate governance in Italy: 10 years after the Consolidated Law on Finance", Rome, December 2008, http://www.bancaditalia.it/studiricerche/ convegni/atti/corp_gov_it/session1/evolution_ownership_control_structures. pdf (last access July 15 2010).

Bigelli, M., Mehrotra, V., and Rau, R. (2007) Expropriation through Unification? Wealth Effects of Dual Class Share Unifications in Italy, ECGI, Finance Working Paper n. 180.

Comisión Nacional del Mercado de Valores (2007), *Corporate Governance Report of Entities with Securities Admitted to Trading on Regulated Markets 2007*, http:// www.cnmv.es/DocPortal/Publicaciones/Informes/IAGC2007_een.pdf (last access July 15, 2010).

Comissão do Mercado de Valores Mobiliários (2008), *Annual Report on the Corporate Governance of listed companies in Portugal*, http://www.cmvm. pt/NR/rdonlyres/33DE0BB8-6C6F-4170-8726-020E33738A2D/12169/ AnnualReportCorporateGovernanceListedCompaniesPort.pdf (last access July 15, 2010).

Comitato per la Corporate Governance (2006) *Codice di Autodisciplina*, http:// www.borsaitaliana.it/borsaitaliana/ufficio-stampa/comunicati-stampa/2006/ codiceautodisciplina_pdf.htm (last access July 15, 2010).

Corporate Governance Code Monitoring Committee (2007) *Third Report on Compliance with the Dutch Corporate Governance Code*, http://www.commis- siecorporategovernance.nl/page/downloads/Third_report_Dutch_corporate_ governance_code_-_December_2007.pdf (last access July 15, 2010)

Dahya J., McConnell, J.J., and Travlos, N.G. (2002) "The Cadbury committee, corpo- rate performance, and top management turnover" *Journal of Finance* 57, 461–483.

De Jong, A., DeJong, D.V., Mertens, G., and Wasley, C.E. (2005) "The role of self-regulation in corporate governance: evidence and implications from the Netherlands" *Journal of Corporate Governance* 11, 473–503.

Dyck, A., and Zingales, L. (2004) "Private Benefits of Control: An International Comparison", *The Journal of Finance* 59 (2), 537–600.

Faccio, M., and Lang, L.H.P. (2002) "The Ultimate Ownership of Western European Corporations" *Journal of Financial Economics* 65 (3), 365–395.

Nenova, T. (2003) "The Value of Corporate Voting Rights and Control: A Cross- Country Analysis" *Journal of Financial Economics* 68, 325–351.

RiskMetrics Group et al. (2009) "Study on Monitoring and Enforcement Practices in Corporate Governance in the Member States", study commissioned by the European Commission, http://ec.europa.eu/internal_market/company/docs/ ecgforum/studies/comply-or-explain-090923-appendix2_en.pdf (last access July 15, 2010).

Volpin, P. (2002) "Governance with Poor Investor Protection: Evidence from Top Executive Turnover in Italy" *Journal of Financial Economics* 64, 61–90.

Weil, Gothshal & Manges LLP (2002) *Comparative study of corporate governance codes relevant to the European Union and its members*, Final Report (on behalf of the European Commission, Internal Market Directorate General), http://

ec.europa.eu/internal_market/company/docs/corpgov/corp-gov-codes-rpt-part1_en.pdf (last access July 15, 2010).

Werder, V.A., and Talaulicar, T. (2008) "2008 Code Report: The Acceptance of the Recommendations and Suggestions of the German Corporate Governance Code" *Der Betrieb* 61 (16).

Zingales, L. (1994) "The Value of the Voting Right: A Study of the Milan Stock Exchange Experience" *Review of Financial Studies* 7, 125–148.

12
Sources of Risk and Return in Different Bank Business Models: Comparing Poland with Global Trends

Ewa Miklaszewska and Katarzyna Mikolajczyk

1. Introduction

The deregulation and globalization of financial markets over the last two decades has dramatically influenced the scale and complexity of banking firms. In the pre-crisis period, there were many studies which advocated the development of new strategies which focused on bank efficiency arising from expansion into new markets and new sources of profits and on the adoption of new models for conducting banking activities, based on product synergies, scale and scope benefits and global coverage (Acharya at al 2010). While large scale and in many cases complex organizational structures, with a high dependence on non-interest income and non-depository funding, allowed for dynamic expansion, they nevertheless constituted new sources of risks. The global financial crisis of 2007–2009 forced banks and regulators to rethink strategic and competitive issues in banking. Banks, which for decades had been leaders in global efficiency or expansion, turned out to be most affected, requiring massive public stabilization funds and in some cases rescue by direct government intervention. Investment and global wholesale banks suffered particularly badly. Thus in the post-crisis literature, new techniques, focusing on predicting banks' default probability have been developed or brought back for review, such as the index of bank distance to bankruptcy (Z-score).

Although the crisis affected the whole world, for the first time the leading industrialized nations were most affected, in this respect making the crisis unique (IMF, 2009a). For many Central and East European Countries (CEE), the crisis was secondary in nature, as their economies were hit by sluggish exports and plummeting currencies, partially as a result of a massive withdrawal of foreign investment. In all CEE countries the presence of foreign capital in banking is excessively high and stands today at 70–90 per cent of total assets on average, as opposed to 5 per cent in 1995 (Naaborg 2007), and this creates a strong potential for contagion (ECB 2008). Austrian, Italian and Swedish banks dominate, and UniCredit, Raiffeisen and KBC operate in more than ten countries (The Economist 2009b). From 2004, the dynamic growth of branches of foreign credit institutions has been an important factor. However, most banks are still licensed and supervized by national monetary authorities (95 per cent of banking assets in Poland). The extent to which CEE countries were affected by the global crisis differs (Table 12.1). Initially, countries like Poland and the Czech Republic were affected to a lesser degree than smaller CEE economies, although the long term impact of the global crisis may turn out be more negative for all CEE countries in terms of curbing of the dynamic expansion of local financial markets and of the reduction of innovations and technological progress in banking.

Thus the aim of this chapter is to contribute to the discussion on how the financial crisis has changed the perception of what the main sources of bank risk and return are, and to look at the question of what constitutes an efficient and stable business model for global banks. In particular, it addresses the hypothesis that the financial crisis has redefined the strengths and weaknesses of bank business models by highlighting the riskiness of the universal (conglomerate) model, in which bank expansion is based on non-depository funding and focused on non-interest income. It also suggests that, in many cases, the benefits from diversification away from traditional banking have been overstated. The chapter compares recent research papers centred on advanced economies with the results of various models of regression for major Polish banks in the period 2000–2008. The econometric analysis is based on a model developed by Stiroh (2004) and Demirgüç-Kunt and Huizinga (2009), who analysed returns measured by ROA and risk by Z-score and Sharpe ratio. The main conclusion of the empirical part is that despite differences in market development and structure similar tendencies concerning efficiency and risk in different bank models were also characteristic of Polish banks. The structure of the chapter is as follows. Section 2 analyses the evolution of bank organizational structures in the pre crisis period. Section 3 describes the recent empirical evidence on sources of risk and returns in universal and specialized bank business models. The

Table 12.1   Bank profitability in selected countries: ROE (%)

Country	2003	2004	2005	2006	2007	2008*	2009**
A Advanced economies							
Japan	–3	4	11	8.5	6	–7	–
US	15	13	13	12	8	0,4	2
Switzerland	12	14	18	18	15	5	–
B Monetary Union countries							
Austria	7	15	15	17	17	3	–
Belgium	14	16	18	22	13	–36.5	15.5
Finland	11	12	10	11	14	11	–
France	8.5	11	12	14	10	–1	–
Greece	9	6	16	13	15	3	–
Italy	8	9	10	14	13	5	–
Portugal	14	13	14.5	17	15	10	–
Slovak Republic	11	12	17	17	17	14	4
Slovenia	12	12	14	15	16	9	–
Spain	15	15	17.5	21	21	14	–
UK	9	11	9	11	6	–11	–
C Emerging Europe							
Czech Republic	24	25	26	23	25	22	23
Hungary	19	25	25	24	18	12	15
Poland	6	17	21	22.5	22	21	16
Bulgaria	23	20	21	25	25	23	16
Estonia	14	20	21	20	30	13	9
Latvia	17	21	27	26	24	5	–20
Lithuania	11	13	14	21	27	16	–1
Romania	20	19	15	14	11.5	18	–
Ukraine	8	8	10	13.5	13	8.5	–24.5

Note: * Countries for which 2008 dataw are not available are excluded; ** last available data.
Source: IMF (2009b), 228.

selection of a proper business model is a major issue not only for global giants, but also for banks in the transition countries, which have undergone major transformations during the post-EU accession period. It is therefore interesting to investigate how various bank business models perform in the Polish market, which is analysed in section 4, followed by regression results in section 5. Finally, we provide some concluding remarks in section 6.

2. Rethinking the bank business model

The past decades of deregulation and globalization of financial markets resulted in the increasing complexity of banks and the expansion of conglomerate structures, which generated synergies between banking (regulated) business and relatively unregulated investment activities and offered both new sources of income and new areas of risk. While increased scale and scope provided better access to funds, diversification of assets and more efficient management, this development posed new areas of risk, namely operational problems resulting from geographic expansion and difficulties with liquidity in global non-depository firms. In the fight for high returns, there was negative arbitrage from non-banking firms, principally hedge funds, as a consequence of which banks moved assets from banking (regulated) activities to those which were less regulated. The business model of the traditional bank was built around specialized business lines with similar risk profiles (Bessis 2002) or asset diversification in the universal bank. The globally active financial institutions selected new strategic models, based on synergies and a global operating scale (Slager 2006), as illustrated in Table 12.2.

The global financial crisis of 2007–2009 clearly demonstrated that scale and complexity increased sensitivity to risk and that the benefits from synergies and global scale were in many cases overstated. It also highlighted problems with stability in large global institutions (systemic risk). Initially, the institutions worst affected were large, specialized banks, with the investment industry leaders disappearing (Bear Stearns taken over by JP Morgan Chase, Merrill Lynch by the Bank of America, Goldman Sachs and Morgan Stanley converted to BHC and Lehman Brothers went bankrupt). Specialized global banks, such as UBS, active in the pre-crisis era in securities trading and the securitization of assets, also recorded huge losses. All this might suggests that the universal bank model is better equipped to cope with a crisis. However, ultimately, almost all global banks recorded immense losses and became subject to public assistance (Figure 12.1).[1] This new crisis-related empirical evidence

Table 12.2 Evolution of bank organizational structures

Traditional specialized model (business lines)	Universal bank model	New strategic models of global bank
Commercial banking retail/wholesale oriented	Synergies between various commercial and investment business lines	Financial supermarket retail oriented (*GE Money, Santander, HSBC*)
Investment banking (advisory services, M&A, interbank market, securitization)		Conglomerate model based on synergies (*Citigroup*)
Trading (equity, fixed income, derivatives)	Trading subsidiaries	Global specialized banks (*UBS, Goldman Sachs*)
Private banking (asset management)	Insurance subsidiaries	

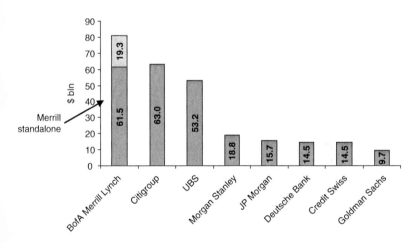

Figure 12.1 Total assets write-downs, 2007–1Q2009
Source: Adapted from Horwood (2009).

has forced many banks to rethink the impact of their business model on risk and return. Many of them have been returning to core business, downsizing their investments, decreasing their scale of operations and simplifying their organizational structures. However, some banks, such as JP Morgan, still operate successfully in commercial and investment banking and asset management (Euromoney 2009).

Moreover, large global banks were not a simple extrapolation of old-style universal banks, but institutions bearing new specific risks (Jones and Nguyen 2004) and generating high risk exposure (Kaufman 2009), which contributed to global systemic instability. Citigroup, until 2008 the largest financial institution, epitomizes the problems stemming from complexity. Its strategy evolved from that of being a simple commercial bank (the McDonald's of finance) to becoming a complex conglomerate servicing 200 million clients in over 100 countries. However, in the crisis it had to be rescued by the US government, which acquired almost 40 per cent of its capital. With hindsight, the most crisis-resistant banks turned out to be retail oriented, global banks with a relatively simple "supermarket" model, such as HSBC, Santander and GE Money. For them, the main source of risk remains scale and non-depository sources of income.[2] The president of HSBC expressed this by saying: "it is now clear that model that depend on wholesale market for funding does not work...and profit is not as important now as balance sheet" (Lee 2008).

3. Sources of risk and return in different business models: empirical evidence

Since the 1990s, the dominant tendency in banking strategies has been that of the universal bank (Fiordelisi and Molyneux 2006). The controversies about the costs and benefits derived from the universal bank model are difficult to resolve, even in the light of post-crisis experience. The problem becomes more manageable if it is narrowed down to the question of the costs and benefits arising from the diversification of traditional bank assets to non-interest incomes. This trend is very clear for most countries (although not for all) for the pre-crisis period (Table 12.3). In some countries asset risk was also increased by the existence of a large proportion of off-balance sheet assets.[3]

During the years of economic boom, this strategy led to a significant increase in income and profits. Bank expansion was additionally supported by large proportion of non-depository funding in global banks. The financial crisis has prompted many questions about this strategy, although some studies had pointed to the riskiness of this strategy long before. Stiroh (2004), researching the US market for the period 1970–2001, found out that non-interest incomes are more volatile than interest-related ones, and are positively related to the probability of default as measured by Z-score. He observed that the strategy of income diversification towards non-interest activities may actually

Table 12.3 Net non-interest income as a percentage of total net income in selected countries

Country	1980–1984	1985–1989	1990–1994	1995–1999	2000–2004	2005–2007
Austria		23	31	44	50	57
Belgium	16	21	23	35	43	50
Czech Republic			61	79	59	45
Denmark	37	22	3	34	41	50
Finland	40	49	52	31	47	36
France		20	32	52	60	71
Germany	18	21	24	26	31	33
Greece*			59	51	32	27
Hungary*				-15	26	32
Ireland				34	38	34
Italy	25	25	22	29	31	36
Luxembourg	18	22	33	44	48	51
Netherlands	25	26	30	38	43	50
Norway	20	25	21	26	26	31
Poland			28	29	44	43
Portugal*	35	19	21	30	33	44
Slovak Republic				46	35	41
Spain	15	17	21	29	31	35
Sweden	26	29	38	46	51	62
Switzerland	46	49	50	60	57	63
US	30	31	31	36	41	41

*Data for commercial banks only.
Source: OECD database.

increase bank riskiness, which would make the long-term benefits of universalism and diversification dubious. Acharya et al. (2002) studied the effect of specialization versus diversification of assets on the return and risk of Italian banks over the period 1993–1999. Their results were similar; they found out that there is no guarantee that a diversification in bank assets will produce superior performance and/or greater safety for banks. Heimeshoff and Uhde (2007), researching the impact of bank concentration on national markets on financial stability in 25 EU countries for the period 1997–2005, found that increasing market concentration also has a negative impact on financial stability, as measured by Z-score.

If banking risk can be defined as adverse impacts on the profitability of several sources of uncertainty (Bessis 2002), its main part is made up of solvency risk, that is of being unable to absorb losses generated by all types of risks with the available capital. Z-score, an index of bank sensitivity to risk (default) measured by standard deviation, can approximate this kind of risk. It points up the riskiness of volatility of returns and is based on the notion that the source of default lies in losses which are not covered by adequate capital. Thus Z-score can be interpreted as the distance from a default, measured by standard deviation of profits expressed by ROA (Lown et al. 2000). The higher on average ROA and CAR (capital/assets) are in a given period, and more stable the returns, the higher the Z-score, and the safer the bank.

$$Z - score = \frac{\frac{1}{n} * \sum_{t=1}^{n} \frac{\pi_t}{A_t} + \frac{1}{n} * \sum_{t=1}^{n} \frac{E_t}{A_t}}{\sigma_{ROA}} = \frac{ROA + CAR}{\sigma_{ROA}} \qquad (1)$$

where: A_t – average assets in a period t,
π_t – net profit in a period t,
E_t – average bank equity in a period t,
σ_{ROA} – standard deviation of ROA,
n – number of researched periods (years).

New insights into the discussion on bank business models have been provided by the research paper by Demirgüç-Kunt and Huizinga (2009), in which they analysed sources of bank risk and return in universal and specialized banks, based on a group of 1334 publicly quoted banks in 101 countries in the period 1995–2007. In their sample, universal banks constituted the dominant group (70 per cent); the other three groups were composed of investment banks, non-banking credit institutions and other banks. Their research focused on the implications of bank activity (business model) and short term funding strategies on bank risk and return. They looked in particular at the traditional bank model (deposit/loans oriented) versus new models based on an expansion to non-interest incomes and financed by non-depository sources of funds. As with Stiroh (2004), they tested the hypothesis that traditional banks, which have a large proportion of interest income and depository funding, are low risk and that their expansion to non-interest incomes financed by non-depository funds may offer some diversification benefits, but nevertheless is very risky. Asset diversification was measured by share of non-interest income (NII) and diversification of financing by the share of short term non-depository funds (NDF) while bank returns were measured by ROA and risk by Z-Score. They used the following explanatory variables: scale of activity, asset growth, CAR, level of costs, assets diversification and diversification of sources of funds.[4] In their basic regressions, the impact of NII and NDF on ROA was U-shaped: traditional banks (with a dominance of interest income) had the highest RoA, but so too, at the other end, did banks with a low level of such income, while diversification of assets in universal banks brought lowest profitability. Looking at the funding structure, the impact of NII and NDF on Z-score was inversely U-shaped: the safest banks were those with diversified sources of financing, while banks depending heavily on one source of finance, too, increased their riskiness (had a low-Z-score). Thus the diversification of assets in a universal bank did not significantly increase profitability, and relying heavily on non-depository funding significantly increased the riskiness of a bank. Moreover, banks with a non-traditional asset structure tended to have non-traditional sources of funding.

4. Risk and return by bank types: Polish empirical evidence

In Poland, as in other CEE countries, a dramatic inflow of foreign capital took place in the pre-EU accession period: between 1998 and 2000 foreign bank assets in relation to total assets increased from 17 to 70 per cent. Since 2004, an important factor has been the dynamic growth of branch networks of foreign credit institutions, reaching 18 in 2008 (but constituting only 5 per cent of bank assets), compared to 52 commercial banks licensed in Poland (KNF 2009). The inflow of foreign capital has sharpened the competitive environment and improved the efficiency of banks, but has at the same time created new challenges for the banks and for the Polish regulator, which in 2008 underwent transformation into an integrated model. Polish banks, although predominantly owned by global foreign groups (see Appendix A 12.1) have tended to be traditional in terms of products and business lines. When analysing Polish banks, the main research question was as follows: "to what extent did bank expansion from a traditional to a universal model, represented by an increasing proportion of non-interest income and non-depository funding, influence bank risk and return?" Returns were measured by ROA and risk by Z-score and

Table 12.4   Groups of analysed banks, according to bank business models

Business model	Selection criteria: deposits and loans as a percentage of totals assets	No. of banks in a group
Traditional	deposits > 50; loans > 50	14
Universal (depository)	deposits > 50; loans < 50	8
Corporate (non-depository)	deposits < 50; loans < 70	9
Specialized, loan-oriented (non-depository)	deposits < 50; loans > 70	11
Others:	– 100% state-owned, of special character – affiliating cooperative banks	1 3
Total		46

Sharpe ratio. To procure a stable, homogenous group, the researched sample consisted of the 46 largest banks operating in Poland for at least five years in the period 2000–2008. We analysed banks both as one group and as sub-groups, representing different business models with different assets and financing structures, according to the criteria presented in Table 12.4. The detailed list of analysed banks is enclosed in Appendix A 12.1.

The selection criteria reflect a specific characteristic of the Polish banking market, i.e. the lack of typical investment banks or a large group of banks which are non-depository institutions (often subsidiaries of foreign groups) and concentrate almost solely on retail loans. Four banks ("*others*") were excluded from further analysis. Banks were not divided according to capital of origin, as the majority of them were foreign owned. However, all of the banks analysed were fully licensed and independently capitalized subsidiaries. The calculations were based on a dataset of the 50 largest Polish banks between 2000–2008, as published in special editions of BANK (2000–2009). In some cases, the data were individually adjusted by the authors, reflecting the rapid transformation of the Polish banking market, particularly waves of M&As. In the analysis of bank business models, asset diversification (universalism) was represented by the percentage share of non-interest net income (NINI) in total net income from banking operations, while diversification of funding was represented by the percentage share of non-depository funding (NDF) in total liabilities. For NINI, specialized loan oriented

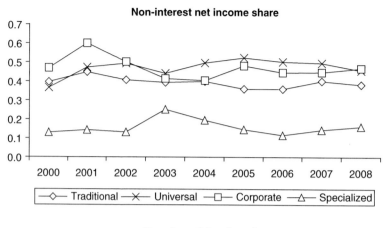

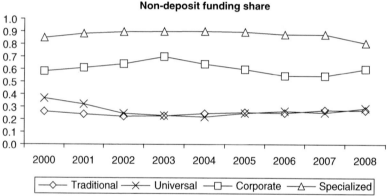

Figure 12.2   Non-depository funding share and non-interest net income share by bank type

banks formed a clearly distinct group; other banks had a rather similar, diversified asset structure. For NDF, loan oriented specialized banks have a distinctly different strategy, as do, to a lesser degree, corporate banks. The traditional and universal banks had a similar, deposit-based funding strategy (Figure 12.2).

In analysing the impact of NINI and NDF on ROA (Figure 12.3), we see that both independent variables have an L-shape (inverted for NDF), where extreme points represent the highest returns. For NINI, a strong concentration on loans is the most profitable strategy, while increasing universalism (moving to the right of the graph) results in low profitability, with an investment banking strategy giving the worst result. On

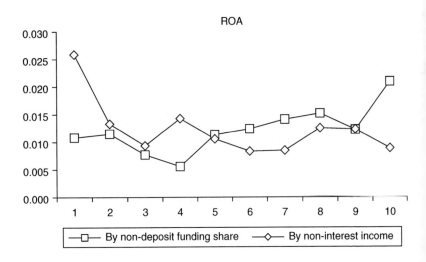

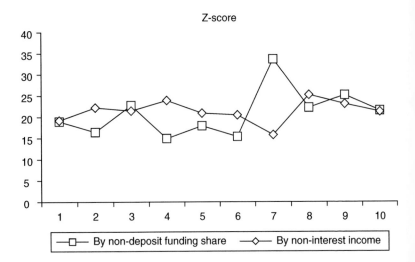

Figure 12.3 Non-depository funding share and non-interest net income share: impact on ROA and Z-score

Note: On the horizontal axis each step is every 10 bins, each containing 10 % of the observations in increasing order.

the other hand, an increasing level of non-depository funding brings higher profitability. For the Z-score the impact lines for both variables are rather flat.

Risk adjusted returns were also measured by the Sharpe ratio (reward-to-variability ratio), which characterizes how well the return on an asset compensates the investor for risk taken. An asset with a higher Sharpe ratio gives a higher return for the same risk. It is calculated as a mean ROE divided by the standard deviation of ROE. In our study the average Sharpe ratio was similar in traditional, universal and corporate models and much higher for banks specializing in loans. The relationships between the Sharpe ratio and NINI share and NDF share seem to be slightly U-shaped (Figure 12.4).

Figures 12.5–12.7 illustrate the impact of NINI and NDF on risk and return in different bank business models. The biggest differences in bank returns were for the boom period 2002–2006, whereas bank results in the last two years have tended to converge, regardless of business model. On average, specialized, loan oriented banks had the highest ROA and ROE and corporate banks the lowest. However, the lowest returns of corporate banks were offset by their higher Z-score, illustrating the trade-offs between risk and return. Loan oriented specialized banks also had a relatively high Z-score, high capitalization (CAR) and on average the highest Sharpe ratio. This, together with their superior

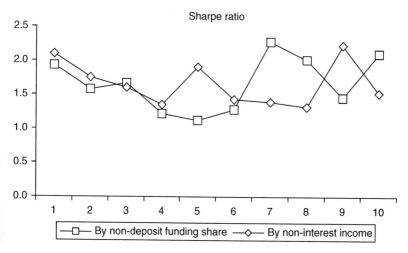

Figure 12.4 Non-depository funding share and non-interest net income share: impact on the Sharpe ratio

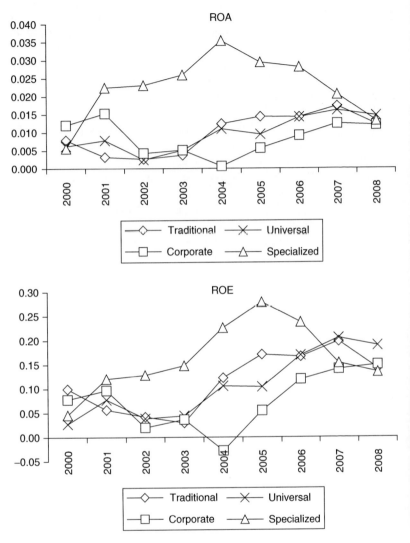

Figure 12.5   Trend of ROA and ROE by bank type

profitability, makes them risk/return leaders. Hence the Polish data support the hypothesis that universalism is not necessary a superior strategy. For the CEPR study (Demirgüç-Kunt and Huizinga 2009) the optimal strategy was that of traditional banks with a more diversified funding structure. Polish loan oriented banks follow this strategy to an

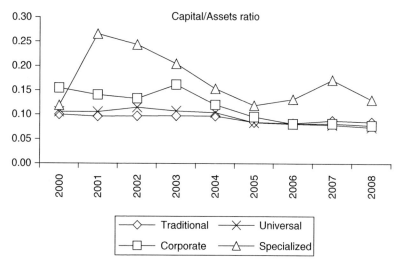

Figure 12.6 Trend of CAR by bank type

extreme, having as they do a very high proportion of loans and very small proportion of deposits (or no deposits at all) and getting superior risk-return results.

5. Regression results for the Polish banks

The next step was to analyse regressions models, adapted from Demirgüç-Kunt and Huizinga (2009). We estimated two basic regressions, using linear and squared forms, which had the return (ROA) and risk (Z-score) as dependent variables and explanatory variables such as size (log of assets), asset growth, CAR, overhead costs to assets, non-interest net income as a share of total net income and non-depository funds as a proportion of total external funds. Dummy variables (0/1) for an additional two regressions were added, representing the bank business model. Table 12.5 shows that NINI has a negative and significant correlation with ROA and NDF, and a positive (but insignificant) one with Z-score. Hence asset diversification negatively influences profitability, while it has almost no impact on increasing safety – a result which is in line with the previously mentioned studies. NDF is positively, although not very strongly, correlated both with ROA and Z-score. The correlation between RoA and Z-score is negative, demonstrating trade-offs between risk and return, however weak and statistically insignificant.

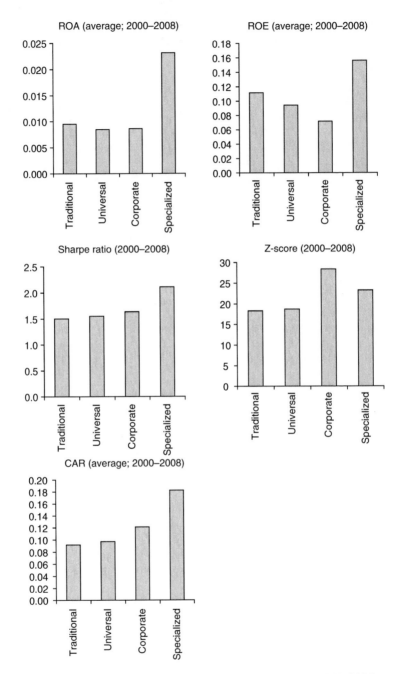

Figure 12.7   Average ratios for different bank business models (2000–2008)

Table 12.5 Correlation matrix

	NON_ INTEREST_INC	NON_ DEPOSIT_ FUND	ROA	Z_SCORE
NON_INTEREST_ INC	1			
NON_DEPOSIT_ FUND	−0.446***	1		
ROA	−0.436***	0.290*	1	
Z_SCORE	0.057	0.187	−0.133	1

*** and * denote significance at 1 % and 10 % respectively.

Tables 12.6 and 12.7 present the results of four models of regression. The basic findings are that scale has a positive and significant impact on returns (ROA), but a negative one on Z-score, indicating that the profitability of large banks is higher than in smaller banks, while at the same time bank stability is reduced. The process of expansion (asset growth) is insignificant for risk, but significant and negative for returns, and this may be interpreted as a consequence of expenditure connected with growth. In our models, the increase in the capitalization ratio (CAR) positively influences returns and Z-score, and this can be seen as an argument for adequate capital base. Additionally, an increase in costs has a strong negative impact on Z-score. The increase in non-interest net income share has a negative impact on ROA, so the strategy of diversification away from loans is not necessarily a profitable one. The higher the share of non-deposit funds in a bank's liabilities, the higher the returns will be (statistically significant in one model). However, the structure of income and liabilities (NINI, NDF) has no significant impact on risk (Z-score). In the analysis of bank types, only for specialized, loan oriented banks was there a significant and positive impact of NINI and NDF on returns; in one model there was a positive impact of the corporate model for Z-score. The above results are not always consistent with those of Stiroh (2004) and Demirgüç-Kunt and Huizinga (2009), i.e. that movement away from the traditional model towards a universal one increases risk, with no significant effect on profitability. For Z-score in particular, our results do not form a clear pattern. In our regressions, adequate capitalization has a positive impact on Z-score, while size and operational costs have a negative one. More similar results were obtained when analysing returns. In the regressions

Table 12.6   Regression results: ROA

	Model 1a	Model 1b	Model 1c	Model 1d
LN_ASSETS	0.003***	0.003***	0.003***	0.003***
	(0.001)	(0.001)	(0.001)	(0.001)
CAR	0.049***	0.028**	0.049***	0.028**
	(0.012)	(0.012)	(0.012)	(0.012)
ASSETS_GROWTH	−0.001*	−0.002**	−0.001*	−0.002**
	(0.001)	(0.001)	(0.001)	(0.001)
OVERHEAD_A	0.099**	0.066	0.103**	0.067
	(0.049)	(0.048)	(0.050)	(0.048)
NINI	−0.015***	−0.009**	−0.020***	−0.017***
	(0.003)	(0.004)	(0.005)	(0.005)
NDF	0.011***	0.001	0.016	0.018
	(0.003)	(0.003)	(0.012)	(0.012)
NINI_SQ			0.007	0.013*
			(0.007)	(0.007)
NDF_SQ			−0.005	−0.016
			(0.011)	(0.011)
CORPORATE_dummy		0.001		−0.001
		(0.002)		(0.002)
SPECIALIZED_dummy		0.015***		0.016***
		(0.003)		(0.003)
UNIVERSAL_dummy		0.000		−0.001
		(0.002)		(0.002)
R-squared	**0.167**	**0.245**	**0.170**	**0.258**
Adjusted R-squared	0.153	0.226	0.151	0.235

Notes: Dependent variable: ROA; method: Least Squares; Sample: 414 (55 observations are excluded).
***, ** and * denote significance at 1 %, 5 % and 10 % respectively. Standard errors are in parentheses.

Table 12.7   Regression results: Z-score

	Model 1a	Model 1b	Model 1c	Model 1d
LN_ASSETS	–3.034 *	–2.745	–3.262 *	–3.155 *
	(1.803)	(1.866)	(1.883)	(1.880)
CAR	83.459**	81.549	92.143 *	89.866*
	(41.372)	(50.665)	(45.990)	(53.045)
ASSETS_GROWTH	4.485	4.562	3.873	3.102
	(3.839)	(4.138)	(3.979)	(4.197)
OVERHEAD_A	–363.687**	–341.735**	–386.790**	–387.231**
	(161.799)	(172.077)	(167.443)	(172.499)
NINI	13.223	9.144	32.124	42.861
	(11.703)	(13.043)	(31.196)	(31.906)
NDF	–11.631	–12.321	–29.351	–67.472
	(9.852)	(12.224)	(41.667)	(46.972)
NINI_SQ			–24.521	–44.952
			(42.502)	(43.692)
NDF_SQ			15.730	47.032
			(34.921)	(38.614)
CORPORATE_dummy		6.008		11.715 *
		(5.985)		(6.846)
SPECIALIZED_dummy		0.275		2.029
		(9.668)		(9.618)
UNIVERSAL_dummy		0.786		1.417
		(5.633)		(5.584)
R-squared	**0.281**	**0.307**	**0.295**	**0.360**
Adjusted R-squared	**0.171**	**0.133**	**0.142**	**0.152**

Notes: Dependent variable: Z-score; method: Least Squares; Sample: 46.
***, ** and * represent significance level of 1 %, 5 % and 10 % respectively. Standard errors are in parentheses.

for Poland, returns are positively correlated with scale, adequate capital and high interest income share, which suggests that profitability is highest in large, universal banks or smaller, loan oriented specialized banks.

6. Conclusions

In the post-deregulation period of the 1990s, the best results were obtained by large and complex global banks – a fact which has frequently been attributed to synergies between their commercial activities, asset management and investment activities. The financial crisis of 2007–2009 has brought a new perspective: not only of a profitable but also of a responsible market participant which is adequately capitalized, not too big to fail and not dependent on government for rescue funds. This new perspective stresses the soundness of bank activities, and advocates a proper analysis of risk, as opposed to concentrating solely on returns. In post-crisis literature, a return to a universal banking model has at times been advocated, with this being viewed as more stable because of risk diversification. The aims of this chapter were to contribute to the discussion about how the financial crisis has influenced the selection of bank business models and to analyse what the relevant trade-offs between risk and return are. Both in the empirical studies reviewed and in the empirical part concerning the Polish banking market we present evidence suggesting that the selection of the universal bank model may not be the optimal choice, as it frequently offers increased risk, with no significant impact on return. Bearing the recent research in mind, the return to a traditional bank model might be advocated, with an emphasis on more diversified sources of funding. For Poland, this model has proved very profitable, particularly in its "extreme" manifestation. The best results (high profitability with moderate risk) were achieved by specialized, loan oriented, non-depository banks. Corporate banks, with the highest Z-score (low risk of default), turned out to be the least profitable. Thus the regressions for the Polish banks support the assertions about the virtues of traditional banking,

Appendix A12.1 List of analysed Polish banks, by bank types

Bank	Main shareholder	Per cent of equity	Last year obs.	End year Assets (000 PLN)	Average in 2000–2008 Loans/ Assets	Deposits/ Assets	Z-score	Sharpe ratio	NDF	NINI
Type: corporate										
Deutsche Bank Polska	Deutsche Bank AG	100.00	2008	6,332,670	0.18	0.28	52.09	2.35	0.67	0.76
WestLB Bank Polska	WestLB AG	100.00	2008	1,972,567	0.27	0.25	29.32	2.62	0.74	0.55
Credit Lyonais (now: Calyon Bank Polska)	Calyon Global Banking S.A. (owned by Credit Agricole)	100.00	2004	1,907,283	0.31	0.48	17.01	1.32	0.43	0.75
Rabobank	Rabobank International Holding B.V.	100.00	2008	8,138,480	0.39	0.08	28.93	1.40	0.91	−0.01
BNP Paribas Oddział W Polsce	BNP Paribas	100.00	2006	4,776,276	0.47	0.37	22.23	3.49	0.53	0.51
DZ Bank Polska	DZ Bank AG	99.13	2008	2,853,637	0.48	0.48	27.63	0.72	0.47	0.46
BRE	Commerzbank Auslandsbanken Holding AG	71.19	2008	82,605,579	0.49	0.49	8.39	0.65	0.46	0.57
Bank DnB Nord	Bank DnB NORD	100.00	2008	7,256,005	0.55	0.26	66.71	1.93	0.67	0.24
Eurobank	Société Générale	98.97	2008	7,507,155	0.58	0.49	3.22	0.27	0.44	0.14

Continued

Appendix A12.1 Continued

Bank	Main shareholder	Per cent of equity	Last year obs.	End year Assets (000 PLN)	Loans/ Assets	Deposits/ Assets	Z-score	Sharpe ratio	NDF	NINI
Type: specialized, loan oriented										
BPH Bank Hipoteczny (now: PKO Bank Hipoteczny	Bank Pekao S.A. (owned by Unicredito Italiano)	99.96	2008	1,919,582	0.76	0.01	33.00	1.46	0.99	0.23
AIG Bank Polska	AIG Consumer Finance Group Inc	99.92	2008	8,075,898	0.84	0.26	6.44	1.64	0.71	0.07
BRE Bank Hipoteczny	BRE Holding Sp. z o.o (owned by Commerzbank)	75.71	2008	4,675,104	0.86	0.04	53.32	1.64	0.95	0.34
DaimlerChrysler Bank	DaimlerChrysler AG – Stuttgart	100.00	2007	339.017	0.89	0.01	25.65	2.18	0.99	0.15
Volkswagen Bank	Volkswagen Financial Services AG	60.00	2008	2,431,595	0.89	0.41	20.22	3.59	0.56	0.14
Toyota Bank	Toyota	100.00	2008	929,512	0.91	0.07	24.58	1.01	0.89	0.13
Santander Consumer Bank	Santander Consumer Finance SA (owned by Banco Santander Central Hispano)	100.00	2008	10,080,639	0.91	0.01	22.55	2.16	0.99	0.26
Fiat Bank Polska	Fiat Bank Germany GmbH.	100.00	2008	1,224,063	0.92	0.03	19.82	1.75	0.95	−0.16

Bank	Parent/Owner	%	Year	Assets						
FCE Bank Polska	FCE Bank plc	100.00	2007	338,263	0.93	0.09	23.89	3.13	0.89	−0.01
GE Money Bank	GE Capital Corporation, Stamford, USA	90.00	2008	23,285,916	0.94	0.02	9.72	2.11	0.98	0.31
GMAC Bank	GMAC LLC	100.00	2007	569,079	0.94	0.03	16.82	2.57	0.96	0.08
Type: traditional										
BPH	UniCredito Italiano S.A.	71.03	2008	15,827,149	0.50	0.62	9.79	1.18	0.30	0.49
Getin	Getin Holding S.A. (Polish capital)	99.56	2008	23,306,151	0.51	0.71	21.71	3.71	0.23	0.33
Bank Millennium	Banco Comercial Portugues SA	65.50	2008	47,144,922	0.52	0.60	15.61	1.53	0.36	0.58
PKO BP	Polish Treasury	62.30	2008	134,755,177	0.52	0.83	14.34	4.08	0.10	0.35
Bank Gospodarki Zywnosciowej	Rabobank International Holding B.V.	59.35	2008	24,034,870	0.52	0.76	10.93	0.48	0.19	0.31
INVEST-BANK	Polaris Finance BV	30.35	2008	2,337,564	0.53	0.77	20.75	0.26	0.14	0.24
BISE	Bank DnB NORD	100.00	2006	2,654,959	0.55	0.69	53.52	1.41	0.26	0.48
Raiffeisen Bank Polska	Raiffeisen International Bank-Holding AG	100.00	2008	24,074,317	0.59	0.64	13.30	1.76	0.32	0.63
Kredyt Bank	KBC Bank N.V.	85.53	2008	38,730,676	0.59	0.62	3.62	0.03	0.32	0.45
Fortis Bank Polska	Fortis Bank SA/NV (owned by BNP Paribas)	99.87	2008	19,869,004	0.65	0.53	23.33	1.90	0.40	0.43

Continued

Appendix A12.1 Continued

Bank	Main shareholder	Per cent of equity	Last year obs.	End year Assets (000 PLN)	Loans/ Assets	Deposits/ Assets	Z-score	Sharpe ratio	NDF	NINI
Dominet Bank (now: merged with Fortis Bank Polska)	Fortis Bank SA/ Fortis Bank NV (owned by BNP Paribas)	99.87	2007	1,838,633	0.65	0.74	18.40	0.22	0.17	0.19
Lukas Bank	Lukas S.A.	100.00	2008	11,158,604	0.69	0.67	8.31	2.27	0.23	0.27
Bank Ochrony Srodowiska	The National Fund for Environmental Protection and Water Management	77.27	2008	11,158,789	0.69	0.74	31.54	1.73	0.19	0.37
Nordea	Nordea Bank AB	98.38	2008	15,764,109	0.73	0.60	11.47	0.46	0.30	0.38
Type: universal										
ABN AMRO (now: RBS BANK POLSKA)	ABN AMRO Bank N.V. (owned by The Royal Bank of Scotland Group plc.)	100.00	2005	3,496,310	0.28	0.65	30.87	3.27	0.32	0.48
Bank Pocztowy	Polish Post Office	75.00	2008	2,697,837	0.29	0.69	17.21	1.57	0.25	0.44
Bank Handlowy w Warszawie	Citibank Overseas Investment Corporation	75.00	2008	41,520,843	0.35	0.51	27.01	1.46	0.40	0.56
ING Bank Slaski	ING Bank N.V.	75.00	2008	69,610,475	0.39	0.76	21.82	1.73	0.18	0.53
Bank Współpracy Europejskiej										

(now: Meritum Bank)	Innova Financial Holding S.a.r.l.	90.17	2006	415,965	0.40	0.60	6.72	-0.59	0.36	0.57
Deutsche Bank PBC	Deutsche Bank Privat- und Geschaftskunden AG	95.58	2008	15,566,639	0.42	0.61	11.90	-0.19	0.32	0.34
Pekao	UnioCredito Italiano SpA	52.87	2008	132,030,453	0.47	0.73	19.46	3.35	0.19	0.43
BZ WBK	AIB European Investments Limited	70.50	2008	57,838,074	0.50	0.73	15.05	1.83	0.19	0.52
Type: others										
Bank Gospodarstwa Krajowego	state-owned bank	100.00	2008	34,311,678	0.53	0.35	8.49	2.71	0.65	0.26
Mazowiecki Bank Regionalny	cooperative bank	100.00	2008	2,334,123	0.25	0.06	8.27	0.84	0.94	0.31
Bank Polskiej Spółdzielczości	cooperative bank	95.30	2008	11,273,205	0.28	0.14	11.11	1.29	0.85	0.45
Gospodarczy Bank Wielkopolski	cooperative bank	97.50	2008	5,767,467	0.29	0.07	15.56	1.63	0.92	0.41

but only when conducted by a relatively small bank which undertakes
a significant funding risk.

Notes

1. In the US, in 2008 the Fed assisted JP Morgan in taking over Bear Stearns and
   Washington Mutual and bailed out AIG; US$125 of TARP money recapital-
   ized Citigroup, Goldman Sachs, Wells Fargo, JP Morgan Chase, BoA-Merrill
   Lynch, Morgan Stanley, State Street, Bank of NY-Mellon and another US$300
   recapitalized Citigroup (Saunders et al. 2009).
2. Consequently, GE Holding declared that it will downscale financial operations from 50 to 30 per cent of profits. (The Economist 2009a).
3. In the US, as much as 40 per cent of banks' assets are estimated to be off-
   balance sheet ones, see Acharya et al. (2009).
4. Other regressions included such macroeconomic variables as inflation, GDP
   and regulatory variables based on (Barth 2004) and binary variables representing bank type.

References

Acharya, V., Hasan, I., and Saunders, A. (2002) The Effects of Focus and
   Diversification on Bank Risk and Return: Evidence from Individual Bank Loan
   Portfolios, CEPR Discussion Paper no. 3252.
Acharya, V., Richardson, M., and Walter, I. (eds) (2010) *Real Time Solutions for
   Financial Reform*, NYU Stern School, New York e-book (http//govtpolicyrecs.
   stern.nyu.edu/doc/whitepapers_e-book, last access January 15, 2010).
Acharya, V., Wachtel, P., and Walter, I. (2009) "International Alignments of
   Financial Sector Regulation" in: Acharya, V., and Richardson M. (eds), *Restoring
   Financial Stability: How to Repair a Failed System*, Hoboken, NJ, Wiley.
BANK (2000–2009) "50 największych banków w Polsce" (annual special issues).
Barth, J.R., Caprio, G., and Levine, R. (2004) "Bank Supervision and Regulation:
   What Works Best?" *Journal of Financial Intermediation* 13.
Bessis, J. (2002) *Risk Management in Banking*, Chichester, Wiley.
Demirgüç-Kunt, A., and Huizinga, H. (2009) Bank Activity and Funding
   Strategies: the Impact on Risk and Return, CEPR Discussion Paper 7170.
The Economist (2009a) *GE Losing its Magic Touch*, March 19.
The Economist (2009b) *Ex-communist economies: The whiff of contagion*, February
   26.
ECB (2008) *EU Banking Structures*, Frankfurt, October.
Euromoney (2009) *Has the Asset Management Love Affair Ended?*, August.
Fiordelisi, F., and Molyneux, P. (2006), *Shareholder Value in Banking*, New York:
   Palgrave Macmillan.
Heimeshoff, U., and Uhde, A. (2007) Consolidation in Banking and Financial
   Stability in Europe: The Case of Promoting Cross-Border Bank Mergers,
   Working Paper, Ruhr-University of Bochum.
Horwood C. (2009) "Credit Swiss Rebuilds its Model" *Euromoney*, July.
IMF (2009a) World Economic Outlook, Washington, DC, April.

IMF (2009b) Global Financial Stability Report: Navigating the Financial Challenges Ahead, Washington, DC, October.

Jones, K., and Nguyen, Ch. (2004) Increased Concentration in Banking: Megabanks and their Implications for Deposit Insurance, FDIC Research Paper.

KNF (Polish Financial Supervision Authority) (2009) *Banking Sector – Key Data,* Warszawa, March.

Lee, P. (2008) "How HSBC made it to the top" *Euromoney,* July.

Lown, C., Osler, C., Stragan, P., and Sufi, A. (2000) "The Changing Landscape of the Financial Services Industry: What Lies Ahead?" *FRB NY Economic Policy Review,* October.

Naaborg, I.J. (2007) *Foreign Bank Entry and Performance with a Focus on Central and Eastern Europe* Rijksuniversiteit Groningen.

Saunders, A., Smith, R., and Walter, I. (2009) "Enhanced Regulation of Large Complex Financial Institutions" in Acharya, V., and Richardson, M. (eds) *Restoring Financial Stability: How to Repair a Failed System,* Hoboken, NJ, Wiley.

Slager A. (2006) *The Internationalisation of Banks: Patterns, Strategies and Performance* Basingstoke, Palgrave Macmillan.

Stiroh, K. (2004) "Diversification in Banking: Is Noninterest Income the Answer?" *Journal of Money, Credit and Banking* 36.

13
Does Board Composition Affect Strategic Frames of Banks?[1]

Alessandro Carretta, Vincenzo Farina and Paola Schwizer

1. Introduction

Board composition choices and the appointment of a new board member are key organizational decisions with important consequences for firms' strategies and outcomes.

This study examines how board composition affects strategic frames (i.e. the knowledge structures used by top decision makers in formulating strategic guidelines) in the banking industry. Do larger boards and/or boards with more executive directors and/or more interlocking directors make differences in formulating more complex strategies?

Based on a sample represented by 27 listed Italian banks in 2007, our results highlight that higher number of board members, higher number of non-executive directors and higher numbers of interlocking directorates all increase the complexity of strategic frames. Moreover, the results show that larger banks are associated with more complex strategic frames, since their greater size exposes them to a broad range of competitive options.

Our chapter contributes to the existing literature in two ways. First, its results have important implications the activities of "corporate governance committees" inside the board of directors by focusing on the existing relationship among board composition and the complexity of strategic frames. Second, we propose a procedure to measure strategic frames in banking industry that may stimulate other studies in different contexts. In the remainder of this chapter, Section 2 presents our theory and hypothesis, Section 3 describes our method, Section 4 describes the measures used, Section 5 describes the analysis and results and Section 6 includes a discussion and conclusions.

2. Theory and hypothesis

Strategic frames are the shared mental models that influence how firms' top decision makers understand/perceive the business environment and, consequently, firms' strategies (Huff 1982; Lyles and Schwenk 1992; Thomas et al. 1993; Weick 1995; Nadkarni and Narayanan 2007). They allow the scanning, the diagnosis and the choice of alternatives (Nadkarni and Narayanan 2007): (1) by acting as filters for the information considered relevant for strategy formulation, (2) by enabling decision makers to assume cause and effect relations along with ambiguous information and (3) by influencing firms' responses to environmental opportunities/threats.

The complexity of a strategic frame reflects the breadth or variety of environmental, strategy and organizational concepts embedded in the frames and the degree of connectedness among these concepts. Thus, complex strategic frames are indicative of a diverse set of strategy solutions that allow firms to notice and respond to more stimuli, which in turn increases their adaptability (Weick 1995). In synthesis, if it is true that more complex strategic frames do not necessarily lead to superior performance (in fact, firms may use only few and simple concepts, but they may be the most relevant and effective ones), complexity may foster firms' strategic flexibility (Nadkarni and Narayanan 2007).

Many actors may participate in the strategy definition process, but the point at which information converges for the final choice of strategies is supposed to be at the top levels of firms (Lyles and Schwenk 1992; Thomas et al. 1993). In this regard, we will focus on the impact of the board of directors on strategy.

First, focusing on board size, some authors (Lipton and Lorsch 1992; Yermack 1996; Eisenberg et al. 1998) maintain that when a board has too many members, these inevitably take on a purely symbolic role and their activities become disjointed from the management processes. However, Zahra and Pearce (1989) and Dalton et al. (1999) claim that large boards may more effectively control the executive bodies (because of the greater difficulty for the latter to influence the directors) and enlarge the breath of perspectives in the planning process as a result of their larger pool of expertise and skills (Lorsch and MacIver 1989).

Forbes and Milliken (1999) maintain that the board may be viewed as a "black box" within which the principal processes take place. The directors' competencies and cultural outlook are directly related to the overall quality of the processes. In other words, the accumulation of skills translates into various ways of perceiving and implementing corporate processes. Conner and Prahalad (1996) assert that the differences existing in terms of competencies and experience (in terms of both breadth and depth) among directors may either facilitate or hinder the board in the exercise of its functions. When, in fact, the environment in which a firm operates features a high degree of complexity and dynamism, the breadth and depth of the skills of the individual directors play a key role, because they allow a better understanding of the competitive environment and more effective and efficient decision making. As a rule, the heterogeneity of the skills of the board members is an important element which is capable of facilitating the learning processes and strategic flexibility.

Second, with regard to the board's monitoring functions, Sapienza and Gupta (1994) stress the information asymmetry that may affect performance monitoring capacities. This asymmetry could also be the result of a lack of competence among those responsible for monitoring the senior management and can translate into monitoring shortcomings. In this sense, a more limited set of skills may entail higher transaction costs with respect to the agents' monitoring activities. Thus:

Hypothesis 1a: The higher the number of board members, the higher the complexity of strategic frames

Hypothesis 1b: The higher the number of board members, the lower the complexity of strategic frames

With regard to non-executive directors' contribution, on one side some authors argue that as market for corporate control is limited, they are essential to mitigate potential agency problems (Eisenhardt 1989; Mahoney 1992; Mahoney and Mahoney 1993; Kor 2006). In this sense, agency problems that arise from strategies that are subject to high levels of risk may be mitigated by the presence of outside directors, and all the better if they are independent of the CEO's influence (Mork et al. 1989). Regarding this concern, boards are less likely to exert control over strategic decision making on behalf of shareholders when they lack formal or social independence from the CEO and management. In fact, Wade et al. (1990) suggest that non-executive directors elected to the board during a CEO's tenure may feel a personal sense of obligation or loyalty to that CEO and thus neglect their role as guardians of shareholders' interests. The separation of the roles of the chairman of board and CEO could mitigate this problem.

Moreover, Lipton and Lorsch (1992) maintain that many boards often work badly and rarely adopt a critical position with respect to the management's decisions. This is primarily as a result of the influence exercised by the senior management in the selection of non-executive directors. Shivdasani and Yermack (1999) support this point of view and observe a negative link between the senior management's influence in the director recruitment process and the board's monitoring capacity.

On the other side, an alternative view considers that the limited time available to the non-executive directors (generally 1 or 2 days per month) makes it extremely difficult for them to influence strategies (Goold and Campbell 1990; Mintzberg 1990). Thus:

> *Hypothesis 2a: The higher the number of non-executive directors, the higher the complexity of strategic frames*

> *Hypothesis 2b: The higher the number of non-executive directors, the lower the complexity of strategic frames*

Last, interlocking directorates have important implications for the structure and effective functioning of boards, which in turn have an important role to play in corporate governance and company performance (Hermalin and Weisbach 2003).

From one perspective, interlocking directorates allow the use of knowledge structures developed from directors' experience on other boards and provide an important source of information about the business practices and policies of other firms (Carpenter and Westphal 2001; Farina 2009). Moreover involvement at board level with firms following different strategies or/and operating in different environments provides directors with greater knowledge about a broad range of potential strategic alternatives (Carpenter and Westphal 2001). A different perspective maintains that serving on boards in multiple firms makes it difficult for directors to gain an adequate understanding of the issues facing any one firm, so directors with multiple appointments have no way to influence strategy (Mintzberg 1990). Thus:

> *Hypothesis 3a: The higher the number of interlocking directorates, the higher the complexity of strategic frames*

> *Hypothesis 3b: The higher the number of interlocking directorates, the lower the complexity of strategic frames*

3. Method

To test our hypotheses we use data on all the banks (27) listed on the Italian Stock Exchange at the end of 2007. The information needed to construct board size and the presence of non-executive directors and interlocking directorates, is hand picked from the banks' "Relazioni sulla Corporate Governance" for the year 2007. Data on banks' total assets are collected from the banks' annual reports for the year 2007. Moreover, the source of data for measuring the strategic frames' complexity is the management report published by each bank in its annual report. Although top decision makers may have little role in preparing annual reports, some authors (Schwenk 1989; Barr 1998; Barr et al. 1992; Nadkarni and Narayanan 2007) maintain that they have the final supervision on the document.

In order to extract strategic frames from annual reports and measure their complexity we employ a methodology based both on computer aided text analysis (CATA) (Stone et al. 1966; Roberts 1997) and social network analysis (Mitchell 1969; Wasserman and Faust 1994). In particular we applied the following steps:

- First we identify some verbs or terms indicating strategic actions. In order to detect the different inflected forms we use the root of each verb or term followed by the symbol "*". The root represents the semantics not reducible and common to more than one word in the same family (Table 13.1).
- Second we define eight fields for strategic actions and a series of terms or synonyms associated with them. In this case, too, in order to detect the different inflected forms we use the root of each term and synonym followed by the symbol "*" (Table 13.2).
- Third we use the software of text analysis Hamlet II (Brier and Hopp 2009) in order to: (1) map for each bank the comprehensiveness (or the total number of strategic fields) of strategy on the basis of the co-occurrence matrix for the verbs indicating strategic actions and the relative field of application of strategic actions[2] (M&A, Distribution, Organization, Human Resources, Pricing, Advertising and Technology) and (2) create for each bank the relationships (edges) between a generic strategic field (node x) and a generic strategic field (node y) inside an adjacency matrix, wherein cell xy was coded "1" if there was a link and "0" otherwise.
- In addition, in order to measure the complexity of strategic frames, using a social network analysis software, UCINET VI (Borgatti et al. 2002), allows us to calculate the total number of linkages (edges) divided by the total number of strategic fields (nodes) in the adjacency matrix.

Table 13.1 Roots of verbs or terms indicating strategic actions

Acquis* (Acquire)	Introd* (Introduce)
Cambia* (Change1)	Investi* (Invest)
Chang* (Change2)	Leader* (Leadership)
Consolid* (Consolidate)	Miglior* (Improvement)
Crescit* (Growth)	Prom* (Promote)
Disinv* (Disinvest)	Raggiun* (Reach)
Downs* (Downsize1)	Razional* (Rationalize)
Downsiz* (Downsize2)	Semplif* (Simplify)
Entra* (Entry)	Sfrutt* (Exploit)
Espans* (Expand)	Snell* (Lean)
Evoluzion* (Evolution)	Sostit* (Substitute)
Fonder* (Merge)	Strateg* (Strategy)
Innov* (Innovate)	Svilupp* (Develop)
Integr* (Integrate)	Taglia* (Cut)
⇨	Turnar* (Turnaround)

4. Measures used

In our analysis, we use two conventional measures of complexity (Carley and Palmquist 1992; Calori et al. 1994; Nadkarni and Narayanan 2007):

- Comprehensiveness (COMPLEX1): the total number of strategic fields within a strategic frame (NSF);
- Connectedness (COMPLEX2): the total number of linkages in a causal map divided by the total number of strategic fields in the map (NL/NSF).

We measure board size as the total number of directors on the board of directors (BOARDSIZE). In the case of dualistic systems of corporate governance, in counting directors we consider both management and supervisory boards.

We measure the number of non-executive directors (NED) as the total number of directors without delegation or an executive appointment within the banks to which they belong. In the case of dualistic systems, in counting directors we consider both management and supervisory boards.

Table 13.2 Fields for strategic actions and roots of associated verbs or terms

M&A	Distribution	Organization	HR	Pricing	Product	Advertising	Technology
Acquisi* (Acquisition)	Canal* (Channel)	Organizz* (Organization)	Capacit* (Skill)	Prezz* (Price)	Prodott* (Product)	Pubblicit* (Advertising)	Tecnolog* (Technology)
Fusio* (Merger1)	Distribuz* (Distribution)	Reengin* (Reengineering)	Competen* (Competency)	Pricin* (Pricing)	Serviz* (Service)	Brand* (Brand1)	Autom* (Automation)
Internazionalizz* (Internationalization)	Vendit* (Sell)	Restruct* (Restructuring)	Creativ* (Creativity)		Strument* (Instrument)	Identit* (Identity)	Erp (Erp)
Joint* (Joint)		Ristrutt* (Restructuring)	Cultur* (Culture)			Immagin* (Imagine)	Informati* (Information)
Merger (Merger2)		Struttur* (Structure)	Esperien* (Experience)			Marchi* (Brand2)	
M&A (M&A)			Motivaz* (Motivation)				
			Person* (Personnel)				

Table 13.3 Descriptive statistics

	N	Minimum	Maximum
COMPLEX1	27	−2.36057	0.82620
COMPLEX2	27	−1.54293	1.96237
SIZE	27	−1.72797	2.16824
BOARDSIZE	27	−1.26172	2.66299
NED	27	−1.54902	2.06302
ID	27	−2.40331	1.80834

Note: Mean = 0; Variance = 1

Table 13.4 Correlations

	COMPLEX1	COMPLEX2	SIZE	BOARDSIZE	NED
COMPLEX1	−				
COMPLEX2	0.281	−			
SIZE	−0.014	0.586***	−		
BOARDSIZE	−0.067	0.407***	0.708***	−	
NED	−0.034	0.231	0.588***	0.804***	−
ID	0.173	0.160	0.297	0.119	0.064

* Correlation is significant at the 0.1 level (2-tailed); **Correlation is significant at the 0.05 level (2-tailed); *** Correlation is significant at the 0.01 level (2-tailed).

We measure interlocking directorates (ID) as the average number of directors' appointments on other boards, taken from the "Relazioni sulla Corporate Governance".[3] In this case, too, that of dualistic systems, in counting directors we consider both management and supervisory boards.

Lastly, bank size (SIZE) is used as a control variable and is measured by the natural logarithm of the banks' total assets. Since larger banks are exposed to a large amount of information from multiple environments, they are more likely to possess the internal capabilities needed to manage organizational and environmental complexity (Hambrick 1982).

In order to perform cluster analysis, all variables are normalized to zero mean and unit variance. In fact, since cluster analysis groups elements such that the distance between groups along all clustering variables is maximized, variables where elements are separated by large distances are given more weight in defining a cluster solution than those with small ranges. As a result, in this way a subset of variables can dominate the definition of clusters. To avoid this, the normalization allows variables to contribute equally to the definition of clusters.

We present the descriptive statistics for our normalized variables in Table 13.3 and the bivariate correlation coefficients among them in Table 13.4.

5. Analysis and results

In order to validate our hypotheses, we subject our normalized variables to a cluster analysis using the SPSS Quick Cluster routine (Norusis 1988). Since no initial cluster centres are specified, this routine proceeds by selecting k cases with well separated, non-missing values as initial centres with which to begin classifying cases, where k is the number of clusters requested.

As cases are added to each cluster, the program updates the selection criteria to the value means for the cases (banks) thus far placed in a cluster. The program uses a squared Euclidian distance measure to assign a company to its nearest cluster.

The following tables summarize the initial cluster centres of the banks and the iteration history (Tables 13.5 and 13.6). The cluster profiles show the differences in the board composition for different levels of complexity of strategic frames.

Two cluster profiles are defined[4] (Table 13.7): the first cluster, consisting of 19 banks, is characterized by lower complexity levels; in contrast,

Table 13.5   Initial cluster centres

	Cluster	
	1	2
COMPLEX1	−0.76719	0.02951
COMPLEX2	−0.41944	1.15345
SIZE	−1.37734	2.06915
BOARDSIZE	−0.31979	2.19203
NED	0.35205	1.30259
ID	−2.40331	0.89771

Table 13.6 Iteration history

	Change in cluster centres	
Iteration	1	2
1	2.560	1.807
2	7.266E-02	0.265
3	0.000	0.000

Note: Convergence achieved as a result of no or small distance change. The maximum distance by which any centre has changed is 0.000. The current iteration is 3. The minimum distance between initial centres is 5.753.

Table 13.7 Final cluster centres

	Cluster	
	1	2
COMPLEX1	−0.13822	0.32827
COMPLEX2	−0.36504	0.86696
SIZE	−0.43322	1.02889
BOARDSIZE	−0.47678	1.13235
NED	−0.46841	1,11248
ID	−0.20125	0.47797

the second cluster, consisting of eight banks, is characterized by higher levels of complexity.

In particular, the results highlight that the higher the number of board members, the higher the complexity of strategic frames, thus confirming hypothesis 1a.

Moreover, from cluster analysis we may observe that the higher the number of non-executive directors, the higher the complexity of strategic frames, thus confirming hypothesis 2a.

Again, hypothesis 3a also seems to be confirmed, since from cluster analysis it emerges in a certain measure that the higher the number of interlocking directorates, the higher the complexity of strategic frames.

Finally, it seems unsurprising that larger banks are associated with high levels of strategic frames' complexity, confirming that their complexity exposes them to a broad range of competitive options.

6. Conclusions

The knowledge structures used by top decision makers in formulating firms' strategic guidelines reflect the breadth or variety of environmental, strategy and organizational concepts. Thus, complex strategic frames accommodate a diverse set of alternative solutions in strategic decision making, allowing firms to notice and respond to more stimuli, which in turn should increase their adaptability.

This study contributes to governance literature by investigating the relations existing among board composition and strategic frames based on a sample represented by all of the banks (27) listed on the Italian Stock Exchange at the end of 2007.

In more detail, the results highlight that higher numbers of board members (Hypothesis 1a), higher numbers of non-executive directors (Hypothesis 2a) and higher numbers of interlocking directorates (Hypothesis 3a) all increase the complexity of strategic frames. Moreover results show that larger banks are associated with high levels of strategic frames' complexity since their complexity exposes them to a broad range of competitive options.

Our chapter has some important theoretical and practical implications. First, our results highlight the strategic role of boards according to a variety of perspectives and show that an effective contribution of board members to strategy requires an appropriate board composition. In this case, the activities of "corporate governance committees", because of their important role in the board composition choices, should have important repercussions for enhancing directors' contributions.

Second, we propose a reliable procedure to measure strategic frames in the banking industry that may stimulate other studies in different contexts. We extracted strategic frames from management reports of banks based on CATA (computer aided text analysis) methodologies with the following advantages: (1) reproducibility, (2) stability and (3) accuracy of results. Moreover, we used social network analysis methods to measure the complexity of strategic frames.

This study does have some limitations. In fact, on one side, the small size of our sample (27 banks in total) classifies this study as exploratory. On the other, we are unable to control for the impact of boards' individual factors (such as directors' competencies, experience and cognitive styles) affecting strategic frames. Future research could examine this important issue in order better to understand how cognitive processes in boards may affect strategic framing.

Notes

1. The authors are grateful to Prof. Roberto Rocci for his useful comments and advice.
2. As a context unit for the search of the various terms, we consider sentences delimited by these characters: ".!?".
3. Missing ID data for the "Banca Popolare dell'Emilia Romagna" is replaced on the dataset with the series mean method of SPSS.
4. We obtained similar results with non-normalized variables.

References

Barr, P.S. (1998) "Adapting to unfamiliar environmental events: A look at the evolution of interpretation and its role in strategic change" *Organization Science* 9 (6), 644–669.

Barr, P.S., Stimpert, J.L., and Huff, A.S. (1992) "Cognitive change, strategic action, and organizational renewal" *Strategic Management Journal* 13, 15–36.

Borgatti, S.P., Everett, M.G., and Freeman, L.C. (1992) "Ucinet IV: Network analysis software" *Connections* 15, 12–15.

Brier, A., and Hopp, B. (2009) "Quantitative Analysis of Textual Data with HAMLET II new generation" Southampton University and University of Cologne. (http://apb.newmdsx.com/hamlet2.html, date of last access: June, 2010).

Calori, R., Johnson, G., and Sarnin, P. (1994) "CEOs' cognitive maps and the scope of the organization" *Strategic Management Journal* 15 (6) 437–457.

Carley, K., and Palmquist, M. (1992) "Extracting, representing and analyzing mental models" *Social Forces* 70, 601–636.

Carpenter, M.A., and Westphal, J.D. (2001) "The strategic context of external network ties: Examining the impact of director appointments on board involvement in strategic decision making" *Academy of Management Journal* 44, 639–660.

Conner, K.R., and Prahalad, C. (1996) "A resource-based theory of the firm: knowledge versus opportunism" *Organization Science* 7 (5) 477–501.

Dalton, D.R., Daily, C.M., Ellstrand, A.E., and Johnson, J.L. (1998) "Meta-analytic reviews of board composition, leadership structure, and financial performance" *Strategic Management Journal* 19 (3) 269–290.

Eisenberg, T., Sundgren, S., and Wells, M. (1998) "Larger board size and decreasing firm value in small firms" *Journal of Financial Economics* 48, 35–54.

Eisenhardt, K.M. (1989) "Agency theory: an assessment and review" *Academy of Management Review* 14 (1) 57–74.

Farina, V. (2009) "Banks' centrality in corporate interlock networks: evidences in Italy" Paper presented at 2009 FMA European Conference, Turin, 3–5 June 2009.

Forbes, D.P., and Milliken, F.J. (1999) "Cognition and corporate governance: Understanding boards of directors as strategic decision-making groups" *Academy of Management Review* 24 (3), 489–505.

Goold, M., and Campbell, A. (1989) "Brief case: Non-executive directors' role in strategy" *Long Range Planning* 23 (6), 118–119.

Hambrick, D.C. (1982) "Environmental scanning and organizational strategy" *Strategic Management Journal* 3, 159–174.

Hermalin, B.E., and Weisbach, M.S. (2003) "Boards of directors as an endogenously determined institution: a survey of the economic literature" *Economic Policy Review* 9 (1), 7–26.

Huff, A.S. (1982) "Industry influences on strategy reformulation" *Strategic Management Journal* 3 (2) 119–131.

Kor, Y.Y. (2006) "Direct and interaction effects of top management team and board compositions on R&D investment strategy" *Strategic Management Journal*, 27 (11), 1081–1099.

Lipton, M., and Lorsch, J.W. (1992) "A modest proposal for improved corporate governance" *Business Lawyer* 48, 59–77.

Lorsch, J.W., and MacIver, E. (1989) *Pawns or potentates: the reality of America's corporate boards* Harvard Business School Press, Boston, MA.

Lyles, M.A., and Schwenk, C.R. (1992) "Top management, strategy and organizational knowledge structures" *Journal of Management Studies* 29, 155–174.

Mahoney, J.M., and Mahoney, J.T. (1993) "An empirical investigation of the effect of corporate charter antitakeover amendments on stockholder wealth" *Strategic Management Journal* 14 (1) 17–31.

Mintzberg, H. (1990) "The design school: Reconsidering the basic premises on strategic management" *Strategic Management Journal* 11, 171–195.

Mitchell, J.C. (1969) "The concept and use of social networks" in Mitchell, J.C. (ed.), *Social Networks in urban situations* Manchester University Press.

Morck, R., Shleifer, A. and Vishny, R.W. (1989) "Alternative mechanisms for corporate control" *American Economic Review* 79, 842–852.

Nadkarni, S., and Narayanan, V.K. (2007) "Strategic schemas, strategic flexibility and firm performance: The moderating role of industry clockspeed" *Strategic Management Journal* 28 (3), 243–270.

Norusis, M.J. (1988) Statistical package for the social sciences (SPSS-PC) (SPSS Inc., Chicago, IL.

Roberts, C.W. (1997) *Text analysis for the social sciences: Methods for drawing statistical inferences from texts and transcripts* Lawrence Erlbaum, Mahwah, NJ.

Sapienza, H.J., and Gupta, A.K. (1994) "Impact of agency risks and task uncertainty on venture capitalist-entrepreneur relations" *Academy of Management Journal* 37, 1618–1632.

Schwenk, C.R. (1989) "Linking cognitive, organizational and political factors in explaining strategic change" *Journal of Management Studies* 26 (2), 177–187.

Shivdasani, A., and Yermack, D. (1999) "CEO Involvement in the selection of new board members: An empirical analysis" *Journal of Finance*, 54 (5), 1829–1853.

Stone, P.J., Dunphy, D.C., Smith, M.S., and Ogilvie, D.M. (1966) *The general inquirer: A computer approach to content analysis* MIT Press, Cambridge, MA.

Thomas, J.B., Clark, S.M., and Gioia, D.A. (1993) "Strategic sensemaking and organizational performance: Linkages among scanning, interpretation, action and outcomes" *Academy of Management Journal* 36, 239–270.

Wade, J., O'Reilly, C.A., and Chandratat, I. (1990) "Golden parachutes: CEOs and the exercise of social influence" *Administrative Science Quarterly* 35, 587–603.

Wasserman, S., and Faust, K. (1994) *Social network analysis* Cambridge University Press, Cambridge.

Weick, K.E. (1995) *Sensemaking in organizations* Sage, Thousand Oaks, CA.

Yermack, D. (1996) "Higher valuation of companies with a small board of directors" *Journal of Financial Economics* 40, 185–212.

Zahra, S.A., and Pearce, J.A. (1989) "Board of directors and corporate financial performance: A review and integrative model" *Journal of Management* 15, 291–334.

14
In Search of an Optimal Board of Directors for Banks

Pablo de Andrés-Alonso, M. Elena Romero-Merino, Marcos Santamaría-Mariscal and Eleuterio Vallelado-González

1. Introduction

The remarkable growth of literature about corporate governance during recent years is evidence of the importance that this issue has gained in the business world. The topic "corporate governance" is beginning to take the important place it deserves in the economics of organizations.

However, it is quite unusual that, as Charreaux (2004) shows, the theories of governance have not generally been focused on the study of the way the managers *govern*, but on the way they *are governed*. This differentiation is significant because these theories emphasize the *control* instead of the *management*. As Salas (2003) reveals, whereas management is about the application of the business judgement rule to decision making (decisions that can be wrong or not), governance is related to getting over the problems of adverse selection and moral hazard. So, at least at the first step, the definition of corporate governance can be confined to "a set of mechanisms through which outside investors protect themselves against expropriation by the insiders" (La Porta et al. 2000: 4). And, with this focus on *control*, the board of directors plays a key role, as Jensen (1993: 18) points out: "the problems with corporate internal control systems start with the board of directors. The board, at the apex of the internal control system, has the final responsibility for the functioning of the firm. Most importantly, it sets the rules of the game for the CEO".

Following these lines, research on corporate finance of the three last decades embarked on the hunt for an optimal structure for the board that would minimize discretionary managerial behaviour and, as a consequence, would maximize corporate value. So then the relationship between the board characteristics – such as its size, the proportion of outsiders or CEO duality – and the performance of the firm was extensively analysed. The results until now have been conclusive for neither board size (Chaganti et al. 1985; Yermack 1996; Eisenberg et al. 1998; Kiel and Nicholson 2003) nor its independence (Vance 1964; Hill and Snell 1988; Rosenstein and Wyatt 1990; Kiel and Nicholson, 2003).

Still, the need for answers – in view of the business scandals that have occurred – has been translated to listed companies in shape of good governance codes. And so, firms have been recommended to have boards with a reduced number of directors and a majority of non-executive directors, and with no duality between the CEO and the chairman of the board.

However, the question about the optimal composition of a board is far from being closed. This is even truer in the financial sector. The financial storm experienced in the banking industry during the last two years has shown up the practices of corporate governance that the banking entities were implementing. The successive bank bankruptcies and the financial aid that the financial sector has received from the monetary authorities in most developed countries are a very good example of the governance failure of these entities. As the OECD Report "The corporate governance lessons from the financial crisis" (Kirkpatrick, 2009: 2) points out "the financial crisis can be to an important extent attributed to failures and weaknesses in corporate governance arrangements". This report suggests "a need for the OECD to re-examine the adequacy of its corporate governance principles…". It is crystal clear that it is time to change corporate governance and, especially, the financial entities' governance. The difficulty lies in defining the best course to follow. Regarding this, we raise in this chapter two issues that, in our opinion, should be borne in mind.

On the one hand, it is necessary to go on studying the problem of corporate governance but taking into consideration the special characteristics of the financial entities. First, that banking entities are characterized by a high opacity, which relates to higher information asymmetries and the complexity of bank business (Levine 2004). Second, the major providers of financial resources in the banking industry are depositors who lack both the motivation and experience to monitor the banks' management (Freixas and Rochet 1997). Third, banking entities have a very high debt ratio, which exposes them to a major risk of insolvency in case of a bank run (Macey and O'Hara 2003). These three characteristics and the externalities related to bank bankruptcies explain why the financial institutions are subject to intense regulation. Moreover, these differences between the banking entities and the non-financial ones justify the need to develop specialized studies that may lead to the adoption of some specific governance recommendations for financial entities. As the Walker Report on Corporate Governance in UK Banks (2009: 43) says, "the combination of complexities in setting risk strategy and controlling risk and the potentially massive externalities involved in failure of a major financial entity means that the need for industry experience on banking boards is greater than that in non-financial business...". We can also observe some similar action in other countries that have just enacted their codes of good governance for their financial entities as a result of the financial crisis (that is in the cases of the Netherlands and Italy).

On the other hand, it is essential to increase the level of study of the role of the board of directors. In complex industries, such as the banking business, the role of the board becomes more significant as a result of the limited competition, intense regulation and high informational asymmetries. But this research about boards must be increased not only from the traditional disciplinary or monitoring approach, but also from an advisory or managerial one. For this purpose, the advisory role of the board consists of providing the CEO with expert counsel and access to information and resources. This is so because the key to the firm's value creation does not lie only in the governance mechanisms that monitor the managerial team and solve agency conflicts but also on the governance mechanisms that induce learning and stimulates the managerial team to imagine, to perceive and to generate new investment opportunities. This change in the concept of the board means a move from the disciplinary model of governance to the cognitive model of governance – a model that emphasizes qualitative coordination, the alignment of cognitive schemes and anticipatory models. From this approach, the role of the board of directors is valued not only as a disciplinary mechanism but also as an advising mechanism to help the managers to make the best decision on each occasion (Raheja 2005; Adams and Ferreira 2007; Andrés and Vallelado 2008).

However, this theoretical approach guides us to a deeper reflection about an optimal board composition (effective in its monitoring and advisory roles) to be used for every financial entity. The underlying idea is that the idiosyncrasy of an entity will determine the balance between its monitoring and advisory needs so that in the end this will lead to a different optimal configuration for each bank. For instance, it seems comprehensible that a priori an international bank will not have the same advisory needs as another that works only in a single country. In the same way, the monitoring role of the boards will be more intense in banks where there is no substitute governance mechanism. So, the size of the bank, its complexity, its age and the ownership structure or the legal framework of the countries where it works, among other issues, are variables that can determine the configuration of the board of directors. The board has recently begun to be considered as an endogenously determined mechanism, and it has been mainly studied in the non-financial sector (Boone et al. 2007; Coles et al. 2008; Lehn et al. 2008; Linck et al. 2008). Literature on this subject for the financial sector is very scarce (Adams and Mehran 2008; Belkhir 2009). Thus, this work supposes an important contribution to understanding banking boards as a governance mechanism by studying the determinants of the board composition for an international sample of commercial banks. To do so, in Section 2 we describe the main board characteristics of the banks included in our sample. Then, we analyse the possible endogenous relationships between the entity's idiosyncrasy and the board's composition. Finally, in Section 3 we conclude the chapter with some considerations about the results we have presented.

2. Endogenous board composition in international banking entities

Our sample includes 74 listed commercial banks from seven OECD countries during the period 1996–2006. The database contains an unbalanced panel data with 662 bank-year observations of commercial banks from civil-law countries (France, Italy, the Netherlands and Spain) and common-law countries (Canada, the UK and the US). Specifically, about 40 per cent of the banks (30) were founded in a civil-law country, while the other 60 per cent (44) were constituted in a common-law country. Although our sample includes only listed banks, and it represents only the 32 per cent of the total number of banks in the seven countries, they hold about 80 per cent of the banking assets and equity.

Most of our data was obtained from the Spencer & Stuart database, although we have also used the banks' websites to complement information on boards for the most recent periods, Compustat Global Vantage database to obtain financial statements of banks and BankScope and Thomson One Banker to obtain full data about ownership structure.

2.1. Board composition and functioning across countries

In the following lines we describe the main dimension of the banking boards (size and independence) in our data. The basic descriptive statistics are in Table 14.1.

Table 14.1 The main statistics of banking boards

Variable	Mean	Std. Dev.	Min.	Max.
BOARD SIZE	15.7	4.41	6	32
BOARD OUTSIDERS	12.6	4.51	0	28
(%) BOARD OUTSIDERS	79.6	14.8	0	100

Note: BOARD SIZE is the total number of directors; BOARD OUTSIDERS is the number of outsiders in the board; (%) BOARD OUTSIDERS is the percentage of outsiders in the board.

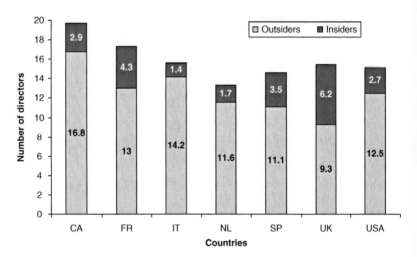

Figure 14.1 Banking board composition and functioning across countries

When looking at the boards of banks in the different countries we observe some clear divergences in their composition. As we can see in Figure 14.1, the mean of the board size varies between 13 and 20 directors, while the global mean stands in the region of 16 members (exactly 15.7). All of the countries have banking boards mostly composed of outsiders. However, we find the most independent boards in Italy (90 per cent), the Netherlands (88), and Canada (85). These figures are in line with those of Belkhir (2009) and Adams and Mehran (2008), who present an average banking board size of 14 and 18 members, respectively, and a percentage of outsiders of 70 and 80 per cent, respectively.

2.2. Endogenously determined boards

After this brief description of the boards' composition, we explore if these changes have been endogenously determined. As we have previously shown, recent research on boards has begun to explain their optimal configuration based on efficiency. These studies consider the two main functions of the board – advising and monitoring – and which firm specific internal and external characteristics will result in these functions creating value (Boone et al. 2007; Guest 2008; Lehn et al. 2008; Linck et al. 2008).

With regard to the advisory role of the board, theoretical studies show that this is more efficiently performed by a larger and more independent board that can provide more important connections and greater information, knowledge and expertise (Fama and Jensen 1983; Guest 2008).

According to previous studies, advisory needs are positively related to a firm's size (Denis and Sarin 1999; Baker and Gompers 2003; Kim et al. 2007; Coles et al. 2008; Guest 2008; Iwasaki 2008; Lehn et al. 2008; Linck et al. 2008), complexity (Denis and Sarin 1999; Coles et al. 2008; Iwasaki 2008; Linck et al. 2008) and age (Boone et al. 2007; Coles et al. 2008; Guest 2008; Linck et al. 2008).

Moreover, in the banking industry boards are a key mechanism for advising managers on strategy identification and implementation (Andrés and Vallelado 2008). As we show in Figure 14.2, our data evidence a clear connection between board size and some of the banks' characteristics, such as size, financial complexity and age (see the left column of the figure). However, we cannot find a clear relationship between board independence and the bank's size or leverage. On the contrary we observe a confusing negative relationship between the bank's age and the board's independence (see the right panel of the figure).

The monitoring role of the board is especially important when there is no other mechanism to reduce the governance problem between investors and managers. Although banking entities, because of their idiosyncrasy, have been subject to intense regulation, the basic dimensions of the governance problem have not changed, except for the inclusion of depositors as the main risk bearers (Caprio et al. 2007), and banking opacity, which is related to higher information asymmetries and more difficulty in monitoring (Prowse 1997a, 1997b; Caprio and Levine 2002; Macey and O'Hara 2003; Salas 2003; Levine 2004).

To solve the governance problem between investors and managers, there are some alternative mechanisms for reducing agency conflicts,

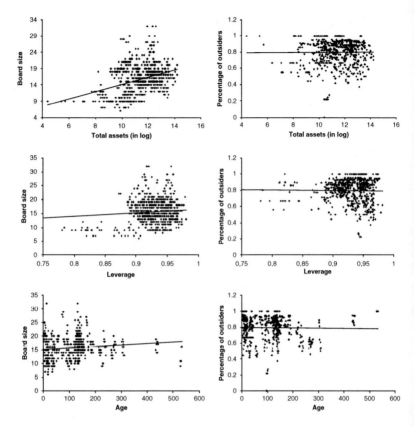

Figure 14.2 Relationships between banks' characteristics and their boards' composition

such as legal protection of the investors' rights, ownership concentration or the board of directors. Thus, whenever there is a substitute governance mechanism that guarantees effective monitoring, there is no need for the board to include more outsiders to enhance its monitoring role.

With regard to the legal protection of investors' rights, civil-law countries are characterized as having a lesser degree of protection for investors' legal rights in comparison with the situation for investors in common-law countries (La Porta et al. 1998). It is expected that those banks located in civil-law countries cope with a potential problem of investors' expropriation by using the board as a substitute governance mechanism of corporate governance. As we can observe in Figure 14.3,

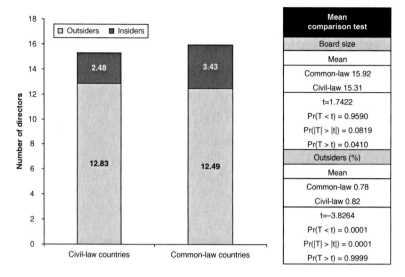

Figure 14.3 Board composition in civil-law countries vs. common-law countries

boards in the civil-law countries are significantly more independent than those of common-law countries and they are notably smaller, so as to avoid coordination and free rider problems (Jensen, 1993; Yermack, 1996). The differences that can be observed in Figure 14.3 are statistically significant for both board size and independence.

Besides the legal protection of the investors' rights, there exist other governance mechanisms, such as ownership concentration, that can also substitute for the board in its monitoring role and define its composition, too. When there is a blockholder, the board does not need to be configured as an effective monitoring mechanism. According to our data, the percentage of ownership of the major shareholder is negatively related to both board size and independence (see Figure 14.4). These facts agree with previous researchers who state that the existence of a blockholder supposes a decrease in the number of directors in order to diminish decision making costs (Kieschnick and Moussawi 2004) and a drop in the percentage of board outsiders as their monitoring abilities are not needed (Belkhir 2009).

In addition to the substitution phenomenon, the configuration of a board as a monitoring mechanism depends on the monitoring costs. When monitoring costs increase, boards reduce their monitoring role, which leads them to diminish their size and the percentage of outsiders (Raheja

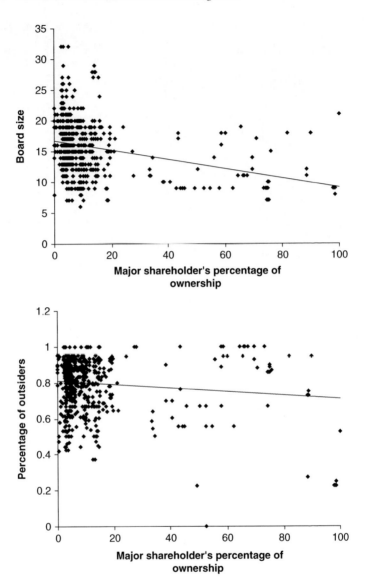

Figure 14.4   Relationships between ownership structure and board composition

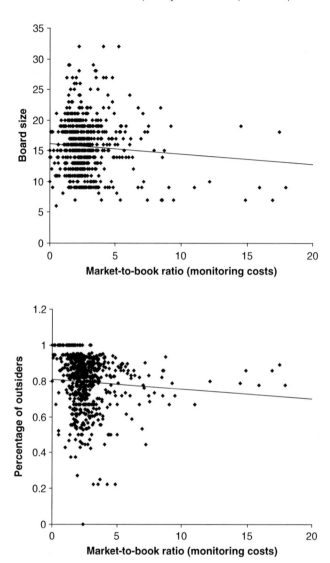

Figure 14.5 Relationships between market to book ratio and board composition

2005). In this research, and following previous literature (Denis and Sarin 1999; Boone et al. 2007; Guest 2008; Lehn et al. 2008; Linck et al. 2008), we expect to find that monitoring costs are related to firm growth (proxied by a high Tobin's Q) and negatively connected to board size and outsider proportion (Boone et al. 2007; Guest 2008; Linck et al. 2008). As we can observe in Figure 14.5, our data confirm these expectations.

In conclusion, according to our data, the board cannot be considered any more as an exogenous mechanism of governance. The bank's characteristics, the existence of an alternative governance mechanism and the costs of monitoring of each entity are connected to the characteristics of the board of directors, all of which ultimately supposes that future research on the boards' effect on the banks' performance will need to cope with this endogeneity.

3. Final remarks

The issue of the board of directors as a simple mechanism to monitor the managerial team is too restrictive. At that point, the cognitive approach can help us to understand better the role of the board and to assemble the puzzle of its optimal composition as an efficient mechanism to both *control* and *advise* the firm. This consideration favours a broader definition for *Corporate Governance*.

Our study shows that there exist important differences in banking board composition across countries. This is because financial entities adapt their boards of directors to their own characteristics and the environment in which they work. Descriptive analysis shows that large boards are related to larger banks, with a high leverage and age. Thus, the larger, older and more leveraged banks need more advisory input from their boards to give them the level of expertise and knowledge required to run such complex institutions. This fact would also explain, in contrast to what is found in the theoretical literature, the absence of a robust relationship between these variables and board independence, because knowledge and expertise can also be derived from insiders.

We also find that the ownership percentage of the major shareholder and the monitoring costs are negatively connected to both the board's size and independence. When there is a major shareholder who can undertake the monitoring role or when the costs of controlling the managers are too high, the bank's board reduces its own monitoring role, which means that fewer members and outsiders are required.

These results make it difficult to provide general recommendations to configure optimal boards of directors. Then, each bank needs a specific board of directors. Some developments in recent codes of good practices for banking organisations confirm our sentence. The UK Combined Code on Corporate Governance published in June 2008 recommended boards with a reduced size. However, the recent Walker Report points out that: "In practice, however, decisions on board size will depend on particular circumstances, including the nature and scope of the business of an entity, its organisational structure and leadership style. [...] So there can be no general prescription as to optimum board size and no recommendation is made in this report" (Walker 2009: 41). In addition, the Central Bank of Italy, in the Report on supervisory provisions concerning banks' organization and corporate governance (2008: 11) points out that: "The number of members of the governing bodies must be adequate to the bank's size and organizational complexity in order to ensure effective oversight of all its operations as concerns management and control". Therefore, we conclude that the questions about an optimal banking board composition are now more open than ever before.

References

Adams, R.B., and Ferreira, D. (2007) "A Theory of Friendly Boards" *Journal of Finance* 62 (1), 217–250.

Adams, R.B., and Mehran, R., (2008) "Corporate Performance, Board Structure, and their Determinants in the Banking Industry" Staff Reports 330, Federal Reserve Bank of New York.

Andrés, P., and Vallelado, E. (2008) "Corporate Governance in Banking: The Role of the Board of Directors" *Journal of Banking and Finance* 32 (12), 2570–2580.

Baker, M., and Gompers, P. (2003) "The Determinants of Board Structure at the Initial Public Offering" *Journal of Law and Economics* 46, 569–598.

Belkhir, M. (2009) "Board of Directors' Size and Performance in the Banking Industry" *International Journal of Managerial Finance* 5 (2), 201–221.

Boone, A.L., Field, L.C., Karpoff, J.M., and Raheja, C.G. (2007) "The Determinants of Corporate Board Size and Composition: An Empirical Analysis" *Journal of Financial Economics* 85, 66–101.

Caprio, G., and Levine, R. (2002) "Corporate Governance of Banks: Concepts and International Observations" Global Corporate Governance Forum Research Network Meeting, April 5.

Caprio, G., Laeven, L., and Levine, R. (2007) "Governance and Bank Valuation" *Journal of Financial Intermediation* 16 (4), 584–617.

Central Bank of Italy (2008) *Supervisory provisions concerning banks' organization and corporate governance* (available at http://www.bancaditalia.it/vigilanza/banche/normativa/disposizioni/provv/en_disposizioni_040308.pdf, last access July 15, 2010).

Chaganti, R.S., Mahajan, V., and Sharma, S. (1985) "Corporate Board Size, Composition and Corporate Failures in Retailing Industry" *Journal of Management Studies* 22, 400–417.

Charreaux, G. (2004) Corporate Governance Theories: From Micro Theories to National Systems Theories Working Paper of Fargo N° 1040101, Université de Bourgogne.

Coles, J.L., Daniel, N.D., and Naveen, L. (2008) "Boards: Does One Size Fit All?" *Journal of Financial Economics* 87, 329–356.

Denis, D.K., and Sarin, A. (1999) "Ownership and Board Structure in Publicly Traded Corporations" *Journal of Financial Economics* 52, 187–223.

Eisenberg, T., Sundgren, S., and Wells, M. (1998) "Larger Board Size and Decreasing Firm Value in Small Firms" *Journal of Financial Economics* 48, 35–54.

Fama, E.F., and Jensen, M.C. (1983) "Separation of Ownership and Control" *Journal of Law and Economics* 26, 301–325.

Freixas, X., and Rochet, J.C. (1997) *Microeconomics of Banking* MIT Press, Cambridge, MA.

Guest P.M. (2008) "The Determinants of Board Size and Composition: Evidence From the UK" *Journal of Corporate Finance* 14, 51–72.

Hill, C.W., and Snell, S.A. (1988) "External Control, Corporate Strategy, and Firm Performance in Research-Intensive Industries" *Strategic Management Journal* 9, 577–590.

Iwasaki, I. (2008) "The Determinants of Board Composition in a Transforming Economy: Evidence from Russia" *Journal of Corporate Finance* 14 (5), 532–549.

Jensen, M.C. (1993) "The Modern Industrial Revolution, Exit, and the Failure of Internal Control Systems" *Journal of Finance* 48 (3) 831–880.

Kiel, G.C., and Nicholson, G.J. (2003) "Board Composition and Corporate Performance: How the Australian Experience Informs Contrasting Theories of Corporate Governance" *Corporate Governance: An International Review* 11 (3) 189–205.

Kieschnick, R., and Moussawi, R. (2004) The Board of Directors: A Bargaining Perspective, Working Paper, University of Texas at Dallas.

Kim, K.A., Kitsabunnarat, P., and Nofsinger, J.R. (2007) "Large Shareholders, Board Independence, and Minority Shareholder Rights: Evidence from Europe" *Journal of Corporate Finance* 13 (5), 859–880.

Kirkpatrick, G. (2009) "The Corporate Governance Lessons from the Financial Crisis" *OECD Journal: Financial Market Trends* 96 (1).

La Porta, R., López-De-Silanes, F., and Shleifer, A. (1998) "Law and Finance" *Journal of Political Economy* 106, 1113–1155.

La Porta, R., López De Silanes, F., Shleifer, A., and Vishny, R.W. (2000) "Investor Protection and Corporate Governance" *Journal of Financial Economics* 58 (1–2), 3–27.

Lehn, K., Patro, S., and Zhao, M. (2008) Determinants of the Size and Structure of Corporate Boards: 1935–2000, CEI Working Paper Series, No. 2008–13.

Levine, R. (2004) The Corporate Governance of Banks: A Concise Discussion of Concepts and Evidence, World Bank Policy Research Working Paper, No. 3404.

Linck, J., Netter, J., and Ang, T. (2008) "The Determinants of Board Structure" *Journal of Financial Economics* 87, 308–328.

Macey, J., and O'Hara, M. (2003) "The Corporate Governance of Banks" *FRBNY Economic Policy Review*, April.

Prowse, S. (1997a) "Corporate Control in Commercial Banks" *Journal of Financial Research* 20, 509–527.

Prowse, S. (1997b) "The Corporate Governance System in Banking: What Do We Know?" *BNL Quarterly Review* Special Issue, March, 11–40.

Raheja, C.G. (2005) "Determinants of Board Size and Composition: A Theory of Corporate Boards" *Journal of Financial and Quantitative Analysis* 40 (2), 283–306.

Rosenstein, S., and Wyatt, J.G. (1990) "Outside Directors, Board Independence and Shareholder Wealth" *Journal of Financial Economics* 26, 175–191.

Salas V. (2003) "El Gobierno de la Empresa Bancaria desde la Regulación" *Revista de Estabilidad Financiera* 5, 197–228.

Vance, S. (1964) *Boards of Directors: Structure and Performance*, University of Oregon Press, Eugene, OR.

Walker, D. (2009) *A review of corporate governance in UK banks and other financial industry entities*, Interim Report HM Treasury, London.

Yermack, D. (1996) "Higher Market Valuation of Companies with a Small Board of Directors" *Journal of Financial Economics* 40, 185–211.

15
Value and Governance in the Exchange Industry: the Case of Diversified Conglomerate Exchanges

Maurizio Polato and Josanco Floreani

1. Introduction

The way in which exchanges operate and compete is rapidly changing in connection with an extensive process of consolidation which is contributing to a reshaping of the exchange industries' structure. Technological developments and regulatory reforms have contributed to the falling of national barriers and gave rise to growing competition from peers and new operators which forced incumbents to react with cross border mergers.

This has given rise to cost and revenue synergies leveraging on the joint use of common trading platforms and the development of cross selling opportunities, respectively. In turn, cross border mergers are redefining governance arrangements and giving rise to a widespread network of relations between operators which modify the industry structure. Nevertheless, mergers hide some threats as cuts in earnings and cash flows resulting from increasing competition may adversely affect both goodwill and the capital base for exchanges going forward with sizable acquisitions.

The aim of this work is to examine changes in the business models of exchanges as consolidation goes forward and their effects on industry structure and competition. In Section 2, we first look at governance reforms in the exchange industry; then in Section 3 we identify the major economic drivers for exchange value. Finally, we identify the main threats lying behind mergers and implications for the governance of networks. Section 5 offers our conclusions.

2. Governance reforms and incentives to consolidation

In recent years, most security markets have experienced fragmentation, and this changes the concept of trading securities as traditional stock exchanges are no longer the only venues for buying and selling securities. Increasing competition in the securities industry led to substantial changes in exchange governance, starting with the demutualization and subsequent listing of most exchanges.

As pointed out above, there were strategic and technological reasons underlying the demututalization process. Technological development and the liberalization of capital markets contributed to the falling of monopolies by eliminating geographical barriers and promoted competition by fostering product and process innovation. Moreover, as national boundaries are blurring, restrictions for issuers to list abroad are falling as well (Macey and O'Hara 1999). Keeping up with an increasingly competitive environment implied the need to reduce the control of local intermediaries over the strategic positioning of exchanges (Steil 2000; Aggarwal 2002), thus forcing demutualization. The incentive problem is also analysed in Serifsoy and Tyrell (2006) where it is shown how a mutual exchange, facing competition from a for-profit, foreign owned platform, can survive only by adopting a similar governance structure.

Above all, technological development contributed to diminishing the role of financial intermediaries (Mishkin and Strahan 1999; Allen et al. 2002). The aforementioned developments put a great pressure on exchanges to list (Fleckner 2006) and to negotiate alliances in order to cope with increasing competition in trading services. What is new is that exchanges are exposed to even greater competitive pressures from electronic communications networks (ECNs that, with their efficient technology endowments, are able to take away important streams of liquidity from exchanges.

Despite many alliances consisting of simple co-operation agreements between legally separated entities the most recent changes in the securities industry structure were driven by a great number of mergers on a cross border scale.

Exchange mergers in almost all cases involve a widening of the business model and are targeted to exploit economies of scale, economies of network and cross selling opportunities.

Since exchanges operate to a great extent with a fixed cost structure, they may reduce average costs by enhancing liquidity. As pointed out by prominent research, the exchanges industry shares the typical features of network industries (Economides, 1993), so alliances among stock exchanges permit the exploitation of economies of network, both direct and indirect. This is a problem of both competition and coordination. Competition should be promoted, since users should have the right to access all the services related to exchange trading, choosing for each of these the provider offering better conditions. Coordination is assured as long as exchanges adhere to common standards (compatibility) assuring equal access to users (Economides and Flyer 1997); it is, therefore, a precondition for a proper competition in the market.

Business diversification is aimed at counteracting the cyclical dynamics in trading activity. Here the rationale is to engage in high growth businesses with a limited correlation to cash markets in order to lower the volatility of revenues and margins. To this end, derivative trading and post trading services are traditionally seen as a counterweight to cash trading; these businesses experienced fast growing volumes, revenues and profitability even during periods of declining trading volumes in cash markets. Moreover, investors and issuers can now access exchange related services more easily than in the past. Therefore, maintaining a competitive advantage in the securities industry requires exchanges to strengthen their relations with clients by granting them access to a wide set of business services.

The most recent wave of consolidation involved major global exchanges embracing different jurisdictions and entailed new challenges for regulators, in particular as regards mutual recognition issues (Tafara and Peterson 2007). In almost all cases, the mergers involved heterogeneous exchanges as to business model, geographical extension, governance arrangements and trading volumes. The most interesting case is the one that resulted in the formation of NYSE Euronext. The NYSE Group, which was traditionally focused on the cash trading business, merged with Euronext in order to gain access to European markets and, particularly, to Euronexts' activities in the derivatives business. The London Stock Exchange (LSE) presented its merger with Borsa Italiana as an opportunity to leverage on the latter's activities in the derivative business and post trading services.

Whereas homogeneous mergers involve similar exchanges as regards business model but with complementary geographical location, heterogeneous mergers are aimed at leveraging on both geographical and product (or process) complementarities.

A few global exchanges with a different degree of business diversification emerged, which reinforced their oligopoly in cash trading and, at least, in one other business line or market segment (which could be derivatives trading or post trading services). It is, however, on derivative trading that the phenomenon assumes the major breadth . Derivative markets appear to be more concentrated then cash markets and more heterogeneous as regards products traded. Here, major players tend to concentrate on few trading segments.

As long as exchanges become involved in businesses characterized by a strict connection with trading activities they end up reinforcing their control within the securities industry value chain. However, the implications for the economics of exchanges are not clear. Few works have addressed the issue of efficiency for multi-business exchanges. The results are affected by the concept of efficiency adopted and do not provide definitive insights on this issue (Schmidel 2001, 2002; Serifsoy 2007). Neither have the threats for traditional exchanges deriving from new competitors been extensively studied. The phenomenon is a recent one, at least for European markets. However, high speed trading platforms operated by ECNs have proved successful in capturing wide streams of exchange order flow.

3. Measuring value in exchange mergers

The competitive advantage for stock exchanges depends on the combination of three factors: the business model, which affects the volatility of revenues, governance arrangements, which affect the incentives for the company's management, and liquidity.

Cross border mergers and business diversification raise the question of what exchanges are worth. At first sight, an exchange's value depends on its revenue base and cost structure. The cost structure reflects the predominance of fixed costs, with average costs declining as volumes traded increase (Figure 15.1). This rigidity is only softened in US exchanges, which foresee rebates to brokers which are directly connected to trading volumes.

As exchanges are now forced to lower the costs of their operating infrastructure and speed up trading, investments in technology are crucial. In this way, we expect investments in IT being an important fraction of total costs. This is particularly true for traditionally listed exchanges (for example, Deutsche Börse and the LSE). In contrast, NYSE and NASDAQ have both a lower incidence of IT costs on total costs and a higher incidence of IT costs on free operative cash flow (Table 15.1).

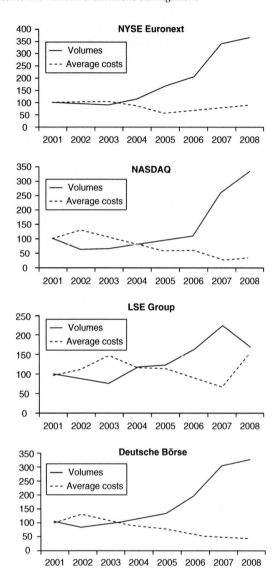

Figure 15.1   Volumes traded and average costs in major exchanges

Source: Our elaboration on exchanges' financial reports and World Federation of Exchanges (WFE) statistics. Volumes traded and average costs equal to 100 in 2001.

Table 15.1 Financial ratios and cost structure for major exchanges

	Leverage (%)	EBITDA (%)	EBITDA/ Interest coverage	Debt/ EBITDA (%)	FOCF/ EBITDA (%)	IT costs/ Total costs (%)	IT costs/ FOCF (%)
NYSE Euronext	44.3	26.7	8.4	188	57.4	6	44
NASDAQ OMX	46.9	20.1	8.5	472	55.6	6.6	13.3
LSE Group	45.4	55.9	5.7	157	60	–	–
Deutsche Börse	53.4	59.1	5.9	550	77.7	9.1	9.4
Chicago Mercantile Exchange	37.2	71	32.1	608	65.8	11.4	9.4

Source: Our elaborations on exchange reports (2008). Data on IT costs on total costs for the LSE are not available.

Governance status appears to affect financial performance as well, with traditionally listed exchanges reporting growing profitability ratios and cash flows (Table 15.2).

Financial performances vary across business lines. Although reporting by segment shows high margins for derivative markets (for example, Chicago Mercantile Exchange and Eurex) and post trading services, the figures do not confirm the dominance of such businesses.

Actually, in some cases cash trading business margins match derivative ones. Deutsche Börse's cash segment reports high profitability margins. However, the London Stock Exchange, traditionally focused on cash trading services, reports high growth margins. However, it is a matter of fact that high growth derivative business constitutes a great reason for stock exchanges to diversify.

Revenue function differs across the various business units with cash trading revenues increasing with trading volumes whereas derivative trading revenues are, generally, dependent on number of contracts traded. While cash trading tend to follow market cycles, in derivatives markets number of contracts traded and revenues has been continuously growing since the last years even during periods of declining trading volumes in equity markets. Tables 15.3 and 15.4 report the trends in trading volumes and revenues for main cash markets and number of contract exchanged and revenues for main derivative markets.

Table 15.2   Some performance measures

	2002	2003	2004	2005	2006	2007	2008
EBITDA %							
NYSE Euronext	–	40.4	34.7	9.0	15.6	27.9	26
LSE Group	39.4	44.2	45.3	51.4	53.1	61.7	55.8
NASDAQ OMX	25.5	5.5	15.6	20.5	17.2	16.6	20
Deutsche Börse	34.9	39.4	39.6	46.8	54.8	55.2	59
Chicago Mercantile Exchange	43.5	47.3	56.4	61.1	63.7	67.7	71
Operative cash flow per share (US$)							
NYSE Euronext	–	–	–	–	1.37	2.64	2.63
LSE Group	0.47	0.65	0.56	0.85	1.34	1.28	1.21
NASDAQ OMX	–	1.34	1.49	1.08	1.39	1.14	2.01
Deutsche Börse	4.12	5.40	4.89	8.61	5.36	5.96	9.36
Chicago Mercantile Exchange	4.8	5.8	9.8	10.1	13.5	15.2	18.02

Source: Our elaborations on financial reports of exchanges considered.

Table 15.3   Trading volumes and revenues in main cash markets

	2001	2002	2003	2004	2005	2006	2007	2008
NYSE Group								
Trading volumes	100	98.3	92.3	110.7	170.2	207.7	285.1	320.7
Revenues	100	102.8	103.6	98.3	86.2	169.9	306.9	463.5
Deutsche Börse								
Trading volumes	100	85.1	91.2	108.2	134.5	192.3	303.8	171.3
Revenues	100	91.9	111.2	124.1	141.3	182.9	275.6	183.8
LSE								
Trading volumes	100	107.8	121.8	138.3	186.8	257.1	590	409
Revenues	100	108.6	117.3	124.7	154.3	213.7	255.5	228

Source: Our elaborations on financial reports of exchanges considered and Wfe statistics. 2001 figures equal to 100.

Table 15.4 Number of contracts traded and revenues in main derivative markets

	2001	2002	2003	2004	2005	2006	2007	2008
Eurex								
Number of contracts	100	118.8	150.5	158.1	185.2	226.5	401.1	470.6
Revenues	100	167.5	206.7	255.3	253.9	313.9	445.1	629.7
Euronext Liffe								
Number of contracts	100	112.6	112.3	91.5	97.9	117.9	153.3	169.5
Revenues	100	364.9	283.1	525.1	546.2	657.5	763	1018.6
CME								
Number of contracts	100	135.6	150.6	191.2	254.5	325.7	546.5	725.8
Revenues	100	114.4	135.8	185.4	229.8	281.5	453.6	661.5

Source: Our elaboration on financial reports of exchanges considered and WFE statistics. 2001 figures equal to 100.

Table 15.5 Average EV/EBITDA multiples in recent mergers

	All deals	European markets	US markets	Derivatives markets
Average EV/EBITDA multiple	27	25.3	28.5	27.6

Source: Our elaborations on financial reports of exchanges and prospectuses related to the mergers considered.

Exchanges combining cash and derivative trading would, therefore, succeed in the attempt to lower the volatility of revenues. In heterogeneous mergers, however, pricing requires the evaluation of the contribution to the exchanges' value of each business activity, which may turn out to be difficult. Moreover, the network of links between market operators as a result of cross border mergers introduces complexity within the exchange industry and may hinder the full exploitation of synergies. Our purpose is to try to identify the main assumptions implied in the pricing of merging exchanges and how the business model of exchanges affects the pricing.

A useful starting point would be to rely on the analysis of multiples (Table 15.5). By segmenting stock exchanges by business activity and geographical location we can draw some interesting considerations.

Analysing multiples in recent deals some interesting considerations can be drawn. In particular:

- US exchanges trade at higher multiples than their European competitors. Moreover multiples are higher among derivatives exchanges. Since the deals examined for the US mainly concern derivatives exchanges, we have to conclude that the market values the derivatives business more than it does cash trading markets.
- It should be taken into account that most recent developments within the securities industry have witnessed the extension of the consolidation process at level of post trading organizations.[1]
- Multiples at which recent deals have been settled far exceed average multiples of European securities exchanges in the last few years. According to the data for the period 2002–2007, the main exchanges traded at average EV/EBITDA multiples ranging from 10x to 11x.

The exchange industry relied to a great extent on mergers. If we Compare the implied multiples in the main mergers, some interesting findings emerge. As a reference, we consider the London Stock Exchange (NASDAQ's bid), NYSE (NYSEs' bid for Archipelago), Euronext (NYSE Group's bid) and the Borsa Italiana (LSE's bid). Table 15.6 compares the valuation of exchange targets with the estimated value on the basis of the multiples for comparables and comparable transactions respectively.

At the announcement of the NYSE-Archipelago merger, the former was valued at a 69 per cent premium against NYSEs' estimated value applying to an implied 19.5 EV/EBITDA multiple in the NASDAQ offer on the LSE. When the two companies issued the joint prospectus, the implied premium was 30 per cent on seat price which corresponded to a 37x EBITDA multiple.

It is worth noting that the NASDAQ offer for the LSE valued the latter at lower multiples than those applied to the generality of mergers and slightly more than the share price of the LSE on the date of announcement. The LSE's management rejected the bid on the basis that the price offered was only just equal to the company's stand-alone value. Whether NYSE was overvalued or the LSE undervalued is arguable.

In the NYSE Group-Euronext merger, Euronext was valued at 23.5 times the EBITDA margin corresponding to a premium of 31 per cent[2]

Table 15.6   Exchange value: some comparisons

Bidder	Target	Announce date	Implied price	Comparables	Comparable transactions	Share price
NASDAQ	LSE*	11 April 2006	£11.75	£6.2613	£14.9–22.1	£10.3
NYSE**	Archipelago	19 April 2005	US$49.3	US$11.9–26.9	US$37.6–48.3	–
NYSE Group	Euronext***	19 May 2006	€92.5	€63–74.8	€74.8–102.4	€65.2
LSE	Borsa Italiana****	23 June 2007	€100.7	€111.3–132.1	€132.1–180.9	€19

Notes: Share price: for LSE this is its value at the announcement date whereas for Euronext it reflects the average price over 30 days before announcement.
*Comparables: we assumed the 2005 NASDAQ and Deutsche Börse EV/EBITDA multiples. Comparable transactions: an EV/EBITDA range of between 25 (average multiples of transactions announced in 2005) and 37 (the NYSE's multiple) is assumed. ** Comparables: an EV/EBITDA range between 9 (the LSE multiple in 2004) and 20 (average NASDAQ multiples) is assumed. Comparable transactions: an EV/EBITDA range between 19.5 (NASDAQ's bid for the LSE) and 28 (average multiple of deals involving American exchanges as target) is assumed. ***and**** Comparables: an EV/EBITDA range between 16 (the LSE multiple in 2006) and 18 (the Deutsche Börse multiple in 2006) is assumed. Comparable transactions: an EV/EBITDA range of between 19.5 (the lowest multiple for transactions announced in 2006) and 26 (the average multiple of all 2006 transactions) is assumed.

Source: Our elaborations on exchanges' annual reports and prospectuses.

on its share price immediately before the deal was announced. It is worth just noting that NYSE offer on Euronext included a 17 per cent premium price over the average Euronext share price registered in the 30 preceding days, whereas the average premium price in similar transactions was 12.1 per cent.

Borsa Italiana was valued, in the merger with London Stock Exchange, at €1.1 billion or 14.3 times the EBITDA margin, with an implied value of €100.7 for each Borsa Italiana share whereas its book value per share was €19.

Now, it is difficult to make comparisons between multiples in different transactions. In fact, varying business models across exchanges make it difficult to identify comparable peers. For exchanges operating with a diversified business model the issue to be dealt with refers to the contribution of each business area to the exchange's value. Considering the exchange as a portfolio of activities, its value could be expressed as the sum of estimated values for each business area on the basis of the multiples ordinarily observed for each business unit. Using this methodology, we estimated the stand alone value for Euronext and Borsa Italiana and the expected synergies (Table 15.7). The pro forma value of NYSE Euronext and the LSE Group is also presented, with the allocation to Euronext and Borsa Italiana shareholders respectively.

Estimating expected synergies is subject to even more degrees of uncertainty as regards both the identification of their sources and the

Table 15.7   Estimated post merger values for NYSE Euronext and the LSE Group

	Low	High		Low	High
Euronext stand alone value (€ per share)*	59.5	62.1	Borsa Italiana stand alone value (€ per share)*	55	67
Eurnext market capitalization (€)	7.4	8.7	Borsa Italiana market capitalization (€)	0.9	1.1
NYSE Group market capitalization (€)**	9.1	10.4	LSE market capitalization (€)**	5.2	6
Synergies***	3.4	3.4	Synergies***	0.6	0.6
NYSE Euronext pro forma value****	17.5	20.1	LSE Group pro forma value	6.7	7.7
Value for Euronext shareholder*****	9.6	10.6	Value for B. I. Shareholder*****	1.8	2.2
Premium on stand alone value	29.1 %	21.6 %	Premium on stand alone value	105 %	100 %

Notes: * Stand alone value estimates are based on the following hypothesis as regards the multiple applied to each business unit: 1) for cash markets we applied the average past multiples for exchanges focused on that business: the London Stock Exchange is assumed as a benchmark; 2) for derivative trading services we applied an EV/EBITDA multiple comprised in the range 19x-27x, corresponding to the multiples at which main derivative markets traded in recent years; 3) post trading services are valued according to the implied multiple in the proposed DTCC-Clearnet merger (2.74 x); 4) as for data dissemination services, we applied an EV/EBITDA multiple comprised in the range 12x-17x, corresponding to the past multiples for the major information providers (i.e. Thomson and Reuters); 5) for IT services, we applied a 12x-15x EV/EBITDA range, corresponding to the past multiples for IT services providers for the financial sector such as Fiserv, a Nasdaq listed company; 6) due to the low trading volumes of Borsa Italiana when compared to its competitors, a smaller range was applied for the EV/EBITDA multiple.
** The estimate for NYSE Group value is based on an EV/EBITDA multiple ranging from 23.5x to 27.5x. The estimate for LSE value is based on an EV/EBITDA multiple ranging from 19 to 22. ***We estimated synergies assuming a P/E multiple of 25 at a 10 per cent discount rate. Such were the parameters adopted by the NYSE and Euronext when estimating the effects of synergies on value. **** Comprises 2.4 billion € of cash distribution. *****Euronext shareholders held 41 per cent of the post-merger group's share capital. Borsa Italiana shareholders had a right to 28 per cent of the resulting group's share capital.

Source: Our elaborations. Data are expressed in billions of € except for per share prices.

estimation of an appropriate discount rate that takes into account the risks to which stock exchanges are exposed. This task is made more difficult by the rapid structural changes taking place in the stock exchange industry, which reduce the level of future certainty. There is no doubt, however, that recent mergers have been settled at prices implying high cost and revenue synergies, thus suggesting that the securities industry is relying to a great extent on consolidation to improve the profitability of stock exchanges.

The LSE offer seems to overestimate the value of the Italian exchange. Actually, such a conclusion calls us to define the relative value of an exchange.[3] At the time of the LSE-Borsa Italiana merger the magnitude of competitive pressure was, probably, not fully understood.

4. Cross border mergers: risks and governance implications

While cross border mergers end in strengthening the oligopoly power of exchanges, market dynamics still expose them to some relevant risk factors both in their core business and, more generally, in all the stages related to trading along the value chain. This risks refers to:

- Exogenous factors such as cyclical downturns in economic activity and increasing cross border competition.
- Endogenous factors such as the concentration of trading activity. When trading volume is concentrated among a few stocks, a company moving to another exchange would cause the exchange to lose an important fraction of its volumes.

Economic downturns may cause drops in exchange trading volumes as happened during the 2008 financial crisis, but they also impact on the business of financial services companies as well.

Moreover, even though major exchanges can leverage on a substantial market power, new competitors are emerging which have proved to be successful in capturing large shares of exchanges' order flow. It is right to consider the case of Chi-X, which gained a straightforward 25 per cent market share in FTSE 100 stocks, in order to understand the magnitude of the phenomenon.[4] Obviously, increasing competition forces exchanges to drop tariffs, for example, and introduce incentives for traders in an effort to fend off competition from new entrants.

Risks for securities exchanges derives from concentration in trading activity as well. According to WFE's statistics (Table 15.8), US markets are less concentrated compared with European ones. For example, the

Table 15.8 Market concentration

	5 % trading volume	Number of companies
US exchanges		
NYSE Euronext	30.3 %	95
NASDAQ OMX	33.1 %	136
European exchanges		
Borsa Italiana	83.2 %	15
LSE	97.3 %	121
Euronext	63.3 %	44
Deutsche Börse	51.1 %	39
OMX Exchanges	78 %	41

Source: WFE statistics (2008). The table shows the part represented by 5 % of the most traded domestic shares compared to domestic share trading value.

most traded 5 per cent of NASDAQ companies (156 companies) account for 33.1 per cent of volume traded on the exchange. The most traded 5 per cent LSE companies account for 97.3 per cent of domestic trading volume, but are represented by 121 companies. This factor, obviously, would reinforce exchanges' incentives to merge reducing, by this way, the risk of losing turnover.

Not all exchange related services are exposed to risks of losing trading volumes to the same extent. Apart from derivative trading which, as we have seen, experienced a constant growth in contract traded and revenues, data dissemination and post trading services are conditioned by declines in trading volumes to a lesser extent.

During recent years, the market foresaw substantial uncertainty about future developments in the exchange industry and the sustainability of past growth rates. After a period of steep rises in share prices, a sharp decline starting at the end of 2007 saw an expected decline in exchanges' profitability. Yet, the decline had started before the deepening of the financial turmoil. It was interesting to observe, during 2008, the contrast between exchanges reporting increasing trading activity and falling share prices. We can observe that declines in cash flows may not only impair the ability of exchanges to support investments but also threat the consistency of their equity bases. For exchanges moving forward with sizable acquisitions weak economic performance may induce large goodwill impairments. For such exchanges, the total tangible equity is often severely negative. Obviously, it is difficult to evaluate the sensitivity of the value of exchange to these events. It is also reasonable to assume that sensitivity to risk factors would vary across different business segments.[5]

It is true that both the recent financial turmoil and regulatory responses may turn out to be opportunities for exchanges. Let us consider the regulators' pressures to expand the use of clearing in OTC markets in order to strengthen the financial system, making CCPs among the most prized assets within the securities industry. Notwithstanding this, in some circumstances, the complexity of relations within the exchange industry may hinder the full exploitation of all potential benefits from business diversification. The prime example is that of the LSE, which integrated the post trading services of Borsa Italiana while maintaining its relevant interests in LCH.Clearnet.

As a result, the governance structure in the stock exchange industry reflects the network of relations between operators and is related to the conditions under which investors can buy the bulk of exchange related services.

It could be argued that governance mechanisms are irrelevant in situations where the exchange has to face strong competition. However, assuming an industry wide perspective, the nature of incentives is now changing in the light of growing interdependences between exchanges and post trading infrastructures, and this requires the governance of networks to be addressed properly. Obviously the exchange industry is a field in which combining the strategic goals of exchanges and right of users to access market infrastructures under fair conditions requires the functioning of external governance mechanisms such as those envisaged by the free action of market forces or, alternatively, by an extensive intervention of regulation.

For example, regulation could encompass some form of tariff control, set limits on share investments in post trading bodies of the stock exchanges, require forms of administrative and accounting separation between the various business segments or – at an antitrust level – place restrictions on mergers between exchanges and post trading infrastructures.

We could highlight the fact that there is a close relationship between how the exchange is regulated and the trading volumes it manages to attract. According to a market perspective, the engagement of regulators should be aimed at coordinating and liberalizing exchanges services since this would benefit both exchanges and users, with the former being able to offer their services in other jurisdictions under same conditions as domestic peers while the latter would have access to a greater variety of services.

Within this framework the conjunction of market forces and regulation should promote non-discriminatory access to exchange industry services. The objective is to render the network effect fully operative, guaranteeing the user ample possibilities to access the various operators and allowing them eventually to acquire "individual" elementary services from various operators. Therefore, the effects of transactions between stock exchanges and their users are becoming of particular importance. To this end, it is useful to concentrate on non-contractual governance mechanisms and, in particular, the effects deriving from so called network embeddedness (Rooks et al. 2006), which defines the conditions under which users may turn to alternative services suppliers (exit network).

Indeed, exchanges have to face the threat of potentially losing their competitive advantage. However, fierce competition discloses new opportunities as well since exchanges are no longer constricted by national boundaries. In recent times the SEC proposed a mutual recognition regime among US and European exchanges for which SEC would negotiate on a case by case basis a regime of substituted compliance with foreign regulators. This mutual recognition regime would be based upon a set of agreed minimal regulatory standards. On this basis, European exchanges and investors would be able to access US markets without additional regulatory burdens.

5. Conclusions

Consolidation in the securities industry underlies some opportunities related to cost reductions as trading volumes increase. From a strategic standpoint, exchanges are able to expand their offer and control almost all of the phases related to exchange trading. Mergers are not only aimed at improving liquidity but also at diversifying the business model (i.e. sources of revenues). Diversifying the business model permits exchanges to stabilize revenues and exploit cross selling opportunities. However, in some cases observed mergers seems to respond to opportunistic goals of controlling shareholders rather than to clear economic and strategic needs. In any case, the multiples observed appear to overestimate future profitability of exchanges as they become even more exposed to fierce competition.

Notes

1. In 2008, the Depository Trust and Clearing Corporation launched a bid on the 100 per cent share capital of LCH.Clearnet Group at €10 € per LCH.Clearnet share, corresponding to a 2.74x EV/EBITDA multiple for the company.

2. The merger between NYSE Group and Euronext NV was based on a public takeover bid in which for every Euronext NV share the acquirer would offer €21.32 in cash and 0.98 NYSE Euronext shares. Subsequently, the NYSE Group merged with the new holding company by exchanging NYSE Euronext shares with NYSE Group shares at a value of 1 to 1. On the basis of the share exchange agreement proposed by NYSE Euronext, the French stock exchange's share price was set at €93.06, according to the share price of the NYSE Group on 2 January 2007.
3. As reference, recall that the value of trading on Borsa Italiana was €45.9 billion in March 2009 whereas that on Chi-X was 57.1 billion in the same month. Despite these figures, we cannot conclude that Chi-X is worth more than Borsa Italiana. However, they reveal how relative value has shifted very quickly over time.
4. We recall just the trading volumes gained in UK securities; in this regard the 25 per cent market share in FTSE 100 stocks could appear straightforward. However, it is worth noting that NYSE has to face increased competition as well (its share of trading in NYSE listed securities declined from 60.5 per cent in 2007 to 45 per cent in 2008). It is clear that if the growth in NYSE's overall trading volume does not offset any significant reduction in its trading share, companies' operating results may be adversely affected.
5. The LSE estimated a negative impact of roughly 17 per cent in value in the use of cash trading cash generating units and 13 per cent in value in use of post trading cash generating units deriving from a 5 per cent reduction in revenues.

References

Aggarwal, R. (2002) "Demutualization and Corporate Governance of Stock Exchanges" *Journal of Applied Corporate Finance* 15 (1) 105–113.

Allen, F., McAndrews, J., and Strahan, P. (2002) "E-Finance: an introduction" *Journal of Financial Services Research* 22 (12) 5–27.

Andersen, A. (2005) *Essays on stock exchange competition and pricing*, Helsinki School of Economics, Doctoral Dissertations.

Economides, N. (1993) "Network economics with application to finance" *Financial Markets Institutions and Instruments* 2 (5) 89–97.

Economides, N., and Flyer, F. (1997) Compatibility and market structure for network goods, Stern School of Business, Discussion Paper, EC-98–02.

Fleckner, A.M. (2006) "Stock exchanges at the crossroad" *Fordham Law Review* 74 (5) 2541–2620.

Macey, J.R., and O'Hara, M. (1999) "Globalisation, exchange governance and the future of exchanges" Brooking-Wharton Papers on Financial Services.

Mishkin, F.S., and Strahan, P.E. (1999) What will technology do to financial structure?, NBER Working Papers, n. 6892.

Rooks, G., Raub, W. and Tazelaar, F. (2006) "Ex post problems in buyer-supplier transactions: effects of transactions characteristics, social embeddedness and contractual governance" *Journal of Management and Governance*, 10 (3) 239–76.

Schmiedel, H. (2001) Technological development and concentration of stock exchanges in Europe, Bank of Finland, Discussion Paper, 21.

Schmiedel, H. (2002) Total factor productivity growth in European stock exchanges: a non parametric frontier approach, Bank of Finland, Discussion Paper, 11.

Serifsoy, B. (2007) "Stock exchange business models and their operative performance" *Journal of Banking and Finance* 31 (10) 2978–3012.

Serifsoy, B., and Tyrell, M. (2006) Investment Behavior of Stock Exchanges and the Rationale for Demutualization – Theory and Empirical Evidence, Wharton Financial Institutions Center, Working Paper, n.17.

Steil, B. (2000) Changes in the Ownership and Governance of Securities Exchanges: Causes and Consequences, Brooking-Wharton Papers on Financial Services.

Tafara, E. and Peterson R.J. (2007) "A Blueprint for cross-border access to U.S. investors: a new international framework" *Harvard International Law Review* 48 (1) 31–68.

Index

abnormal returns, following M&A,
  126–33, 142–3, 144
activity restrictions, 112
agglomerative hierarchical
  clustering, 28
Asian banks, 98
assets, credit institutions, 36
asymmetric information, 59, 92, 248
attitude, 42
average linkage between groups
  method, 28

bank bailouts, 244n1
bank bankruptcies, 261
bank boards, *see* board composition;
  boards of directors
bank business models, 6
  average ratios for different, 234
  impact of global financial crisis
    on, 220, 222–4
  Polish banks, 227–38
  rethinking, 222–4
  sources of risk and return in, 219–44
  universal bank, 224–7
bank concentration, 225–6
bank financial profile, mergers and
  acquisitions and, 153–68
banking industry
  consolidation in, 139–40
  impact of global financial crisis
    on, 219–20
  innovation in, 11–25
  non-interest income in, 224–31
  R&D in, 14–15, 59–85
  strategic frames in, 6–7
banking structure, 26–40
  benchmarks for, 33–4
  empirical results, 28–37
banking system development,
  estimation of, 28–37
bank management, 1–2, 260
  see also boards of directors;
    corporate governance

bank mergers
  see also mergers and acquisitions
    (M&As)
  determinants of likelihood of, 5,
    171–98
  efficiency following, 122–34
  market returns on, 3
bank organizational structures, 219,
  223
bank profitability, 18, 20, 46, 56–7,
  107, 123, 173, 221, 227, 229–35,
  238
  see also profit efficiency
bank risk, *see* risk
banks
  average asset size, by country, 111
  business model for, 6
  impact of board composition on
    strategy, 246–57
  intellectual capital of, 2
  number of, by country, 111
  as portfolio optimizing agents,
    99–102
  separation of corporate and
    investment, 6
Belgian banks, 12, 14, 19
board composition, 6–7
  across countries, 263–4
  affect on strategic frames, 246–57
  in civil-law vs. common-law
    countries, 267
  endogenously determined, 265–70
  market to book ratio and, 269
  optimal, 260–71
  ownership structure and, 268, 270
boards of directors
  see also board composition
  advisory role of, 262, 265
  characteristics of, 260–1
  control by, 260
  monitoring role of, 265, 267, 270
  role of, 262
borrowers, screening of, 92

Borsa Italiana, 11, 282, 284, 287, 289n3
business freedom, 112
business models, of exchanges
   see also bank business models
   of exchanges, 7

Cadbury Code, 203–4, 215n3, 215n4
CAMEL taxonomy, 154, 155, 158
Capital Asset Pricing Model (CAPM), 92–3
capital employed (CE), 42, 43
capital employed efficiency (CEE), 43, 48, 50
capitalization, 178, 188, 196
capital strength, 177–8
Central and East European Countries (CEE)
   foreign capital in, 220, 227
   impact of global financial crisis on, 220
Central European banks, VAIC analysis, 51–2, 53
centroid method, 28
chief executive officer (CEO), 248
Citigroup, 224
cluster analysis, 26–7, 28
collateral, 61–2
commercial banking, literature review, 107–9
competencies, 42
compliance, with codes of corporate governance, 203–16
consolidation, 4–5, 139–40, 153, 275–7
   see also mergers and acquisitions (M&As)
CoRe indicator, 207–15
corporate banking, separation from investment banking, 6
corporate culture
   bank mergers and, 4–5
   impact on M&A results, 139–51
   measurement of, 143
corporate governance, 5–7
   see also boards of directors
   codes, 5–6, 261
   compliance with Italian code of, 203–16

defined, 260
definition of, 270
failures of, 261
for financial entities, 261–2
literature on, 260
role of, 203
self-regulatory codes, 203–5
corporate governance committees, 246
cost efficiency, 114, 115, 116, 128, 180, 195–6
credit institutions
   assets, 36
   number of, per country, 36–7
   number of branches of, per country, 37
   number of employees of, per country, 37
credit rationing, 65
cross-border mergers, in exchange industry, 274, 285–8
cumulative average abnormal returns (CAR), 127, 128–33, 144
customer service, intellectual capital and, 41–58
Czech Republic, 220

Data Envelopment Analysis (DEA) Model, 46, 55, 57, 119n1, 127–8
deregulation, 11, 219, 222
determinants of mergers and acquisitions, 171–98
   conclusions about, 196–7
   dataset and sample, 180
   empirical results, 180–96
   factor analysis, 179–80, 189–93
   free cash flow hypothesis, 176
   growth-resource hypothesis, 177–9, 188–9
   hypothesis development, 174–9
   independent variables in study of, 174–80
   inefficient management hypothesis, 176–7, 188, 196–7
   literature on, 172–3
   logit analysis, 186–9, 193–6
   market to book hypothesis, 198n7
   price-earnings hypothesis, 198n7

determinants of mergers and
  acquisitions – *continued*
  regulatory/institutional hypothesis,
    179, 189, 197
  size hypothesis, 174, 176, 196
  specialization of business
    hypothesis, 177
  study methodology, 173–4
  synergies hypothesis, 188
distribution-free approach (DFA), 119n1
Dutch banks, innovation in, 17

Eastern European banks, VAIC
    analysis, 52, 54
econometric frontier, risk
    measurement in, 99–102
economic freedom, 179
efficiency, 2–4
  bank mergers and, 3–4, 122–34
  of financial institutions, 3
  incorporating risk into analysis of,
    91–104
  in investment banking, 106–19
  as motivation for M&A, 153, 165–6
efficiency models, equity capital in,
    91–5
employees, 2
entrepreneurship, 42
environmental factors, in investment
    banking, 106–19
environmental variables, 111–13,
    116–17
equity capital, 3, 91–5
  cost of, 92–4
Euronext, 11, 276, 282, 284, 289n2
European Association of University
    Teachers of Banking and Finance
    Conference, *see* Wolpertinger
    Conference
European banking systems
  branches of credit institutions, per
    country, 37
  convergence in, 32, 35, 36, 38–9
  credit institutions' assets, 36
  employees of credit institutions,
    per country, 37
  financial structures, 2
  impact of corporate culture on
    M&A results in, 139–51

intellectual capital and, 41–58
  number of credit institutions per
    country, 36–7
  post-merger bank efficiency in,
    122–3, 128–33
  structure of, 26–40
European listed banks
  empirical analysis of, 11–19
  financial figures, 13
  financial innovation in, 11–24
  R&D, 14–15, 19–20
  exchange industry
  business models, 7
  cross-border mergers, 274, 285–8
  governance reforms, 275–7
  incentives to consolidation, 275–7
  M&A activity, 274–89
  market concentration, 286
  performance measurements,
    277–85
  regulation in, 287
  value and governance in, 274–89

factor analysis, of determinants of
    M&A, 179–80, 189–93
finance sources, for traditional
    investments vs. R&D, 62–83
financial crisis, *see* global financial
    crisis
financial freedom, 112
financial industry
  see also banking industry
  consolidation in, 4–5
financial innovation, 1–2, 11–25
  classification, 15–16
  conclusions about, 19–20
  definitions, 11–12
  empirical analysis of, 11–19
  identifying, 12
  life cycles, 16–17
  by year (2005–2008), 16
financial institutions
  see also banks
  efficiency of, 3
financial intermediaries, 275
financial markets, deregulation in,
    219, 222
financial performance, intellectual
    capital and, 44–58

financial system structures, 2
  appraisal of European, 26–40
  benchmarks for, 33–4
  convergence ratios, 32, 35, 36
  data and testing strategies for, 26–8
  empirical results, 28–37
foreign capital, 220, 227
free cash flow hypothesis, in
    determinants of M&A, 176
free disposal hull (FDH), 119n1
French banks, innovation in, 17, 19
frontier efficiency measurement, 127–8

GE Money, 224
geographical distance, in mergers &
    acquisitions, 150
German banks, VAIC analysis, 51–2, 53
global exchanges, 276–7
global financial crisis, 5, 93, 106,
    219–20
  corporate governance and, 261
  impact of, on bank business
      models, 220, 222–4
  impact on innovation, 19
globalization, 219, 222
growth-resource hypothesis, in
    determinants of M&A, 177–9,
    188–9

hedge funds, 222
high-technology exports, 112
HSBC, 224
human capital, 42, 43
human capital efficiency (HCE), 43,
    48, 49, 55

index of bank distance to
    bankruptcy (Z-score), 219, 224,
    226, 231–2, 235, 237
inefficient management hypothesis,
    in determinants of M&A, 176–7,
    188, 196–7
inflation rate, 112
information asymmetry, 60–1, 62,
    69, 92, 248
information transparency, 60
innovation, 1–2, 42, 61
  see also financial innovation;
      technology

in organizational structure, 16, 17
  product, 14, 16–17, 20
  technological, 11
institutional environment, 112
intellectual agility, 42
intellectual capital, 2, 41–58
intellectual capital efficiency (ICE),
    42–3
International Bank Credit Analysis
    Bankscope Database, 111
Internet users, 112
investment banks/banking, 106–19
  core function, 106
  efficiency and environmental
      factors in, 106–19
  efficiency of, 3
  literature review, 107–9
  main businesses in, 108
  regulation of, 109
  separation from corporate banks, 6
investment freedom, 112
investments
  see also research and development
      (R&D) investment; traditional
      investments
  funding of, 59–62
Italian banks, 14
  innovation in, 14–15, 17
  intellectual capital efficiency and,
      47–51
  VAIC analysis, 52
Italian Code of Corporate
    Governance
  compliance with, 203–16
  enforcement of, 206
  introduction of, 206
Italian listed companies, compliance
    with corporate governance
    codes, 5–6, 203–16
Italian manufacturing firms, R&D
    investment in, 59–60

JP Morgan, 223

Latin American banks
  cross-country differences, 154
  M&A activity, 4–5, 153–68
  outcomes from M&A activity,
      156–8

liquidity, 178
logit analysis, factor analysis, 186–9,
    193–6
logit regression, 174, 197n3
London Stock Exchange (LSE), 11,
    276, 282, 283, 285, 287, 289n5

market capitalization, 112
market competition, 153–4
market concentration, 225–6, 286
market power, as motivation for
    M&A, 153–4, 165–6
market to book hypothesis, in
    determinants of M&A, 198n7
market value, intellectual capital and,
    44–58
mergers and acquisitions (M&As)
    among European listed banks, 12
    bank efficiency following, 122–34
    bank financial profile and, 153–68
    corporate culture and, 4–5
    corporate failure and, 158
    cross-border, 274, 285–8
    descriptive statistics on, 184–5
    determinants of, 5, 171–98
    determinants of successful, 146–8
    efficiency motive for, 153–4, 165–6
    in exchange industry, 274–89
    geographical distance and, 150
    growth in, 139–40
    impact of corporate culture on,
        139–51
    in Latin American banks, 4–5,
        153–68
    literature on, 142–4
    market power motive for, 153–4,
        165–6
    market returns on, 3–4
    motives for, 153
    number and value of, by financial
        institutions, 141
    number of, 181–3
    in securities industry, 7
    stock market reaction to, 122–34
multinomial logit model (MLNM),
    154, 155–6, 160

NASDAQ, 282, 283
network embeddedness, 288

non-depository funds, 226–31
non-executive directors, 248–9
non-interest income, 224–31
Northern European banks, VAIC
    analysis, 52, 54
NYSE, 282, 289n2
NYSE Euronext, 276, 282–3, 289n2

official supervisory power, 113
operating efficiency, bank mergers
    and, 3–4
operational inefficiency, 176–7
organizational structure, 16, 17, 219,
    223

pecking order theory, 60
performance measurements
    equity capital in, 91–5
    in exchange industry, 277–85
    incorporating risk into, 91–104
    post-merger, 123–4
physical capital, 41, 44
Poland, 220
Polish banks
    business model structure of, 6
    list of, by bank type, 239–43
    regression results for, 233–8
    risk and return by bank type, 227–33
portfolio optimizing agents, banks as,
    99–102
Portuguese banks, 17, 93–4, 98
post-merger bank efficiency, 122–34
    data for empirical analysis, 125–6
    empirical results, 128–33
    estimation of abnormal returns,
        126–7
    frontier efficiency measurement,
        127–8
    literature review, 123–4
price-earnings hypothesis, in
    determinants of M&A, 198n7
product innovation, 14, 16–17, 20
productivity analysis, incorporating
    risk into, 91–104
productivity decompositions, 95–9
productivity issues, 2–4
profit efficiency, 114, 115, 116, 128,
    165–6, 180, 195
profit maximization, 128

property rights, 112
public subsidies, for R&D, 69, 70–1,
    76, 82

regulation, 112, 287
regulatory/institutional hypothesis,
    in determinants of M&A, 179,
    189, 197
research and development (R&D),
    1, 59
  empirical analysis of, 14–15, 19–20
  financing of, 2
  public funding of, 69, 70–1
research and development (R&D)
    investment, 59–85
  collateral and, 61–2
  compared with traditional
    investment, 62
  credit rationing in, 65
  data and sample analysis, 62–3
  descriptive analysis, 64–9
  finance sources for, 59–83
  funding of, 60–2
  LOGIT model, 75–6
  OLS model, 77–8
  public funding of, 76, 82
  public subsidies and, 62
  return on investment (ROI), 79
  self-financing of, 59–61, 64–5,
    70–1, 76, 79, 82
  SUR model, 80–1
return, sources of, in bank business
    models, 219–44
return on investment (ROI), 69
  of R&D, 79, 82
risk
  deregulation and, 222
  direct measure of, in frontiers,
    99–102
  globalization and, 222
  incorporating into performance
    measurements, 91–104
  measures of, 3
  sources of, in bank business
    models, 219–44
risk assessment, 92
risk diversification, 92
risk management, productivity
    decompositions and, 95–9

risk-return trade-off, 99–102
risk taking, 92
Russian banks, 98, 99

Santander, 224
scale efficiency change, 3, 91
second moment statistics, 3, 91
securities industry
  M&A activity, 7, 274–89
  value and governance in, 274–89
seemingly unrelated regression (SUR)
    models, 59
self-financing, of R&D, 59–61, 64–5,
    70–1, 76, 79, 82
service companies, features of, 2
shadow price of equity, 93–4, 95,
    100–1, 103
shareholder returns, bank mergers
    and, 3–4
Sharpe ratio, 220, 228, 231, 234, 239
size hypothesis, in determinants of
    M&A, 174, 176, 196
small and medium size enterprises
    (SMEs)
  financial preferences, 60–2
  funding of, 59–62
  self-financing by, 59–61
SME Observatory Survey of Italian
    Manufacturing Firms, 62–3
social welfare loss, 154
solvency risk, 226
Spanish banks, VAIC analysis,
    52, 53
specialization of business
    hypothesis, in determinants of
    M&A, 177
stochastic frontier approach (SFA),
    107, 110, 119n1
stock exchanges, *see* exchange
    industry
stock markets, reaction, to bank
    mergers, 122–34
strategic frames
  defined, 247
  impact of board composition on,
    246–57
structural capital, 42, 43, 44
structural capital efficiency (SCE),
    43, 48, 49, 55

supervision, 113
synergies hypothesis, in determinants
    of M&A, 188

technological innovation, 11
technology, 2
    equity capital and, 93
    exchange industry, 275
thick frontier approach (TFA), 119n1
too-big-to-fail policy, 4
total factor productivity change,
    95–9
traditional investments
    credit rationing in, 65
    LOGIT model, 75–6
    OLS model, 77–8
    R&D investments compared with,
        59–83
    SUR model, 80–1
transaction costs, 174
translog functional form, 119n4

UBS, 222
UK banks, 14
    innovation in, 17, 19, 20
universal banks, 224–7
US banks
    M&A activity in, 142
    post-merger bank efficiency in,
        122–3, 128–33
US exchanges, 282
utility maximization, 101

Value Added Intellectual Coefficient
    (VAIC), 42–5, 47–57
variable cost function analysis, 93
Variable Returns to Scale (VRS), 127–8

Wolpertinger Conference, 1
workers' remittances, 112

Z-score, 219, 224, 226, 231–2, 235,
    237